D0811162

# THE COUNTRY LIFE COLLECTOR'S

# POCKET BOOK
# OF GLASS

# THE COUNTRY LIFE COLLECTOR'S

# POCKET BOOK
# OF GLASS

*Written and illustrated by*

## GEOFFREY WILLS

## COUNTRY LIFE

Published by Country Life Books
and distributed for them by
The Hamlyn Publishing Group Limited
London · New York · Sydney · Toronto
Astronaut House, Feltham, Middlesex, England

First published 1966
Revised edition 1979

ISBN 0 600 34091 0

Printed in Great Britain by
Hazell Watson & Viney Limited
Aylesbury

# Contents

# Author's Note

In writing this book I have been guided by the plan followed by the late W. B. Honey in his *Glass*, published in 1946 and long out of print. In that work, the author was restricted for illustrative material to the resources of the Victoria and Albert Museum, in which he was Keeper of the Department of Ceramics for many years. No single collection, not even that admittedly magnificent one, can picture with complete adequacy a subject ranging far and wide over the world and covering a period from the earliest times to the close of the nineteenth century. I have been fortunate in having a very wide choice of examples from which to provide a selection.

1966

For this new edition I have revised the text so as to incorporate facts brought to light since it was first published. At the same time, the opportunity has been taken to change a few of the original illustrations for more appropriate examples and to add two extra ones.

1979

# CHAPTER I

# The Making of Glass

Glass is such a familiar substance that a description of it may be considered superfluous. To most people, indeed, its prominent characteristic is its transparency, but this is not necessarily present; it is usually, but not always, translucent, and some of the deeper-coloured and white varieties are opaque. Whether tinted or colourless, it has been admired and valued for some thousands of years, and in its more artistic forms challenges description in words. While chemical analysis can pin-point its constituents and its shapes can usually be defined, there remain always subtle beauties that defy explanation.

An 18th-century writer listed the following qualities of glass, carefully garnered from what he termed 'learned authors':

1 That glass is an artificial concrete of salt and sand or stones.
2 Fusible by a strong fire.
3 When it is fused it is tenacious and coherent.
4 It does not waste or consume in the fire.
5 When it is melted it will cleave to iron.
6 When it is red hot it is ductile, and may be fashioned into any form; but not malleable, and capable of being blown into a hollowness, which no mineral is.
7 It is frangible when thin without annealing.
8 When it is cold is friable.
9 Diaphanous, whether hot or cold.
10 It is flexible and elastic.
11 It is dissoluble by cold and moisture.

12 It is only capable of being cut with diamond or emery.

13 It will receive any colour or dye, both externally or internally.

14 It is not dissoluble by aqua fortis, aqua regia or Mercury.

15 Neither acid juices, nor any other matter extract either colour, taste or any other quality from it.

16 It will admit of polishing.

17 It will neither lose of weight or substance, by the longest and most frequent use.

18 It will give fusion to metals, and soften them.

19 It is the most pliable thing in the world, and will best retain the form that is given it.

20 It is not capable of being calcined [will not burn to ashes].

21 An open glass filled with water in the summer time will gather drops of water on the outside, so far as water on the inside reaches; and the breath of a man blown upon it will manifestly moisten it.

22 Little balls filled with water, Mercury or any other liquor, and thrown into the fire, as also drops of green glass being broken, will fly asunder with a great noise. [*See* Rupert's Drops, p. 16].

23 Neither wine, beer, or any other liquor will make it musty, or change its colour or rust it.

24 A drinking glass partly filled with water, and rubbed on the brim with a wet finger, will yield beautiful notes, higher or lower as the glass is more or less full, and will make the liquor frisk and leap.

Perhaps the most remarkable property of glass is one that escaped inclusion in the foregoing lengthy list: that man can transform with heat a mixture of sand and ashes to produce one of the loveliest materials known. This is so much taken for granted that it is seldom realised how drab and commonplace are the ingredients of which glass is composed. Its appearance and its fascination were summed up by the late W. B. Honey in these words:

'Its beauty never seems to be wholly the result of calculation. Its forms may be designed and controlled, its colour may be named and secured by a percentage of oxides; but beyond all these there is a quality in the material that defies prediction, and the play of light and colour within it, its insubstantial air, and the "pattern of a gesture" which its form so often records, are only the chief elements, perhaps, in the beauty it may assume at the will of the artist.'

**Constituents.** The basic constituents of glass are silica, used in the form of sand, flint or quartz, heated with an alkaline flux, alternatively potash or soda. Pure silica can be melted and used on its own, but in practice this needs an inconveniently high temperature, and the addition of the alkali causes the material to fuse at a more manageable heat.

The silica used by the Egyptians was the sand that was so plentiful in and around their country; the Venetians employed quartz-like white pebbles, and the 17th-century English glass-makers used calcined and powdered flints. In time, however, the latter found that sand was an excellent and more easily prepared alternative; that from Kings Lynn in Norfolk, Alum Bay in the Isle of Wight, Maidstone in Kent, and more recently, Loch Aline on the Sound of Mull, being preferred. Nevertheless, in spite of the change of ingredients the name 'flint glass' remains to this day obstinately and inaccurately current for much English glassware.

Whichever form of silica was used, it had to be prepared carefully: the sand by washing, and the flints by removal of any of a brown or yellow colour, which denoted the probable presence of iron liable to discolour the finished product. For calcination, the wetted flints were heated in a furnace until they were adjudged white throughout. When this state had been reached, they were removed and put immediately into cold water, which made them break down into flakes suitable for reduction to a fine powder.

The alkaline flux used in glass-making has varied from place to place, as well as from time to time. The earliest makers, those in Egypt and thereabouts, made use of natron: a form of soda found deposited naturally in the beds of dried-up lakes, of which there were a number eighty or so miles to the north-west of Cairo.

Later, soda was obtained from marine plants; notably, that known as Glasswort (*Salicornia herbacea*), a lover of seaside salt marshes, which produced a soda-charged ash when it was burned. The plant grew prolifically in Spain, and quantities of the ash were exported from that country under the name of *barilla*. When sent from the Eastern Mediterranean area it was termed *roquetta*.

Venetian glassmakers used barilla from an early date, and in the 17th century it was imported into England. A traveller in Spain in 1621 wrote back:

'I am noe (thanks be to God) come to Alicant, the chief rendezvous I aymed at in Spain, for I am to send hence a commodity called Barilla to Sir Robert Mansell, for making of Chrystall-Glasse, and I have treated with Signor Andriotti, a Genoa merchant, for a good round parcell of it, to the value of 2000 pound . . . This Barilla is a strange kind of vegetable, and it grows nowhere upon the surface of the Earth, in that perfection as here. The Venetians have it hence, and it is a commodity whereby this Maritime Town doth partly subsist, for it is an ingredient that goes to the making of the best Castile Soap. It grows thus: 'tis a round thick Earthy shrub that bears berries like Barbaries, but 'twixt blue and green, it lies close to the ground and when it is ripe they dig it up by the roots, and put it together in Cocks, wher they leave it dry many days like Hey, then they make a pit of a fathom

10

deep in the earth and with an instrument like one of our prongs they take the Tuffs and put fire to them and when the flame comes to the berries they melt and come into an Azure Liquor and fall down into the pit till it be full, then they dam it up, and some days after they open it and find this Barilla-juice turned to a blew stone so hard that it is scarcely malleable.'

The resultant substance, in the form of bluish-grey stones, was described as being 'full of little eyes or holes'.

**1 and 2. Two types of Glasswort** found growing wild in England. LEFT: Prickly Saltwort (*Salsola nali*). RIGHT: Sea Goosefoot (*Chenopodium maritimum*).

Some varieties of Glasswort are native to the British Isles (Figs 1 and 2), where it is found on seashores, especially if muddy. Attempts were made towards the end of the 18th century to grow it here on a commercial scale, but they did not succeed, in spite of offers of prizes made repeatedly from 1770 to 1800.

An alternative flux was potash or pearl-ash: commercial potassium carbonate made from the ashes of burnt wood, the resultant powder being well calcined until it became perfectly white. It was made in Central Europe, and after about 1760 in North America, and sent to England in barrels. Importers complained that it was frequently adulterated by the addition of common salt, which was no particular detriment in glass-making. However, having paid the higher price of potash the buyers, not unnaturally, felt they were being swindled.

Soda makes a glass of light weight that stays plastic when hot for a longer time than one containing potash. It was the basis of most of the wares made in the Mediterranean area and the Venetians, in particular, exploited its bubble-like properties to the fullest. The Germans were the principal makers of potash glass, and the fact that it was less amenable to manipulation when molten caused it to be formed into vessels with thick walls. These were very suitable for ultimate decoration by means of engraving and cutting.

Two other fluxes were used also: saltpetre (nitre) and borax. The former was the principal alkaline ingredient in English glass, but the latter, which was sent from the East Indies under the name of *Tincal*, was expensive. Its high cost restricted its use except in small quantities or in special circumstances.

Other additions of various kinds were made by individual makers, but one in particular, oxide of lead, was introduced in England in the last quarter of the 17th century, and its general adoption gave the glass of this country a distinction enabling it to overcome all competitors. The oxide, usually in the form known as 'red lead', acted not only as a flux, but resulted in material 'less hard and transparent than that made of salts only. But there is in glass of lead a power of reflecting the rays of light of the same nature with that of diamonds, and gives a lustre and brilliant appearance to vessels of round figure not found in the mere glass of salts, where the too great transparency and want of play occasion a deadness of look when seen by the other.'

For perfecting transparency and removing unwanted tints caused by the presence of impurities or by chemical changes during manufacture, nitre and black oxide of manganese were added. The latter, usually known to glass-house workers incorrectly as *magnesia*, produced a purplish stain in the glass which counteracted effectively the green of irremovable iron. Nitre, on the other hand, dealt with the yellow which resulted from the oxide of lead. Both of these ingredients had to be added in carefully regulated quantities; too much of either would have a bad effect. This was especially the case with the manganese, which made a dye so strong that a slight excess of it would stain the whole mass black. Arsenic was sometimes added, to assist the action of manganese.

Whichever ingredients were employed, it was essential for them to be in a thoroughly dry state and to be mixed with care. A preliminary heating in a moderate furnace resulted in a partly-vitrified mass known as *frit*, which was broken into pieces and ground to a powder. If necessary, further ingredients were added to this powdered frit and the whole placed again in a furnace, but this time the heat was raised to the full.

Old authors give some of the recipes commonly used in English glass-houses during the 18th century. Typical are the following:

'Take of the white sand one hundred and twenty pounds, of red lead fifty pounds, of the best pearl-ashes forty pounds, of nitre twenty pounds, and of magnesia five ounces.'

'Take of white sand one hundred and twenty pounds, of the best pearl-ashes thirty five pounds, of red lead forty pounds, of nitre thirteen pounds, of arsenic six pounds, and of magnesia four ounces.'

'Take of the calcined flints or white sand one hundred and twenty pounds, of the best pearl-ashes seventy pounds, of salt-petre ten pounds, of arsenic half a pound, and of magnesia five ounces.'

One important addition may be mentioned: *cullet*. This is

the name for broken glass, which was remelted and frequently formed a proportion of the new material being made. Its presence helped both the fusing and the final appearance of the product. The gathering of cullet was a minor trade; not only was it conserved within the glass-houses, but it was noted as early as 1697 that 'Many hundreds of poor families keep themselves from the Parish by picking up broken glass of all sorts to sell to the Maker'.

**The glass-house.** The glass-house building was conical in shape and rose to a squat chimney (Fig. 3). Within, there

3. An 18th-century glass-house.

would be one or more furnaces, circular structures (Fig. 4) grouped round and fed to a common central stack, each of which had a number of openings, known as *boccas*, round the circumference. Each bocca framed the mouth of a crucible or *pot* in which the glass was made ready, and by which it might be reached by the workmen. One bocca was of much greater size than the others, and through this both the fuel and the crucibles could be introduced or removed.

While the principal or 'working' furnace was used at a white heat, a more moderate one was used for the preliminary fritting, and a small rectangular furnace served for baking

14

**4. A furnace** with men working at the boccas.

enamelled decoration. One of the latter is shown in Fig. 17, copied from an 18th-century engraving. Further, a moderate-temperature oven or furnace was required for annealing—the process of allowing the molten and manipulated glass to

**5. A glass-house pot.**

cool very gradually to normal temperature. This was called the *leer* or *lehr*, and was sometimes built so that it utilised waste heat from the working furnace. Later, it took the form of a long tunnel, through which finished wares were drawn on wheeled iron trucks, making their slow progress from hot to cool. The time taken for annealing to be complete varied with the wares: thick-walled pieces required longer than thin-walled ones. On an average, it would seem that about 24 hours was the minimum time for articles to be left in the leer.

The reason for annealing is to equalise the tension set up in the walls of a vessel or sheet of glass during manufacture. The strain is due to the fact that the outer sides, being in contact with the air, naturally cool more quickly than the internal portion. Failure to carry out the process, or faulty application of it, would result in a material that proved unstable and might, for instance, fly asunder without apparent cause. The glass pellets known as *Prince Rupert's Drops*, the cause of scientific speculation and popular wonder in the past, clearly demonstrate this effect. The Drops were made by letting the molten glass fall into water, the resulting objects being pear-shaped. If hit on the fatter end there would be no result and the Drop was unharmed, but if the smaller part or stem was chipped or broken the whole exploded into powder.

Glass-makers all began by firing with wood, but in England the early 17th century saw a fast-increasing shortage of suitable timber; much of it of greater importance for ship-building than for providing heat. Encouraged by Parliament, attempts were made to use coal in its place and these quickly proved successful.

The manufacture of glass-making pots was a specialised task. They were formed of selected clay, that from the Stourbridge area of Worcestershire being especially suitable, and it had to be freed from any gravel or stones. After being pulverised and sieved, it was mixed with ground-up material from broken pots, and moulded by hand to the required shape. They were annealed for some days at red heat before being put to use, and their careful making was a matter of great importance. A pot that fractured when full of molten

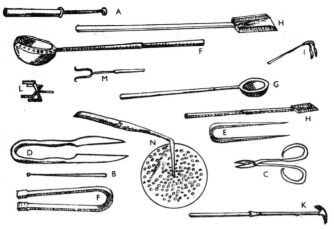

**6. Tools** used by late 17th- and early 18th-century glass-makers.

glass, or *metal*, caused big losses in material, time and money. Fig. 5 illustrates a typical pot, the opening at the upper side being for the entry of raw materials, as well as for the removal of them when melted. It stood about 40 in. in height, with a diameter of some 30 in. at the base.

When a pot was worn out or cracked its removal from the furnace proved a hazardous job, for the fire was not usually extinguished for the purpose. The cover was taken from the large bocca, and the workmen used iron tools as well as their hands at the task. An 18th-century author wrote: 'But before they set about this rough work, those who do it clothe themselves in a sort of skins in the shape of a pantaloon, which they make as wet as possible, and which covers them all over except the eyes; and for them they make use of glass to see to guide themselves. And indeed without such a sort of clothing it would be almost impossible to manage this change of the pots, by reason of the long time it would otherwise take up . . .'

**Making vessels.** The most artistic branch of glass-making is the forming of hollow vessels, which realise the greatest possibilities of the material and at the same time reveal its beauty to the fullest extent. Their creation relies both on the ductility of the molten metal and the skill of the workmen who exploit it. Molten glass becomes not unlike treacle in consistency, and adheres not only to iron, but to itself; also, it retains over a considerable range of temperature a semi-plastic state in which it can be worked. These attributes are exploited fully and form the basis of its manufacturing techniques.

Once a mass of the metal is withdrawn from the pot it begins to cool fairly rapidly to a temperature at which it can be worked. Its property of allowing constant manipulation without signs of stress in the way of cracks and breaks, permits the most complicated results to be achieved with the aid of the simplest tools.

Some of the instruments in use in the late 17th century are illustrated in Fig. 6. They were described at the time as follows:

'The hollow pipe marked A serves to blow the glass; it ought to be of iron, with a little wooden handle on the top.

'The rod marked B ought to be of iron, but not hollow; this serves to take up the glass after it is blown, and cut off the former, so that there remains nothing to do, but to perfect it [this is the *pontil* or *puntee*].

'The scissors marked C are those which serve to cut the glass when it comes off from the first hollow iron (A), when it is given to the master-workman.

'The shears marked D serve to cut and shape the great glasses, as also the lesser, to open them and make them more capacious.

18

'The instruments marked E serve to finish the work [known as *procellas*].

'The great ladle marked F is of iron, the end of the handle being only done over with wood; it is with this you take out the metal of the great pot when it is refined, and put it into the little ones for the work-men.

'The little ladle marked G is also of iron, and covered with wood at the handle; this serves for skimming the metal, and taking off Alcalick Salt which swims on the top.

'The great and little shovels, or peels, marked H, and which are hollow, having the edges turned up all round except at the end, serve only to take up the great glasses.

'The less is called the little shovel, and they make use of one like this to draw out the coals and ashes of the furnace where the fire is made.

'The hooked fork marked I serves to stir the matter in the pots; it ought to be all of iron except the handle.

'The rake marked K is also of iron, and the handle of wood, it serves to stir the matter, as also to move about the frit in the first oven.

'The instrument marked L is for making chamber-pots.

'The fork marked M is made also of iron, and the handle of wood; there are of them of several bignesses, they serve to carry the glass-works into the upper oven [the leer] to cool them. They make use also of forks in glass-houses, when they change the pots in the furnace.

'The great ladle marked N is of brass, and hollow, full of holes about the bigness of a pea; its handle towards the bottom is of iron, and the top of wood. This ladle serves to take off the Alcalick salt from the kettles, as fast as the lee evaporates.'

Also used was the *chair* (Fig. 7), in which the master-workman sat down to his work and used the pair of flat-topped arms on which to rotate pontil or blow-pipe. His tools hung conveniently beside him, and immediately in front was a bucket for cullet.

The constant rotation of the heated 'bubble' of glass was an important feature of its working. The motion given to it

**7. A Gaffer in the Chair.**

by the *gaffer* in the chair effectually prevented it from collapsing under its own weight, and ensured a symmetrical and perfectly circular shape. The term *chair* was applied also to the small team of men who worked together on any job. The

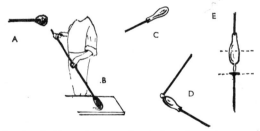

**8. A wineglass in the making.** A: the gather of metal. B: marvering. C: the paraison. D: adding metal for forging the stem. E: ready for cutting from blowing-iron and pontil.

chief of them occupied the chair and was assisted by a *servitor* and a *footmaker* and, in addition, a youngster, known as a *taker-in*, who carried finished work from the gaffer to the leer.

The making of a wineglass is a typical example of the processes involved, which are illustrated here in Fig. 8. The footmaker began by dipping his blow-pipe into the mouth of the pot and withdrawing it with sufficient metal adhering to its end (A). He then blew into it and rolled it to and fro on a table of smooth iron called a *marver* (B): *marvering* it thus to remove inequalities on the surface and to shape the mass roughly, in which form it is known as a *paraison* (C). He blew it into a bubble of the required size, checked the diameter

**9. Wooden clapper, palette or battledore.** **10. Stuck shank glass:** made in three parts. **11. Straw stem glass:** made in two parts, with the stem drawn from the bowl.

with a pair of callipers or other gauge, and adjusted it until it was correct. Then the servitor added a small blob of metal to the end of the bowl and *forged* the stem (D). The process was repeated for making the foot, which was shaped with the aid of a pair of wooden boards (*clappers* or *palettes*, Fig. 9). This resulted in a three-piece or 'stuck shank' glass (Fig. 10), but an alternative two-piece example could be made by drawing the stem from the base of the bowl. This was known as a 'straw stem' (Fig 11).

A pontil was then attached to the foot by means of a dab of metal, and the mouth of the wineglass cut from the blow-pipe by touching it with a drop of water or a wetted metal tool where the break was wanted. A sharp tap on the blow-pipe spread the resultant crack completely around the circumference. The rough edge of the bowl was trimmed accurately with shears, and smoothed by further re-heating at the furnace-mouth. Finally, the pontil was broken off to leave the well-known mark; a mark that is present on any glass made before about 1780 and will be found on many made subsequent to that date (Fig. 208, p. 195).

The entire series of operations was performed with dexterity; as the metal cools it becomes difficult, and finally impossible, to work, and then has to be re-heated. This is done constantly during manufacture, so that the portion of a piece being worked is kept in a conveniently plastic state. Only when it is sufficiently soft can it be drawn, sheared or otherwise managed.

Decoration of various kinds could be added at this stage of the making. Strings of clear or of coloured glass could be 'trailed' on the surface where required, and the familiar rings on the necks of many decanters were applied in this manner (Fig. 12). The ornamentation known in the 17th century as 'nipt diamond waies' was produced with the aid of a pair of tongs, or procellas (Figs 13 and 6E), and applied flat discs, stamped with simple patterns and known as *prunts* (Fig. 14), were a common form of decoration.

**Millefiore.** The making of *millefiore* (literally: thousand flowers) and similar effects was basically simple and relied on the skill of the workers and the properties of the material. Millefiore, which reached its ultimate development with 19th-century French glass paperweights (p. 262), was known to the Egyptians and Romans and was much used by Venetian glass-workers.

The ductility of molten glass allows it to be drawn out into the finest of threads; so fine, indeed, that cloth has been (and is) woven from it. Additionally, if a pattern is introduced

**12. Ringing** the neck of a decanter. **13. An 18th-century English tankard** 'nipt diamond waies.' **14. Prunts on goblet stem.**

prior to the elongation, this pattern will remain constant in scale as the reduction in size continues. The process is, in fact, similar to that for the making of peppermint rock 'with the name all the way through', a sweetmeat that provides one of the pleasures and one of the mysteries of childhood; for how was it made?

The miniature patterns in millefiore glass were each created individually in the form of a rod or *cane* (Fig. 15). They

**15. Two cane patterns.**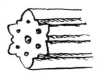

were constructed in the following manner; the central subject was first made from a piece of glass of the selected colour. It was dipped into clear glass, marvered, and to its circumference were added rods at equal distances. A further coating of clear glass returned the cane again to a circular section, and

23

then the shaped rods, which had been made in a mould, were added and a further coating of clear or coloured glass completed the whole. Each separate piece of the pattern could be in a contrasting colour or white, and there was no limit to the number of components that might be assembled in this way. Finally, the whole was re-heated and drawn out until it was reduced in diameter to the size required for the work in hand; a pontil was attached at either end and men holding each of them walked slowly in opposite directions stretching the rod as they went.

**Latticino.** This is responsible for much of the well-merited fame of Venetian glass. A general description of the making of the material, which is also aptly named *lace* or *filigree glass*, is as follows:

'Canes of coloured filigree and transparent colourless glass are arranged around the interior of a circular metal or earthenware mould. They are heated near the furnace, and when they can be touched by hot glass, a bubble of clear glass is blown into the middle; to this the canes adhere, and the whole being taken out of the mould, a band of glass is placed over the canes now forming the exterior surface of the cylindrical mass. It is then fashioned in the fire in the usual way into any form that may be desired. An appearance of greater intricacy could be obtained by welding two cylinders together, the one inside the other, and of which the lines of the canes ran in contrary directions. At each crossing of the canes a bubble of air would be captured, and repeat itself at regular intervals according to the form which the mass would be made to assume.'

The white- and colour-twist stems of wine-glasses were made in a similar manner. The 'twists' being placed equidistantly round a core of clear glass, dipped into more clear metal, and the whole twisted and elongated to produce the desired pattern.

The air-bubble trapped in the upper part of many wine-glass stems is none other than its name implies: an imprisoned air-bubble. It is an ornament that served sometimes as the beginning of another; for from it grew the air-twist stem. This was formed by entrapping a bubble, and drawing and twisting it in the same manner as was done for white- and colour-twist stems.

**Crystallo-Ceramie.** Another type of decoration which, like millefiore, is widely known from its use in the form of glass paperweights, is the *cameo incrustation*; known alternatively as *Crystallo-Ceramie* or *sulphide*. Small figures or other orna-ments were made of a special ceramic composition which, when coated in clear glass, appeared brilliantly mirror-like. The pro-cess was used on the Continent first, and copied in England early in the 19th century. As well as paperweights, goblets and other articles were decorated with sulphides, and were occasionally coloured and inscribed prior to being embedded.

**Moulding.** Moulding as a method of decorating glass was in use from the earliest times, the molten material being pressed onto moulds of stone or clay in which the required pattern was rendered in intaglio. Flat plaques with raised patterns, as well as saucers and bowls, were made in this manner, but all had to be designed so that there was no undercutting to prevent removal of the finished piece from the mould. The Roman glass-workers added raised ribbing to some of their pieces by means of pincers, which were used swiftly and ac-curately before the article cooled. The result is the so-called *pillar-moulding* (Fig. 57, p. 63).

With the introduction of blowing, moulds remained in use and were made in two or three pieces, to be assembled and taken apart as required. Eventually they were of metal and fitted with hinges. The following is an old account of the process as applied to the making of wine-bottles, for which it was particularly suitable:

'Six people are employed at this task; one, called a gatherer, dips the end of an iron tube, about five feet long, previously made red-hot, into the pot of melted metal, turns the rod round so as to surround it with glass, lifts it out to cool a little, and then dips and turns it round again; and so in succession till a ball is formed on its end sufficient to make the required bottle. He then hands it to the blower, who rolls the plastic lump of glass on a smooth stone or cast-iron plate, till he brings it to the very end of the tube; he next introduces the pear-shaped ball into an open brass or cast-iron mould, shuts this together by pressing a pedal with his foot, and

16. A wine-bottle seal.

holding his tube vertically, blows through it, so as to expand the cooling glass into the form of the mould. Whenever he takes his foot from the pedal-lever, the mould spontaneously opens out into two halves, and falls asunder by its bottom hinge. He then lifts the bottle up at the end of the rod, and transfers it to the finisher, who, touching the glass-tube at the end of the pipe with a cold iron, cracks off the bottle smoothly at its mouth-ring. The finished bottles are immediately piled up in the hot annealing arch, where they are afterwards allowed to cool slowly for 24 hours at least.'

The seals found on wine-bottles were made by impressing a small pad of molten glass with an engraved metal disc, in much the same manner as sealing a letter or parcel with wax.

Some impressions of these seals, which were used by the Romans and later in 17th-century England, are so clear that the guide-lines drawn on the brass by the engraver can be seen without difficulty (Fig. 16).

Mould-blowing was employed occasionally for such purposes as forming fluted patterns round the bodies of jugs and decanters. One of its drawbacks was that the interior of a vessel was rendered uneven: the raised pattern on the outside was reproduced as a concavity within. However, it was a step forward in the search for more output with less labour and at a lower price.

**Pressing.** Press-moulding was a mechanical process and greatly accelerated the production of cheap wares. The method was as follows: dies were cut in metal with the shaping and pattern of the inside and outside of the article to be made; they were fitted to the pressing machine, and a pre-determined quantity of molten glass placed between them. When the jaws of the press were closed, the glass was squeezed between the dies and took both shape and pattern from them. Dishes and open bowls were the most popular articles made in this way, and they could be given a passable imitation of cutting. The pattern was often placed on the underside or inside of the pieces and it glittered acceptably when viewed through the smooth front. This was brightened by re-heating at the mouth of the furnace; a process named *fire-polishing*.

The casting of glass was practised from the time of its earliest invention, but the process has not played a significant part in the development of domestic glassware. Pouring the molten metal into shaped or carved moulds had a very limited application until the French used it for the making of plate-glass (p. 40).

**Colour.** Glass was coloured, probably in the first place in attempting to imitate natural stones, from the earliest times. It was found that the addition of certain minerals would produce various tints, and the medieval glass-makers exercised their skill to produce the brilliant effects still to be seen in numerous church windows. The various recipes employed in the past have usually died with their inventors, who kept their knowledge strictly to themselves and did everything possible to ensure complete secrecy.

In 1751 a traveller in the Midlands noted in a letter:

'We came to Stourbridge, famous for its glass manufactures, especially for its coloured glass, with which they make painted windows, which is here coloured in the liquid [i.e. in the molten state], of all the capital shades, and, if I mistake not, is a secret which they have here'.

At about that date instructions for making glass in most of the colours of the spectrum were published by Robert Dossie, who printed recipes for imitating many kinds of stones. He warned his readers that great care was essential when preparing and mixing the ingredients, otherwise disaster might ensue. Dossie related what had occurred a few years earlier when there was a big demand 'for all kinds of ornaments decorated with false stones for the Spanish West-Indian trade', and lapidaries eagerly bought the coloured glass introduced by an English maker in place of material that formerly had had to be imported at a higher cost. However, before very long, 'all turned foul, with a dull scum on the surface, and little specks, which eat down into the substance; and took away the smoothness, as well as the lustre'. As a result, all the work that had been expended in cutting, polishing and mounting the glass 'stones' was completely wasted.

The Romans were adept at covering a vessel with a layer of glass of a contrasting colour; the Portland Vase (Fig. 64, p. 66) being the most noteworthy surviving example of the technique. *Overlaying*, which is known also as *casing* or *flashing*, was revived widely during the 19th century, when a piece might have two or more colours superimposed on the original. One of them would probably be white, which, cut at an angle and between two others, helped the upper and lower layers to gain in contrast with each other. A variation of the process, but one in which only a single colour was overlaid, involved staining the surface, which could then be cut or etched away where needed to reveal the underlying clear crystal.

**Pâte De Verre.** Glass, white or coloured, has also been used in the form of a ground-up powder moistened with water and gum to make a paste. This mixture could then be moulded, or even turned on the wheel like pottery, and when dry could be heated and fused.

**Bottle glass.** One further type of coloured glass deserves a mention at this juncture: bottle glass. This impure material assumed some importance in England during the period of glass taxation; whereas clear 'flint' glass paid duty at the full rate, bottle glass paid only a proportion. The metal could be made from simple ingredients, as the following recipe shows:

'Take of wood-ashes two hundred pounds, and of sand one hundred pounds. Mix them thoroughly well by grinding them. This is the due proportion where the sand is good, and the wood-ashes are used without any other addition: but there are instances of sand of so kindly a nature for vitrification, that a greater proportion may be used.'

Another mixture comprised sand and wood-ashes augmented by a quantity of ground or broken clinkers 'from furnaces or forges'.

## ORNAMENTATION

**Cutting.** The types of decoration already mentioned were added during the actual manufacturing of the article, while the glass was hot, but others were applied to the annealed and finished piece. The most important and best-known is cutting: in which the surface is literally cut into sharply angled patterns that scintillate with light.

An early Victorian author has described cutting methods and materials that vary little, if at all, from those in use during preceding centuries. He wrote the following, which is lengthy, but clear:

'The cutting shop should be a spacious long apartment, furnished with numerous skylights, having the grinding and polishing lathes arranged right under them, which are set in motion by a steam-engine or water-wheel at one end of the building. . . .

'Some [of the different discs for cutting] are made of fine sandstone or polishing slate, from 8 to 10 inches in diameter, and from $\frac{3}{4}$ to $\frac{1}{2}$ in thick. They must be carefully turned and polished at the lathe, not only upon their rounded but upon their flat face, in order to grind and polish in their turn the flat and curved surfaces of glass vessels. Other discs of the same diameter, but only $\frac{3}{4}$ of an inch thick, are made of cast tin truly turned, and serve for polishing the vessels previously ground; a third set consist of sheet iron from $\frac{1}{8}$ to $\frac{1}{2}$ an inch thick, and 12 inches in diameter, and are destined to cut grooves in glass by the aid of sand and water. Small discs of well-hammered copper from $\frac{1}{2}$ to 3 inches diameter, whose circumference is sometimes flat, and sometimes concave or convex, serve to make all sorts of delineations upon glass by means of emery and oil. Lastly, there are rods of copper or brass furnished with small hemispheres from $\frac{1}{24}$ to $\frac{1}{4}$ of an inch in diameter, to excavate round hollows in glass. Wooden discs are also employed for polishing, made of white wood cut across the grain, as also of cork.

'The cutting of deep indentations, and of grooves, is usually performed by the iron disc with sand and water, which are allowed constantly to trickle down from a wooden hopper placed right over it, and furnished with a wooden stopple or plug at the apex, to regulate by its greater or less looseness the flow of the grinding materials. Finer markings which are to remain without lustre, are made with the small copper discs, emery, and oil. The polishing is effected by the edge of the tin disc, which is from time to time moistened with putty and water. The wooden disc is also employed for this purpose with putty, colcothar, or washed tripoli. For fine delineations, the glass is first traced over with some coloured varnish to guide the hand of the cutter.

'In grinding and facetting crystal glass, the deep grooves are first cut, for example the cross lines, with the iron disc and rounded edge, by means of sand and water. That disc is $\frac{1}{6}$ of an inch thick, and more or less in diameter, according to the curvature of the surface, the grooves may be widened. These roughly cut parts must be next smoothed down with the sandstone disc and water, and then polished with the wooden disc about $\frac{1}{2}$ an inch thick, to whose edge the workman applies, from time to time, a bag of fine linen containing some ground pumice moistened with water. When the cork or wooden disc edged with hat felt is used for polishing, putty or colcothar is applied to it. The above several processes in a large manufactory are usually committed to several workmen on the principle of division of labour, so that each may become expert in his department.'

The actual cutting was performed by the medium in use—principally sand and water—and the revolving wheel kept it in motion to do its work. In the same way, the final polish was gained by using the softest of agents. The putty referred to in this connection is not to be confused with the common builders' putty composed of powdered whiting and linseed oil, but was prepared from calcined tin. Colcothar is the pink powder better known as Jeweller's Rouge or Crocus. Tripoli, used also for polishing, was a fine earth found near the North

African town which gave it its name, and was known alternatively as Rottenstone.

**Engraving.** Effective decoration could be accomplished by engraving, or scratching, with a diamond. This did not go far below the surface and was therefore particularly applicable to the bowls of wine-glasses and similarly thin-walled pieces. A variation of the technique was stippling tiny dots, which were applied with great delicacy to form the pattern. This was done in such a way that the rendering of shadows was by leaving the glass untouched in contrast to the diamond-engraved highlights. The effect has been described with some justice as looking as though the design had been 'breathed upon the glass.'

**Etching.** Etching, engraving with acid, was greatly developed for the quick and cheap decoration of glassware during the 19th century. The article was coated with a special varnish, and when it had dried a design was scratched through it. The piece was dipped for a suitable length of time in hydrofluoric acid, the parts bare of varnish would allow penetration and the pattern was eaten into the glass. Finally, the remaining varnish was removed.

**Enamelling.** Glass was painted with specially compounded colours fixed by a re-firing that took place at a low temperature not affecting the article itself. The colours or enamels were prepared in the form of fine powders containing a proportion of borax or some other flux to ensure easy melting, and were mixed with an oil so that they could be applied by brush.

The firing was done in a Muffle Furnace of the type shown in Fig. 17. In this (A) is the ash-hole and draught; (B) the fire-place; (C) iron bars on which the pan (E) rests; (D) opening for the insertion and removal of articles; (E) earthenware pan in which wares rest while firing; and (F) two lids that are cemented (or *luted*) in position when the furnace is working. The 18th-century description of it reads:

'This furnace must be square, of good brick, two foot high, and so much every way, and have three divisions; the undermost for the ashes must be six inches high, the middle one for the fire and to put in the fuel must be six inches high, and have its opening (B) five or six inches broad and four deep, with a good iron grate of three square bars of iron which cross the furnace and divide it in the middle to support the earthen stove (E) hereafter described; the uppermost division

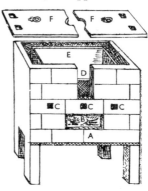

17. **Muffle furnace** for enamelling.

must be a foot high, with a little opening (D) about the middle before of four inches high, and two wide, to put in and draw out the ware a baking, to see if it be well done.

'In this uppermost division must be put the aforesaid stove of good fire-proof crucible earth, the bottom an inch and a half thick, and from thence up to the brim ten inches full; it must be square as the furnace, and have two inches room on all sides, that the fire may flame round about it to bake the work, therefore placed exactly in the middle of the furnace.'

Caution was needed during the firing process to ensure that

no damage was sustained by the articles. Test pieces, small fragments of glass bearing samples of the enamels, were put in with the work and removed from time to time to record progress. As soon as the colours had melted sufficiently the temperature was lowered, either by removing the pieces from the furnace or by letting the fire go out. In either case it was essential for the drop in temperature to be gradual and for annealing to take place either in the furnace itself or in a leer.

**Gilding.** The decoration of glass with gold is highly effective, and has been practised in many countries over a long period of time. Various methods were used, of which one was given in a book published in 1701:

'Moisten the Glass you design to Gild every where with Gum-water; and when half dry, lay on the Leaf Gold, letting it dry.

'This done, wash all the gilded part with Water in which Borax has been dissolved; and so dust it well with impalpable Pouder of white [clear] Glass.

'Afterwards set it into the Furnace, first in a very gentle heat; and encrease the heat by little and little till the Glass becomes red hot, and the Pouder on the Gilding is melted and runs.

'Then draw it leisurely to the mouth of the Furnace, and let it cool leisurely; so will your Glass be admirably Gilded, not to be hurt by Scraping, force of Weather, Heat, Cold or Age it self.'

Alternatively, the gold, also beaten skilfully into the thinnest of leaves, could be applied to a surface painted with varnish. This was not durable, and in course of time the work has usually disappeared. Again, gold in the form of a fine powder could be mixed with honey, painted on, and then lightly fired. Porcelain was often gilded in this latter manner, and not only was it hard-wearing, but it could be given a high polish with an agate or a dog's tooth burnisher.

*Verre églomisé* was made by the Romans and revived at later dates. It takes the form of a piece of glass with a painting drawn on the reverse of it in black outline against a background of shining gold. It was made by affixing gold leaf to the underside of the glass, incising the design with a pointed tool and then painting over the back with black or coloured paint so that this showed through the places where the leaf had been scored. The back was usually protected in one of several ways: with a coat of varnish, by fusing powdered glass over it, or by sticking or fusing over it a piece of thin glass.

It acquired its name towards the end of the 18th century, when a Paris art dealer and auctioneer, Jean-Baptiste Glomy, popularised the framing of prints and drawings within a border of black and gold painted on the inside of the protective glass. Thus displayed, they became known in France as *églomisées*, and the name has been used since then to designate all kinds of engraved gold work executed on the back of glass. The Roman works are known as *fondi d'oro*.

Glasses with a type of *verre églomisé* decoration were made in Bohemia during the first part of the 18th century, and examples are known as *Zwischengoldgläser* (literally: gold-between glasses). For this ingenious work, a specially shaped glass vessel was decorated on the outside with a pattern in engraved gold, and another glass was made so that it fitted accurately outside the first and protected the pattern. The pieces were cemented together and finished with a disc in the base. The work was done with such care and ingenuity that the method of making is scarcely discernible (Fig. 18).

**Mirror pictures.** A different process was used by the mid-18th-century Chinese painters who produced *mirror-pictures*, mainly intended for export to Europe. They took a mirror, in most cases one that had been sent out from the West, and scraped away the silvering from the portion they wanted to paint. On this latter part was painted from the back

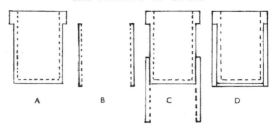

**18. Making Zwischengoldgläser.** A: the inner glass decorated on the outside. B: outer casing to protect the decoration. C: A and B partly assembled. D: Fully assembled and with the disc in the base (*See* also Fig. 170, p. 153).

whatever subject was desired in either water-colours or oils. In most instances the sky of a landscape scene was left in silver to contrast with the brilliantly colourful foreground.

Other Chinese paintings were executed on plain sheets of unsilvered glass, but again from the back. In both types of work it must be remembered that the artist worked in reverse: the embroidery of a costume, for instance, would have to be painted on the glass before the addition of the actual fabric, so as to appear correct when seen from the front. Likewise, the high colouring on a person's cheek would have to be applied before the cheek itself was painted. In normal painting on canvas or paper such detail was added afterwards, and to do this in the opposite order, as well as to reverse left and right, must have needed great patience and considerable skill. Some work of this type was executed in European countries, but it very rarely attained the high standard of excellence of the Chinese.

**Transfer-pictures.** One further method of picture-making deserves a mention: the so-called *transfer-pictures*, or *glass-pictures*. For these, a piece of crown glass with its characteristic 'wavy' surface was coated on one side with varnish. When this had dried to a tacky state, an engraving was placed face downwards on it and smoothed carefully to remove air-bubbles. The whole was left until the varnish hardened completely, and then the paper was wetted and rubbed away gently with the fingers. This process was continued until little more than the ink impression on the surface of the print remained; afterwards, in the words of an instructor of 1680, 'so paint it with your colours as your fancy shall direct you'.

## SHEET AND PLATE GLASS

**Crown sheet.** A number of methods were used for producing sheets of glass for use in house and carriage windows, or for silvering, as looking-glasses. The *Crown* or *Normandy* process involved the blowing of a large bubble on the iron, the bubble was then opened and spread into a flat disc by rotating it rapidly at the furnace-mouth (Figs 19 and 20). This not only increased the diameter of the disc, but the heat of the fire gave it a brilliant surface.

Circular sheets measuring as much as five feet in diameter were made in this manner, but with a central bulge and pontil mark. This portion was known as the *bull's eye* or *bullion* and although used sometimes for glazing purposes it was generally cullet. The remaining area of the glass circle was cut into usable sizes, but it is distinguished by the wavy concentric markings in it caused by the rotation. The complete sheet was known as a *table*, and these were sold by merchants by the *case*; a case consisting of any number from 24 to 45 tables, varying from place to place according to local custom.

Crown glass was used for house windows, in furniture, or wherever thin material could be employed. Its high gloss usually distracted attention from its characteristically uneven surface, and it was too thin to withstand grinding flat. Thus, it was unsuitable for use as looking-glass or where a true plane was essential. The size of piece that could be cut was

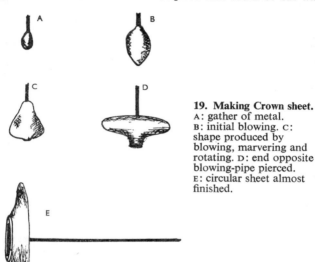

**19. Making Crown sheet.**
A: gather of metal.
B: initial blowing. C: shape produced by blowing, marvering and rotating. D: end opposite blowing-pipe pierced.
E: circular sheet almost finished.

limited by the size of disc that could be manhandled successfully, and by the amount remaining for cutting after the bull's eye had been removed.

**Broad sheet.** *Broad, Lorraine* or *Muff* glass was made as follows:

'The workman first blows the lump of glass into the shape of an oblong pear, the length of which must be nearly equal to the length of the intended plate, and its diameter such that the circumference, when developed, will be equal to the breadth of the plate. He now rests the blowing-iron on a stool or iron bar, while an assistant with a pointed iron pierces a hole into the extreme end of the pear, in the line of the blowing-pipe. This opening is then enlarged, by introducing the blade of a pair of spring-tongs, while the glass is turned round; and by skilful management, the end of the pear is eventually opened out into a cylindrical mouth. The workman

**20. Rotating a Crown sheet** at the furnace-mouth.

next mounts upon a stool, and holds the blowing-iron perpendicularly. The blown cylinder is now cracked off, a punto rod of iron having been previously stuck to its one end, to form a spindle for working the other by. This rod has a flat disc on its end, or three prongs, which being dipped in melted glass, are applied to the mouth of the cylinder. By this as a handle, the glass cone is carried to the fire, and the narrow end being heated, is next opened by spring tongs, and formed into a cylinder of the same size as the other end. The cylinder thus equalised is next cracked or slit down in its side with a pair of shears, laid on a smooth copper plate, detached from the iron rod, spread out by heat into a plane surface, and finally annealed.'

An alternative sequence of operations is shown in Fig. 21.

Advantages of the Broad process were that it produced a material of a greater and more even thickness and with a smoother surface and larger area than the crown method.

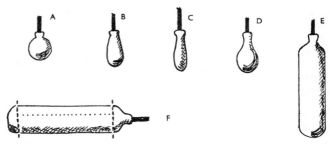

21. (A to F). **Broad sheet**: successive stages in manufacture.

The latter, however, gave a glass with a brilliant sheen that was ready for sale without further processing once it was annealed. Broad glass was dulled from contact with the metal or stone table on which the cylinder was unfurled, and required the further operation of polishing before it could be used.

**Cast plate.** Plate glass was cast, and this process competed with the broad in supplying the thicker varieties used, for instance, for looking-glasses. For casting, the molten material was poured on to a metal-bedded table from a container swung on a jib from the furnace. The table had raised edges the height of which determined the thickness of the glass to be cast. As soon as the molten glass was on the table, it was spread evenly and swiftly by means of a large roller supported on the table-edges, and when sufficiently cooled was removed to the annealing oven. The whole operation was carried out with a military precision, and, in a well-ordered workshop, might take only a few minutes from start to finish.

Again, as with broad glass, the product was dull with an uneven surface, and translucent rather than transparent. To correct this and produce plates with optically correct surfaces, the glass had to be ground and polished. First, however, it was examined carefully for irremovable air-bubbles or other defects, and the remaining perfect areas were cut into suitable sizes.

The percentage of waste during manufacture was often high, but it was possible to make very large plates with success. Although it was claimed that a plate measuring 82 by 48 inches had been made by the broad process, this was quite exceptional and such examples were usually cast.

**Grinding and polishing.** Grinding and polishing were achieved by affixing the rough plate to a flat table by means of plaster, and then rubbing over the surface a mixture of abrasive and water. This was applied by means of a flat piece of glass or wood, and as the process continued the abrasive was made finer. In the end, the softest of polishes, such as crocus, was rubbed on with pads made from hat-felt. Each side of the glass was treated in this manner, and, when correctly done, the surfaces would be perfectly even and highly polished. The work was performed mainly by hand until the 19th century, and although various machines were invented from the 1670s onwards they were seldom completely successful for one reason or another.

**Silvering.** Looking-glass plates, once they were ground and polished, required to be silvered or *foiled*. Methods varied in detail, but these instructions of 1740 were probably followed widely:

'A thin blotting paper is spread on a table, and sprinkled with a fine chalk; and then a fine *lamina* or leaf of tin, called *foil*, is laid over the paper; upon this *mercury* is poured, which is equally to be distributed over the leaf with a hare's foot or cotton. Over the leaf is laid a clean paper, and over that the glass plate.

'The glass plate is press'd down with the right hand, and the paper is drawn gently out with the left; which being done, the plate is covered with a thicker paper, and loaden with a greater weight, that the superfluous *mercury* may be driven out, and the *tin* adhere more closely to the glass.

'When it is dried, the weight is removed, and the looking-glass is complete.'

Bevelled edges were often given to the plate while it was being ground, and when silvering took place these were protected by shaped pieces of wood placed on the table. Unless the edges were supported they were liable to be damaged when the surplus mercury was squeezed out.

After about 1840, a different process was used. It had been discovered that a quicker and cheaper method of silvering resulted from depositing on the glass a thin film of real silver. The finished product was, to all intents and purposes, identical, and the dangers of using mercury were avoided at the same time as costs were reduced.

The making of high-quality sheet for silvering as looking-glasses remained for long a monopoly of the Venetians, who employed the Broad process. By the end of the 17th century, however, the French developed casting sufficiently to oust all competitors (*see* page 258). The high cost of their products, together with import duty and transport charges, led the English to set up their own casting works. This was built at St Helens, Lancashire, and in 1773 the British Cast Plate Glass Manufacturers commenced operating. After various vicissitudes the company was absorbed in 1901 by Pilkington Brothers who, in 1959, introduced a completely new method of sheet glass manufacture. The product is known as Float glass because it is made by literally floating the molten metal on the surface of a bath of molten tin, and by a further process the 130-inch wide ribbon of glass can be coloured by an electro-chemical method.

# CHAPTER II

# Egyptian Glass

The actual discovery of glass, how it might be made and fashioned, is unrecorded. It took place so long ago that not only is the name of the inventor forgotten, but it is not certain exactly where in the then civilised portion of the globe the discovery occurred. Writing in about the year 30 A.D.,

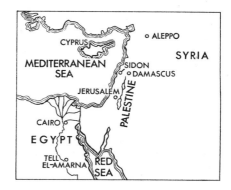

**22. Egypt and the Eastern Mediterranean.**

Pliny, the Greek historian, described some Phoenician merchants who had encamped at the mouth of a river in Syria, where they lit a fire and used some of their ship's cargo of natron (a variety of soda) on which to support their cooking-pot. The heat caused sand and soda to fuse and form glass, and from this completely accidental beginning grew the many varieties of the material that now exist.

43

This story is not accepted in its entirety, but some such happening may well have taken place at an early era in one of the countries of the Middle East. As Pliny wrote more than two thousand years after the suggested event, it is too much to expect that such a lapse of time would leave it unencumbered by additions and emendations.

Alternatively, it has been suggested that the firing of pottery produced a glaze accidentally, and that men then attempted to make a glaze on its own. This was done in the first instance by chipping off the glaze from finished pieces of pottery and re-melting it, until in due course a less involved method was found and glass was made in its own right. The earliest known pieces of glass are coloured, as is the contemporaneous pottery, so it is not impossible that glass manufacture could have started in this manner.

Whatever its start, finds made in Egypt make it not improbable that glass was first made in that country, and if they were not its inventors, then the Egyptians were certainly its earliest exploiters. It has been pointed out that the country enjoyed a long period of freedom from outside interference; the surrounding areas of desert keeping potential marauders at bay, while the southern boundary was narrow and defensible. The land enjoyed greater fertility than it does today; natural irrigation was more widespread and rainfall heavier, trees would have been more plentiful and provided ample supplies of fuel for the furnaces. Not least, sand and soda were at hand.

The oldest surviving examples of glass found in Egypt date from about the year 2,000 B.C., and take the forms of beads and small amulets made in imitation of those previously carved in precious stone. Earlier, pottery beads covered in a blue-tinted glaze—in reality the latter is no more than glass—had been produced successfully, and experiment enabled the makers to omit the clay body and achieve a more convincing effect. In this manner, such prized stones as turquoise, lapis lazuli and cornelian were copied, and for many centuries it is probable that the man-made pieces were esteemed no less highly than the natural ones.

While small amulets were formed simply by pouring or pressing the heated glass into carved stone moulds (Fig. 23), beads were made in a number of different ways, varying in

**23. Moulded turquoise-green mask,**
1500–1400 B.C. Ht 2 in.

method according to their date and their place of manufacture. For the earliest and most simple, pieces of suitable length were cut from a heated glass rod, and after being reheated each bead could be decorated by pressing into it threads and spots in contrasting colours. More ambitious makers formed the decoration into grotesque human faces by suitable arrangements.

Alternatively, layers of glass in different colours were fused together and then carefully wrapped round a piece of iron wire, so that the final product was a bead with a neat zigzag design. As a variation of the last method, coloured glass threads were coiled round a length of wire, and this was done so skilfully that an unbroken surface resulted after polishing. Only when broken specimens reveal the internal coils is it possible to conclude how they were made.

Glass beads vary as much in their colours, and combinations of colours, as in their methods of construction. Owing to their widespread popularity they were exported over great distances; a circumstance aided by their small size and light weight. As it is not unusual to discover specimens many thousands of miles from their probable place of manufacture, discussion and research are often necessary to determine with certainty the origin and date of finds.

Beads first inspired the so-called *millefiori* (literally, 'thousand flowers') technique, known also as *mosaic* (*see* p. 22). When drawn out to the required thickness, lengths were cut off and bored to make beads.

The ancient Egyptians seem neither to have desired nor admired clear glass, or even pale tints, and little of it has survived. Liking rich colour and favouring the imitation of stones like turquoise, red jasper and lapis lazuli, they preferred blues, yellows, reds and browns in strong shades. These were often used in contrast to one another, but the finished product seldom bears an obvious resemblance to any natural material. The liking for the latter shows, however, in the frequent employment of dark and light blues, which were borrowed from lapis and turquoise respectively.

Considering the difficulties of manipulating the molten metal when technical knowledge was so slight, the results were amazingly good and successes were achieved that prove the mastery of the workers in the craft. By the close of the fifteenth century B.C. the Egyptians were making use of four distinct techniques, which were (i) dipping a core into molten glass; (ii) building up sections of rod on a core; (iii) grinding from a solid block of glass; (iv) casting in a mould.

In order to form hollow articles like vases and jugs, the usual method employed was to take a metal rod and affix to it a core probably made of mud and straw shaped to the form of the interior of the required object. This was dipped into molten glass, patterns then being added by dropping on it blobs and trails of contrasting colours; zig-zags being made by combing the trails while they were still plastic and prior to marvering (Fig. 27, p. 48). Details such as neck-rim, foot and handles were added, and finally the rod and as much as possible of the core were removed. The interiors of these small vessels are pitted and rough, often retaining fragments of mud that reveal how they were made.

Alternatively, vessels and dishes were sometimes made by placing short sections of glass rod on a core, doubtless holding them in place with the aid of an adhesive, covering the whole with a shaped mould and then putting it in the kiln. The surface was ground away to remove unevenness and other faults.

**24. Carved blue staff head,**
8th/7th century B.C. Ht $2\frac{3}{8}$ in.

Small articles were occasionally formed from solid blocks of glass by shaping them with a tool of quartz or flint, slowly chipping and scraping away the superfluous material. This was a laborious method, more usually employed with rock crystal or some other natural stone (Fig. 24).

Flat objects could be cast in moulds without difficulty, but bowls and similar vessels could involve a more complex process: the *cire perdue* (lost wax) method. The article was modelled in wax and this was covered in clay, the wax being melted, poured away and replaced by molten glass. Again, imperfections were removed by abrasion.

The types of vessel can be divided into four main shapes: the *alabastron*, of cigar-shape and found both with and without small looped handles (Figs 25 and 26); the *urn*, squat and with a wide mouth (Fig. 28); the *amphora*, tall, pear-shaped and, like the alabastron, with a completely inadequate small base, so that in use it would have to be supported in a stand of wood or metal (Fig. 27); and the *oenochoe*, a jug with a curved handle and a flat practical base (Fig. 29).

**25. Alabastron,** about 500 B.C. Ht about 5 in.  **26. Alabastron,** about 500 B.C. Ht 4 3/16 in.  **27. Amphora,** about 500 B.C. Ht 2¾ in.

All these vessels varied somewhat in shape according to the century in which they were made, and most were little more than six inches or so in height. They were made principally as containers for the oils and other cosmetics used by

**28. Urn,** 1500–1400 B.C. Ht 2½ in.  **29. Oenochoe,** 400–300 B.C. Ht 4¾ in.  **30. Aryballos,** about 500 B.C. Ht 2⅜ in.

ladies in those times. The quality of the glass and the dry soil and climate of Egypt have ensured that surviving specimens are often in remarkably good preservation, but comparatively few are to be seen outside museums.

Small-sized globular bottles (Fig. 30) with strong handles

that have been likened to dolphins, were made for holding essences for use after the bath. With a cord threaded through the handles, they were suspended conveniently from the wrist. Examples were found in the ruins of Pompeii, which was destroyed in 79 A.D., but they had been made long before, and continued in production long after, that date. Because of

**31. Turquoise-green goblet** with the cartouche of Thotmes III, about 1450 B.C. Ht 3⅝ in.

**32. Flask** in the shape of a fish, about 1370 B.C.

their resemblance to the Greek oil-flask, an *aryballos*, they are often referred to by that name.

The earliest datable glass vessels are some which bear the cartouche of Thotmes III (1501–1447 B.C.), preserved in the British Museum, London, the Metropolitan Museum, New York, and the Aegyptische Staatssammlung, Munich (Fig. 31). Of slightly later date is an unusual flask in the shape of a fish, found at Tell el-Amarna and now in the British Museum, illustrated in Fig. 32. The majority of extant specimens are, however, little older than the fifth century B.C.; old enough, perhaps, when it is realised that this gives them an age of nearly 2,500 years.

Specimens of ancient glass from both the Egyptian and Roman periods have been preserved through the ages because of the shared custom of interring their dead with a supply of worldly goods. Until the spread of Christianity this was a common custom, and whether the deceased was given the form of a mummy or was reduced to a mere heap of ashes, the final resting-place usually also contained articles made of glass.

Whereas the custom doubtless began as a serious religious observance, it would seem possible that it degenerated in time until it became no more than a matter of form. At first, a person would have been buried with their actual much-loved and probably costly possessions, but, in due course, as the practice lost its initial significance, goods were doubtless manufactured especially for the purpose.

So many of the pieces of glass found in tombs and graves are utterly impractical that doubts are raised as to whether they can ever have been intended for use. Mr E. B. Haynes wrote of a carafe in his possession, supposed to have been found in Jerusalem, which holds three pints of water—no inconsiderable quantity. It is blown so extremely thinly that the weight of the empty vessel is only $4\frac{1}{2}$ ounces: 'when filled it seems eminently desirable to raise this Syrian carafe with care, and to support the base with one hand lest either the neck come away from the body or the bottom fall out of the whole'. The same writer mentions beakers which are equally fragile, and of which the rims were left rough from the shears and not smoothed at all. This would normally have been performed either by grinding on the wheel or by holding the beaker near the furnace-mouth to let the heat re-melt the rim.

Whether executed summarily or not, these surviving pieces are genuinely old and much has been learned from them. If this burial custom had not been instituted, we would have had only a very slight idea of the appearance of Egyptian and Roman glass. Certainly, there are literary mentions, especially of the latter, but words could hardly convey to us the brilliant hues, pleasing shapes, and technical excellence of what must otherwise have vanished.

Ancient Egyptian core-formed vessels resembling those illustrated have been reproduced in modern times. However, the resemblance to the originals is often no more than superficial, and a careful examination will generally reveal that such objects were made in a mould. In spite of the presence of traces of clay in the interior, which were put there to deceive the unwary, signs of mould-marks on the outside will dispel any doubts.

# CHAPTER III

# Roman and Syrian Glass

Whereas, on the whole, the Egyptians were content to remain within the frontiers of their own country, the Romans formed an adventurous nation wandering far and wide from their homeland. Their successful colonisations are too familiar to need recounting, and wherever they journeyed their ideas spread among the conquered peoples; conversely, they

**33. Workers at a furnace:** from an Egyptian wall decoration, about 3000 B.C.

adopted whatever pleased them in the lands they ruled. This was the case after Egypt fell to Augustus in 30 B.C.: the thriving glass industry was encouraged, and the much-travelled Romans admired and bought the wares of which they had seen hitherto only occasional specimens. In exchange, they were responsible for the dissemination of a completely new manufacturing technique: the art of glass-blowing.

When, in the 19th-century, the decorated rock tombs at Beni Hassan were discovered, dating from the IVth dynasty (3000 B.C.), it was thought that one of the paintings depicted glass-blowers at work (Fig. 33). It was difficult, or impossible,

to reconcile the suggestion with a complete lack of other
evidence that the method had been known at such an early
date, but the argument was waged for some years. It is agreed
now that the men shown at the small furnace are, in fact, not
connected with glass-making at all. They are probably iron-
workers, and the paraison-like bulge at the end of each of their
blowing-tubes is perhaps a lump of clay which, it has been
suggested, acted as a protection against the blast of the furnace.

With the adoption of the new process, the glass article was
less restricted in size as well as shape, and the laborious sand-
core method of making a hollow vessel fell quickly into disuse.
Whoever discovered the art of blowing glass remains unknown,
for although the discovery must have been the result of a
gradual development, someone must assuredly have been the
first to practise it in its perfected form. Not only does this
person remain unidentified, but the time and place of his
existence and of his invention remain equally obscure.

It is most probable that the technique originated at Sidon;
a place long famed for its glassworks relying on the sand at
the mouth of the River Belus. A number of surviving pieces
bear on them the name of their maker and that of the Syrian
city. These, and others of about the same date, were blown
into moulds, and it is possible that the earlier practice of
moulding such flat articles as dishes led to the blowing of
completely hollow articles.

Syria came under Egyptian rule in 1468 B.C., and the art of
glass-making developed slowly there and elsewhere in the
region, but without attaining the artistic heights reached in
Alexandria. The Syrians used moulds of sand and clay, the
ingredients of the Egyptian vase-cores, and onto the shaped
moulds pressed suitably-sized lumps of molten glass. Alternatively, the plastic metal might have been dripped or teased
onto a mould, and this clumsy manipulation have caused
bubbles. The sight of them imprisoned in the body of a piece

could well have been the germ from which sprang the idea of forming a bubble deliberately by blowing through a tube.

Glass wares had for long been sent to Italy from Alexandria, but following the capture of Egypt this trade increased greatly. In addition, very shortly after the birth of Christ glass-houses were established in Rome itself and at places on the Campanian coast. The sand at the mouth of the River Volturno, which flows into the sea just north of Naples, was found to be excellent for glass-making, but there is little doubt that the principal craftsmen employed there came from Syria and Egypt. This was the case, also, with places under Roman occupation throughout Europe, which makes it difficult to be certain exactly where many extant specimens were made; whether they were imported from afar or were local work by emigrants.

The term *Roman Glass* is applied often to pieces made during the lengthy period of the Empire, but it must not be taken to imply that they were made in the city of Rome itself or even in Italy. Equally, *Syrian Glass* is used also in a general sense to cover pieces of accepted Syrian types, that may have been made elsewhere in the Eastern Mediterranean area. *Roman Glass* is used sometimes to include both Syrian and Roman, and is on the whole a description roughly indicative of age rather than origin.

Generally, the simpler blown forms with or without moulded decoration are ascribed to Syria, whereas the more artistic productions showing the use of advanced techniques are given to Alexandria and Rome. All the glass was coloured, more or less; the use of manganese as a decolouriser did not become general until the 2nd century A.D. On the whole, it is said that Syrian glass was thinly blown and a pale blue-green in tint, and that of Alexandria was a definite green colour. Later, both acquired a yellow tone. These are generalisations, and the colour of any particular glass cannot alone determine its origin, which must be gauged from other factors as well: size, shape and decoration all playing their part.

The location of excavated glass is only occasionally helpful in determining its origin and is seldom decisive. The Syrians seem to have been less skilful in their handling of the material, and they used a less stable formula than the Egyptians. For this reason much of their glass is found to have been fused imperfectly and has often disintegrated with age. The decorative trailed patterns have sometimes come away on surviving examples, and this is ascribed to inexperience on the part of the makers. Certainly, the dry soil of Egypt has proved to be remarkably suited to the preservation of man-made works of numerous kinds, not least glass, and apart from any defects that may have been present prior to interment, there can be no doubt that burial in the earth elsewhere has often had a marked deleterious effect. For this reason, it is possible that the Syrian glass-makers have been blamed wrongly sometimes; they have been less at fault than the ground in which their productions lay buried for so long.

The action of damp soil over the centuries, for instance in the Eastern Mediterranean area, tends to cause the surface of glass to decay and separate into thin layers. These laminations break up the light and produce a prismatic effect which is highly attractive. The rainbow-like appearance, or iridescence, is sought eagerly by collectors who consider, with good reason, that otherwise plain and comparatively uninteresting glass is enhanced by it. Although usually limited to the surface, decay of this nature is found on occasion to have penetrated deeply throughout a piece.

It is considered that the earliest blown vessels were formed in clay moulds, and a number of surviving examples bear on them the names or trade-marks of their makers. In some instances only an inscribed fragment has been preserved, and the list includes: *Neicon, Sidon*; *Artas, Sidon*; *Ariston, Nicon,*

*Jason* of Rome; and *Ennion* who possibly began his successful career in Sidon and then transferred his manufactory to Italy.

These vessels, mostly intended for holding perfume or cosmetics, are usually of small size and in glass of various colours. Typical is the ewer in Fig. 34, which is of a shade of blue patterned in a raised design of honeysuckle flowers, fluting and diapers, and with the inscription *Ennion, Sidon*. Similarly made in a mould are bottles with a human head at

**34. Blue glass vase or ewer,** marked *Ennion, Sidon.*, 1st century A.D. Ht 9¼ in.

back and front (Fig. 35), some in the shape of a date and others modelled as a bunch of grapes (Fig. 36). All these remained in current use, on and off, from the 2nd to the 4th century A.D.

The tall beaker moulded with bosses (Fig. 37), which are not only decorative, but provide a functional hand-grip, is probably Syrian, 1st century. A similar example was found in the ruins of Pompeii, which proves that the design was being

**35. Bottle** moulded with two human heads: Syria, 2nd Century A.D. Ht 3½ in. **36. Brown glass flask** moulded as a bunch of grapes: Rome, 2nd Century A.D. Ht 5 in. **37. Beaker** moulded with bosses: probably Syria, 1st Century A.D. Ht 5 in.

produced at some date prior to 79 A.D. when the city was overwhelmed.

A number of pieces, blown in moulds and ornamented with Jewish symbols and made probably for ritual purposes, are ascribed to glass-makers in Palestine. It is not at all improbable that the Jews should have learned of the art when captives in Egypt, or have acquired a knowledge of it from the neighbouring Syrians, and in due course set up glass-houses in their homeland. An example of the productions attributed to them is the small amber-coloured hexagonal flask or bottle in Fig. 38, which has relief decoration of various symbols, including the seven-branched candelabrum (*menora*).

The presence of this ornamentation cannot be taken in itself as evidence of Palestinian origin, for such pieces can equally well have been made elsewhere by Jewish or by non-Jewish craftsmen. Other glass, of greater or lesser age than the preceding, has been found in tombs in Palestine, but is on the whole little different from contemporaneous Eastern Mediterranean types.

Free-blown vessels, those not formed in a mould, take

innumerable shapes which vary somewhat with the years and which have made it possible for a rough chronological order to be plotted. As might be expected, the earliest pieces were of the simplest shapes, and handles, where present, are heavier and usually less elaborately formed than in later examples. The mouths and feet of earlier vessels were of simple construction, and the latter were seldom fashioned separately. Complex threaded or trailed decoration became

**38. Amber-coloured flask:** Palestine, 2nd to 4th Century A.D. Ht 3½ in.   **39. Jug** with trailed handle: Rome, 2nd Century A.D. Ht 3 in.   **40. Jug** with blue trailed ornament: probably Syria, 2nd Century A.D. Ht 4¼ in.

fashionable in the 4th century, A.D., after an earlier and less complicated appearance.

At all times in the past, as today, there has been a demand for both plain and fancy articles, and it is not possible to lay down hard-and-fast rules for dating based solely on design. While daily use required only a severely functional vessel, the wealthy demanded for their tables more elaborate productions. Both would be of the same date, but of contrasting patterns, which can be confusing in assessing age. A typical example is seen in comparing the pieces shown in Figs. 39 and 40. The pale green jug with a small curved handle is of about the same date as the more sophisticated tall one; the latter is also of green glass, but with blue trailed ornament and handle.

The plain, but carefully-shaped cup or beaker in Fig. 41 was doubtless an everyday article in its time. Age has coated its pale green substance with an iridescence which cannot be reproduced adequately in mere black-and-white, and it relies here on its simplicity of form. It was found in Palestine. Slightly later in date are the magenta-coloured two-handled

**41. Cup,** from Palestine: Rome, 1st or 2nd Century A.D. Ht 4⅜ in.
**42. Magenta-coloured jar:** Rome, 2nd Century A.D. Ht 4 in.
**43. Flask** with blue zig-zag ornament: Rome, 2nd Century A.D.
Ht 3¾ in.

jar in Fig. 42, and the green flask with trailed blue zig-zag ornament around the waist in Fig. 43.

The tall bottle or flask in Fig. 45 is a fine example of blowing, its excellent proportions left untrammelled by ornament and its surface now crusted with iridescence from· burial. Nearly comparable in simplicity, but each slightly elaborated in pattern, are the bowl and beaker in Figs. 44 and 46; the former with a neat spreading foot and the latter encircled by a band. A 3rd-century goblet in Fig. 47 stands on a short-stemmed foot and has three trailed rings around the bowl. Metal apart, only its slight assymmetry distinguishes it, and

**44. Bowl:** probably Syria, 2nd Century A.D. Diam. 6¼ in.   **45.**
Bottle or flask: Rome, 2nd Century A.D. Ht 7 in.
**46. Beaker** with central trailed band: Rome, 2nd Century A.D.
Diam. 2⅝ in.

many other pieces of the period, from a modern drinking-
vessel.

The flask or jug in Fig. 48 is of purple glass streaked with
white, and the dark blue trailed handle is placed very low on
the body. This feature points to a Syrian rather than an
Egyptian origin, and a date sometime about the 1st or 2nd
century. Somewhat later is the green glass jug in Fig. 49,
which has a shaped and curled lip outlined in trailed bluish-
green. The same colour was used for forming the handle; a
feature that appears, in this instance, more normally placed
than in the preceding example. Similarly positioned is the blue
handle on the jug in Fig. 51.

The bluish-green glass accepted widely as being of Roman
origin was used for the flask in Fig. 50. This has trailed ornament at the neck, suggested in the first instance, perhaps, by a
cord on a leather vessel, but on a glass one serving a useful
purpose in providing a hand-grip. More complex in pattern

**47. Goblet** with trailed ornament: Syria, 3rd Century A.D. Ht 5 in.
**48. Purple and white streaked jug** with dark blue handle: Syria,
1st or 2nd Century A.D. Ht 4 in. **49. Jug:** Rome, 3rd Century
A.D. Ht 8 in.

**50. Flask** with trailed ornament: Rome, 2nd or 3rd Century A.D.
Ht 8 in. **51. Jug** with blue trailed handle: perhaps Rome, 2nd
or 3rd Century A.D. Ht 2¾ in. **52. Double balsamarium:** Rome,
5th/6th Century A.D. Ht 4 in.

is the double unguent bottle (*balsamarium*) in Fig. 52, which has the appearance of two tubes side by side. It was formed in one piece from a large diameter tube squeezed down the centre while molten, the trailed handles at top and bottom were then added.

The vase-like two-handled flask in Fig. 53 is ornamented neatly with trailed blue rings and a band of zig-zags round the

**53. Two-handled flask** with blue trailed ornament: Rome, 2nd or 3rd Century A.D. Ht 5¾ in. **54. Dark bluish-green sprinkler:** probably Rome, 2nd or 3rd Century A.D. Ht 6½ in.

body. Of more complex design and decoration is the flask in Fig. 54. This has a funnel-hole inside the base of the neck, and the piece was used to sprinkle liquid. The body is decorated with fin-like raised curves, and the base has a series of pointed projections at the circumference.

Trailed ornament of a more ambitious type is seen in the small jar in Fig. 55, and the ointment pot (*unguentarium*) in

Fig. 56. The row of loops encircling the neck of the former is purely decorative, and the bands of zig-zags on the latter are equally without function, but this last piece has the

**55. Jar** with trailed neck ornament: Rome, 4th century A.D. Ht 3¾ in.

**56. Unguentarium** with trailed ornament: Syria, 3rd or 4th century A.D. Ht 3½ in.

addition of a pair of handles and three small feet. Both date from about the 4th century A.D.

In addition to free-blowing, blowing into moulds and ornamenting with trails of the same or a contrasting colour,

**57. Amber 'pillar-moulded' bowl:** Syria, 2nd or 3rd century A.D. Diam. 4½ in. **58. Bowl** with silver pattern handles: probably Egypt, 1st century A.D. Ht 3¼ in.

decoration was attempted with success in a number of other ways. *Pillar-moulding*, the pinching-out of ribs with a tool while the vessel was still plastic, is seen on the Syrian amber-coloured bowl in Fig. 57, and the same technique was applied to other objects. The interiors of pieces decorated in this manner can show corresponding slight ribs, not depressions, as would have been the case if they had been moulded.

Grinding was used for the shaping and polishing of vessels, and seems to have been preferred sometimes to finishing by means of re-heating; which also gave a gloss. The handles on the bowl in Fig. 58 would seem to have been ground out of the solid material, a technique borrowed from carvers of hardstone, whose methods and materials were imitated also on other occasions. Handles of the same pattern are found on a

59. **Cup** with cut decoration, found in Cambridgeshire: Rome, 1st or 2nd century A.D. Ht 5⅜ in.  60. **Jar** with simple cut decoration: Syria, 3rd or 4th century A.D. Ht 5⅝ in.  61. **Flask** incised with a hatched pattern and inscribed PHILE: probably Rome, 4th century A.D. Ht 9½ in.

number of other glass bowls, and owe their origin to Roman silver of the 1st century A.D. in which they were more suitably formed. Flat facets were cut on the surface of rounded objects (Fig. 59), and simple lines or criss-cross patterns were cut or engraved (Figs. 60 and 61). The use of the diamond for glass-engraving would seem to have been appreciated by the Romans, but it is probable that much of their work of this nature was done with flint.

Like the Egyptians before them, the Romans had a liking

**62. Mosaic cup** on domed foot: Egypt, 1st century A.D. Diam. 6⅛ in. **63. Millefiore dish** with striped edging, Rome: 1st century A.D. Diam. 5¼ in.

for coloured glass; partly from a preference for strong colour and partly because of their admiration for minerals. These they attempted to imitate, and successful copies of sardonyx and other stones are known. Much speculation has ranged about the 'Murrhine bowls' mentioned by Pliny and others, which remain unidentified, but it has been suggested that they are made of a natural stone from Parthia (now part of Iran), a type of jade, pottery, or a variety of fluorspar. It is thought that glass bowls and other vessels were made in imitation of this fabulous substance, whatever it may have been, that has been described as 'scented, fragile, and prized for its colouring, which was purple, white or flame-coloured, sometimes iridescent, sometimes opaque or knobbed'.

Apart from the usual pale greens, pale blues, and ambers of which most of the surviving glass of the time was made, many stronger colours were produced. These were blown and cast, cut and engraved, and also used to form mosaic pictures. For this purpose the glass was cut into cubes and set in cement in the same manner as the more usual coloured stones.

Known also as *mosaic glass*, but really a variety of millefiore, are vessels made from fragments of patterned glass fused together. An example is illustrated in Fig. 62, and the portion of a dish in Fig. 63 shows the striped edge that was often added as a finish. This was formed from rods of contrasting colours, softened and twisted together to form a cordlike pattern.

It has been mentioned that the copying of minerals was practised, and this embraced the imitation of cameos of layered stone. The most famous example of Roman glass employing this technique is the Portland Vase in the British Museum (Fig. 64). It was made from a deep blue glass cased

**64. The Portland Vase:** Rome, 1st century A.D. Ht 9¾ in.

in opaque white, either by making a cup of white and blowing a blue paraison into it, or by dipping the blown vase into molten white metal. The outer coating was cut away to form the pattern, and the dark ground showing through the thinned portions gives an effect of depth to the whole. Not only was the work done with grinding wheels, but the more delicate portions necessitated the use of hand-tools, such as small chisels and gravers.

The subject shown in the decoration is the story of the sea-goddess Thetis with whom both Zeus and Poseidon fell in love, but who finally married a mortal, Peleus, and bore him a son, Achilles. In the view, illustrated here, of the vase are seen Peleus (on the left) held by the arm by the seated sea-goddess, Doris, mother of Thetis. Beside her stands her bearded husband, Nereus, with his chin cupped pensively in his hand, and above her hovers Eros.

The vase dates from the reign of the Emperor Augustus (27 B.C. to A.D. 14), and it has suffered grievously with the passage of time. It was originally taller, and the base probably came down to a knob somewhat resembling the amphora in Fig. 27. It is not known when the breakage occurred, nor is it known where the vase was discovered, but by 1642 it was recorded as one of the notable ornaments of the newly-built Barberini Palace in Rome, and some fifty years later the earliest print of it shows that it was then of the shape familiar today. In 1783 it was brought to England and purchased by the Duchess of Portland, an avid collector of rarities, but she died two years later and her collection was sold by auction. The vase became the property of her son, the third Duke of Portland, who loaned it to the potter, Josiah Wedgwood, so that it might be copied in his jasperware.

In 1810 the fourth Duke deposited the vase on loan to the British Museum, where it rested safely for 35 years. Then, in February, 1845, a man, who was apparently suffering from the after effects of a week-long bout of intemperance, picked up an unidentified stone object in the room and smashed the precious vase into more than two hundred pieces. Incredibly, the fragments were re-assembled by one of the Museum officials, and the vase was again placed on exhibition before the end of the year. To complete the story, it was put up for auction at Christie's in 1929, but failed to reach the reserve price, and in 1945 it was purchased by the Museum. Since then it has been taken apart and restored again.

Other cameo vases, probably slightly later in date than the Portland, include the Blue Vase, decorated with amorini feasting and gathering grapes, in the Museo Nazionale, Naples, the Balsamarium Torrita, with a Bacchic scene, in the Museo Archeologico, Florence, and the Auldjo Vase. The latter was discovered at Pompeii in 1834, and the two parts into which it had been broken went to different collectors. In due course, they both reached the British Museum, where they are now re-united.

Comparable in virtuosity with the foregoing are the so-called *cage-cups* or *vasa diatreta* (Fig. 65); the latter term is incorrectly used. The *diatretarii* were Roman glass-cutters, and the word *diatreta* applies to their work whatever its type and not specifically to these cups. Modern usage, however, has tended to assign it to these particular pieces which, whatever they may be called, are described correctly as *tours de force* of glass-cutting.

In most instances, cage-cups take the form of a round-bottomed bowl or cup with the sides and base covered in a network of pierced ornament. Some examples bear an inscription round the upper edge, some are in clear glass and a few are multi-coloured. Most are decorated with geometrical patterns, but some rare ones show mythological scenes. Whatever the ornament, it is raised from the body with only small, barely visible, struts remaining to retain it in position.

It has been suggested that the cups were decorated in this manner by fusing the outer network to the previously-shaped body, but now it is accepted that with incredible patience they were cut from the solid; a task involving the most complicated undercutting in which the slightest error would have wrecked the entire operation. No doubt the work was aided by having the cups moulded in the first place to a shape that would aid the craftsman, but unquestionably the principal credit is due to him and to the consummate skill at his command.

The cups date from the 4th or 5th century, A.D. There has

been much discussion as to their origin: whether they were made by Romans or Syrians working in Rome or elsewhere, or whether they came from Alexandria. At present, opinion is against the latter, but it remains undecided whether Rome or some other Italian town may have housed the workshops whence they came. The fact that some of the cups have been found in graves in the Rhineland has led to the proposal that

**65. Double-walled cup** (*Diatreton*): perhaps Rhineland, 3rd or 4th century A.D. Ht 4¾ in. **66. The Lycurgus Cup:** Rome, 4th or 5th century A.D. Ht. 6⅗ in.

they may have been made in that area, and the city of Cologne has been suggested as the source.

A few of the surviving cups and fragments of cups are of coloured glass, and to this group belong some that change tint according to the light to which they are exposed. The finest example of this is the Lycurgus Cup, long in the possession of the Rothschild family and now in the British Museum (Fig. 66). It shows events in the mythological tale of the Thracian king, Lycurgus, and in the view shown here is seen the god Dionysus with his attendant panther.

The cup, which is in remarkably fine condition considering

its age, was originally of the same shape as the one in Fig.'65. The colour of the surface is pea-green with a patch on one side of a more yellow shade than the remainder, but the remarkable feature of it is that when seen in a transmitted light (i.e. when a light is shone through the glass from within the cup) the colour changes to a wine-red with the yellower part altering to purple. The effect has been attributed to the presence of minute amounts of gold and silver in the metal,

**67. Bowl** with engraved gold decoration: Rome, 1st century A.D.

and the treatment accorded to it in the furnace. The Cup is as outstanding for its material as for its cutting.

Some enamel-painted vessels dating from the 4th century A.D. have survived, and prove that this form of decoration was practised by the Roman glass-makers. Examples have been found in various countries, including Algeria and Denmark, but it has been surmised that it was not much employed and the scarcity of specimens would appear to confirm this.

Glass decorated with engraved gold leaf, *fondi d'oro*, was favoured by the Romans from perhaps as early as the 1st century A.D. Two bowls found in Southern Italy and now in the British Museum (Fig. 67), are outstanding examples of the work and have been dated to that time. Less rare are small medallions, mostly engraved with religious scenes (Fig. 68), but occasionally with secular portraits or figures (Fig. 69), mainly of the 4th century.

A number of these small medallions have been found embedded in the walls of the catacombs in Rome, where they were placed in the wet plaster, together with such objects as coins, pieces of mosaic, beads and bits of twig. This was done perhaps by relatives of the deceased interred there, and may have been to mark the graves for future identification. The glass discs in these circumstances are mostly fragments of larger objects, and were originally in the bases of bowls and

**68. Gold-engraved medallion,** Christ and Lazarus: Rome 3rd or 4th century A.D. **69. Gold-engraved medallion,** a gladiator named Stratonicus: Rome, 3rd or 4th century A.D.

cups possibly broken away deliberately so that they did not project into the narrow passages of the catacombs. There is some doubt as to whether this is the correct explanation for the placing of these objects in the catacomb walls, but no other theory that has been advanced seems to be as satisfactory.

Under the rule of the Romans there were glass-works in both the Rhineland and France, and possibly also in the British Isles. Some of the workers would undoubtedly have been immigrants from Syria and Alexandria who would have tended to make articles in patterns with which they were already familiar. Thus, the glass made in the various provinces of the Empire can be distinguished only rarely from that of

71

Rome and the Eastern Mediterranean. While there was certainly an export trade from east to west, it is not improbable that once the Gallic and Rhenish craftsmen were established their productions circulated in Rome and farther afield.

Just over a century or so ago the archeological world was agog with the reported finding of several lumps of coloured glass, of different tints and varying in size, on the beach at Brighton. These had become worn by the action of the tides until they resembled pebbles, and the discoverer, a Dr Guest, showed them to a local lapidary. This man was unperturbed and showed in turn a further quantity of the same material, varying in colour from amethyst to amber, emerald and deep maroon. He had been cutting and polishing these specimens and using them to inset in jewellery.

The most popular theory advanced to account for the find was that cliff erosion had resulted in the remains of a Roman glass-house falling into the sea. Support for this was said to be the reference by Pliny to *massae*—lumps of glass that were either imported from the Continent or made on the spot to be sent elsewhere for working. The pieces in the Brighton find were tinted, and Pliny's description implied that the *massae* were clear when they left the pot and would be coloured after reaching the final manufactory. This seemed to point to the latter being actually at Brighton, but the lengthy arguments came to a halt when it was pointed out that there was no proof whatsoever that the lumps dated back to Roman times.

Commonly found in European graves are the square and cylindrical bottles, of which an example is shown in Fig. 70. These were used normally for the transport of liquids, but when excavated they usually contain the cremated remains of 2nd and 3rd century individuals. The bottle in Fig. 71 was found in Suffolk and is one of a type of which a few other examples have been discovered in Britain; the ewer in Fig. 72,

**70. Square bottle** found in a grave in Hertfordshire: 1st or 2nd century A.D. **71. Bottle or flask** found in Suffolk: 2nd or 3rd century A.D. Ht 7⅛ in. **72. Ewer or flask:** probably Amiens, 2nd or 3rd century A.D. Ht 5½ in.

found at Amiens, represents a style of vessel thought to have been made in that area.

The 1st century cup in Fig. 74 is moulded with scenes and an inscription commemorating a victory by Cresces in a chariot-race. It was discovered in a grave at Colchester, Essex, and was made perhaps in the Rhône valley in France, or in Switzerland. Others are known which are moulded with prize-fights and with the names of popular gladiators.

A grave near Sittingbourne, in Kent, yielded the flask in Fig. 73. Not only is the body decorated with neat vertical ribbing, but on the front is a glass seal impressed with the head of Medusa. This piece may also have been made in one of the Gallic glass-works, which were established in about 60 A.D. at Namur, Rheims, Amiens and Boulogne.

Positively identifiable as being of Western origin is the bottle in Fig. 75 which is moulded with raised rings at the

top and bottom of the body; under the base is inscribed
FROTI. This is one of the marks of a man named Frontinus
whose glass-works was apparently in Gaul, either at Amiens
or Boulogne. Surviving examples of his productions bear
versions of his name in raised letters spelt (or, rather,

**73. Flask** with a seal on the body: 2nd century A.D.
**74. Cup** moulded with a chariot-race: 1st century A.D. Diam.
3¼ in.　**75. Bottle** with FROTI in raised letters under the base:
Amiens or Boulogne, 3rd or 4th century A.D. Ht 7 in.

abbreviated) variously: FRONTINO, FRON, and FRONTI. He
was active at sometime in the 3rd and 4th centuries.

The Romans were the supreme makers of glass, and the
importance of their contribution to the art cannot be over-
stated. A study of surviving examples cannot fail to corroborate the judgment that 'its artistic achievement and example lie

74

behind most subsequent phases of the history of glass-making in Europe. In glass blown with or without moulds, in the decorative manipulation of the plastic metal, in cut and engraved designs, and even in painted and gilt decoration—in all these departments the glass made under the Roman Empire can show examples hardly surpassed at any later time.'

# CHAPTER IV

# Medieval European Glass

Following the fall of the Roman Empire, the art of glass-making in Europe made little or no progress, but did not entirely cease. In assessing what actually was made there is a comparative shortage of examples from which to draw conclusions, but on the whole the quality of the metal deteriorated and technical skill followed the same path. Once the civilizing and progressive influences of the conquerors were removed there was a long period of semi-darkness; not only did endeavour lessen, but traces of what may have been achieved have proved hard to discover.

One reason, and the principal one, for a present-day scarcity of glass specimens of the period can be put down to a marked change in burial customs. With the spread of the Christian religion the deceased was no longer interred with any of his or her worldly goods, and the preservation of glass and other objects became very much a matter of chance. Fragments of vessels have been found among the remains of ancient building sites or where glass-houses once operated, but both searches and accidental discoveries have produced disappointingly small quantities.

From studies of the surviving pieces it has been possible to gain some idea of the glass made in Europe from about the 5th century A.D. until the Venetian renaissance a thousand years later. The productions of those ten centuries prove, with some few exceptions, to have been little less dull than they are rare. In time, when a greater number of specimens has been brought to light it may be necessary to make adjustments here and there, but the overall picture is unlikely to be altered to a noticeable extent.

Apart from some variations in design from those that had prevailed previously, the principal change was in the metal itself. This was usually of a strong green tint, full of bubbles and markings, but in exceptional instances it was made in shades of greenish-blue and amber. The generally poor nature of the material and consequent uninteresting appearance of pieces made from it no doubt led to a lack of care in using and cherishing such vessels. This fact was perhaps additionally responsible for a shortage of surviving examples; for a work of art, however minor, has a quality about it that beguiles all but the most savage vandal and makes it in some degree self-preserving.

Perhaps the most controversial of all the extant vessels of the 5th to 8th centuries are drinking-cups. These are of tall, conical shape with varied ornament on the body, but all have in common the fact that they are footless (Figs. 76 –78). It has been said that this shows a marked decline in manufacturing technique; that the art of making and affixing a foot to a vessel, known well enough to the Romans, had been forgotten. It can be argued, however, that this was not due necessarily to such a lapse, but that drinking-glasses took their particular form quite deliberately.

Vessels in other materials, notably horn, were also footless, and it is known from drawings in manuscripts of the 10th century that a cup was not then set down on the table. It was handed by a servant, emptied, and then returned to the waiting man. Most probably the same custom prevailed in earlier times, and it may be unjust to blame glass-makers for not achieving what they made no attempt to do.

Typical of the cups is that in Fig. 76, ornamented round the upper part of the bowl with threads which are not only decorative, but give the user's hand a firm grip. The example in Fig. 77 displays the embellishment of vertical trailed loops resembling fluting. Specimens of this type have been found in both Kent and Sussex.

Of more advanced pattern and of distinctive type are the beakers known in Germany as *Rüsselbecher* (from *rüssel*: an elephant's trunk), because of the claw- or trunk- like projections drawn-out from the raised and rounded hollows on

76. **Conical beaker,** 5th century. Ht 4½ in.  77. **Conical beaker** with trailed ornament, 5th century. Ht 10 in.  78. **Claw-beaker** (Rüsselbecher), 5th/6th century. Ht 9⅜ in.  79. **Detail of claw** with notched trailing.

the body (Fig. 78). These rare glasses have a curious appearance, but certainly show skill and individuality on the part of their makers. Variations in design occur, with the numbers of projections ranging between six and a dozen and some having the extra detail of notched trailing (Fig. 79).

Comparable to the claw-beakers, but earlier in date, are some with raised oval bosses which give them a resemblance to the skin of a pineapple (Fig. 82). Again, the ornament

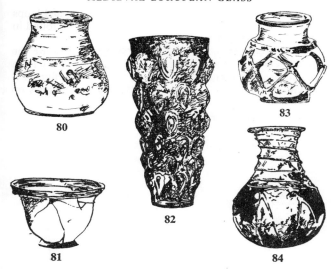

**80. Bag-shaped bowl,** 6th/7th century. Ht about 3½ in.   **81. Bowl** with threaded rim, 6th/7th century. Diam. 3 in.   **82. Beaker** with pineapple bosses, 2nd/3rd century. Ht 8 in.   **83. Vessel** with trailed strapwork, 5th/6th century. Ht 2½ in.   **84. Bottle** with trailed spiral and loop ornament, 5th century. Ht 5 in.

serves the additional purpose of being functional by providing a good surface for gripping the glass. Probably of Syrian or Palestinian manufacture, this type of glass has been excavated in Europe and one example was discovered in the ruins of Pompeii.

The bag-shaped bowl in Fig. 80 has threads looped round the upper part of the body, and the open-mouthed bowl in Fig. 81 has a deep threaded rim. Fig. 83 shows a bowl, cup or vase of somewhat similar outline to that in Fig. 80, but with the addition of applied threads in the form of strapwork. The bottle in Fig. 84 has a threaded neck in widely-spaced spirals, and the bulging body decorated with threads drawn into loops to form a star-like pattern.

The shaped cups with loops of thread around the necks and with the bodies constricted are later types than many of the preceding, possibly dating to as late as the 8th or 9th centuries (Figs 85 and 86). Towards the end of the 18th century

**85. Drinking-vessel**, 9th century. Ht 5¼ in. **86. Drinking-vessel**, 9th century. Ht 4½ in. **87. Bottle** with opaque blue and white trailed ornament, 3rd century. Ht 7⅜ in. **88. Green goblet** with white and gold trailing. 3rd century. Ht 4¾ in.

a cache of no fewer than thirty 9th-century examples was found accidentally in Kent. They had probably formed a trader's consignment from the Continent which had somehow been mislaid and lay undiscovered for about a thousand years. It is said that after they were found the local farmers used them for celebrations of Harvest Home, and before long all were smashed.

Most of the pieces described above were excavated in the

British Isles, but there is little likelihood that they were actually made there. They were imported in the ordinary way of business from makers in Gaul and the Rhineland or brought across the Channel by immigrants and other travellers. The constant movement of peoples from one land to another meant that styles, such of them as were recognisable from each other, would be spread widely, and identification of the characteristics of a particular region made uncertain. Dating often proves equally difficult, as designs changed as little in time as in place.

The Roman glass-makers and decorators were able to create such superb *tours-de-force* as the Portland Vase and the cage-cups. Yet, within no more than a couple of centuries the art had sunk back to a primitive state. Taking into account the ruggedness of life at the time, it is perhaps a wonder that even the most simple glassware should have been manufactured. The hazards of everyday life made only slight allowance for luxury, and it was to be several centuries before more stable conditions in the west of Europe once again permitted the proper development of artistic skills.

That in at least one part of England, the North, glass-making was perhaps non-existent for a time seems indicated in the well-known requests of two of the abbots of Wearmouth. In 676 Benedict sent to Gaul for men to make glass for the windows of the abbey and vessels for his table, and in 758 Cuthbert wrote to as far afield as Mayence, a town situated amid the Rhineland glass-houses, for similar articles. This need not be taken to mean that no glass was being made in England at the time, but only that whatever material was available to them was not to the liking of either of the abbots.

Some European manuscripts of the 9th and 10th centuries refer to the making of glass, but most were content to copy out what had been written earlier by Pliny and add to the formulae such exotic ingredients as fat worms and the blood of fasting goats. Most were concerned with making materials that would counterfeit precious stones, a reflection of the efforts being made by alchemists to turn lead and other base metals into gold. Emerald and sapphire glass was made and often accepted as the genuine natural stone, specimens being mounted in metal and treasured fittingly. An altar-table described as being made from a slab of sapphire was said to have been at Glastonbury in 1126, and the Byzantine Empress Irene, who died in 803, is stated to have given Charlemagne a slab of green glass, known subsequently as 'Charlemagne's Emerald', which is still at the Abbey of Reichenau on Lake Constance, in Switzerland.

Glass of this type was made in the Middle East, and both Alexandria and Fostat (Old Cairo) in Egypt were well known for their fine emerald green. It was perhaps at the former place that a celebrated bowl known as the *Sacre Catino*, in the Cathedral of S. Lorenzo in Genoa, was made in medieval times. It was brought to Italy by a crusader in the year 1101, and has attracted a wealth of legend to itself. Not only has it been named as the Holy Grail, but it was supposed to have been the very dish on which rested the severed head of St John the Baptist and also to have been presented by Solomon to the Queen of Sheba. An 18th-century author wrote of it:

'This wonderful relique is kept under many keys, which are lodged in separate hands, and is never shewn without a decree of the Senate: when this has been obtained, a string is put through the two handles of the vase, and it is hung round a priest's neck, the only situation in which it is exposed to view. By a decree of the Senate made in 1476, the spectator is prohibited, under grevious penalties, from approaching too near it . . .'

The *Sacre Catino* was for long thought to have been carved from a real emerald, but is now known to be of glass. It is in the form of a two-handled six-sided bowl cut with a pattern in the interior and, according to the writer quoted above, measures 14½ inches in diameter, 5¼ inches in height and about a ¼ inch in thickness.

Chronologically out of place, but leading on in design to the following section are the so-called *snake-thread* pieces: bottles, dishes and other articles, ornamented with serpentine patterns trailed in contrasting colours. Examples have been discovered on the Continent, and fragments of them in various parts of the British Isles. Although similar specimens have been found in the Eastern Mediterranean they differ somewhat from Western ones, and it has been surmised that immigrant Syrian glass-workers were responsible for the latter. They probably had employment in the Rhineland during the 3rd century, and brought a whiff of Eastern styling with them. Typical of their work is the bottle in Fig. 87, which is decorated with patterns in opaque white and blue on a clear body. Fig. 88 illustrates a goblet that is uncommon in its combination of colours; the superimposed trailings are white and gold on a body of pale green.

# CHAPTER V

# Islamic Glass

It has been shown how European countries allowed their practice of the art of glass-making to decline rapidly from the heights of Roman inspiration. In contrast, the art to the south and east of the Mediterranean continued to employ, and sometimes to improve, the techniques developed in preceding centuries. The period begins approximately with the rise and spread of Mohammedanism, which dates from the year 622 A.D. when Mahomet fled from Mecca to Medina, and the work of the time is referred to as Mohammedan or Islamic. These names indicate only roughly both place and time, for it is often impossible to be precise either about the actual country wherein a particular piece was made or to be certain within a century or so of when it was produced. It may be added that these strictures apply not only to glass, but to most other works of art, major and minor, surviving from the comparatively poorly-charted area.

The history of the Near East, then as in earlier and later times, is chequered with large and small wars. Dynasties came and went, and the capitals of the component countries were removed sometimes from one land to another or merely from city to city. It is not easy to conjecture the effects of this on the arts after so much time has passed, but each upheaval must have left its mark. In some instances it led to acute and noticeable changes in style, or the introduction of fresh styles, which were adopted from a captured people or from a newly-acquired neighbour. Attempts to trace these influences and their results often lead to no more than opposing theories:

the opinion of one expert against that of another, each being accepted in turn by the outside world.

Briefly, the successive governing dynasties in Egypt, which continued to play a large part as far as glass was concerned, were as follows:

*Tulunid*
from Ahmad b. Tūlūn 868–884,
to Muhammad b. Takin 933.
*Ikshīdī*
from Muhammad b. Tughj al-Ikshīd 933,
to Abu'l-Fawāris Ahmad b. 'Alī b. al-Ikshīd 968.
*Fātimite*
from Mo'izz Abū Tamīm Ma'add (or li-dīn-allāh) 969–975,
to 'Adid (Abū Muhammad 'Abdallah) 1160–1171.
*Ayyūbite*
from Malik al-Nāsir Salāh al-dīn Yūsuf b. Ayyūb (Saladin) 1169–1193.
*Bahri Mameluke*
from Shajar al-durr 1250,
to Mozaffar (Salāh al-dīn Hājjī) 1389–1390.
Followed by the *Burji Mameluke*.

From the 7th century to the 10th, Egypt was a province of the Arab Moslem empire, and its rulers were from one of the various cities which ranked as capitals from time to time. These rulers were able to establish semi-independent dynasties; e.g. the Tulunid and Ikshīdī. The country was conquered again in 969, and the Fatimite Caliph, Mo'izz, became ruler and removed the capital from Mahdia, on the coast of what is now Tunisia, to Cairo. The next important change took place in 1171, when Saladin embodied it once again in the Abbasid empire centred on Baghdad under a Caliph. Saladin founded the Ayyūbite dynasty, and his name remains familiar as leader of the Mohammedan armies which conquered not

85

only Egypt, but also Syria. He was attacked in Palestine by the Christian forces of the West, the Crusaders led by Richard I of England, who regained Jerusalem in 1192.

The vicissitudes of Damascus, with its long-held reputation in the Near East as a centre of glass-making, have led to the attribution to it of pieces bearing decoration traceable to Chinese sources. In 1260 and 1300 the city was raided, first by Mongols and later by Tartars, and Oriental motifs found on glassware from about that time are probably traceable to these invasions. It has not been possible to prove that such pieces were made, or even decorated, in the Syrian city.

The earlier glass with combed decoration either had continued to be produced in Alexandria or elsewhere, or was revived. The later examples lack some of the qualities of those of the days of the Pharaohs. While the colourings of white, blue and black continued in favour as in the past, the shapes of the vessels were changed somewhat and the patterns on them less finely executed (Fig. 89). As the sand-core method was still employed for their manufacture and the composition of the glass remained unchanged, it is sometimes only through subtle stylistic features that their age can be determined. In some instances, however, such changes were very slight, and expert knowledge is required in order to differentiate between old and less old. Equally, the simple kinds of green-tinted glass wares, with and without the addition of trailed ornament, continued to be made as they had been for so long.

Our knowledge of the types of glassware current during the last part of the 9th century owes much to the work of German archaeologists at Samarra in 1912–14. The Abbasid Caliphs, who alleged they were descended from the eldest uncle of Muhammad (Mahomet), Abbas (A.D. 566–652), are known to have removed their Court from Baghdad to Samarra, and to have remained at the latter place only for a short period between the years 836 and 883. Excavations carried out on the site resulted in the recovery of much glass, and also pottery, that has provided highly important knowledge of what was in use during that particular half century.

The Court of the Caliphs was noted for its love of luxury, and there can be little doubt that it attracted imported goods from many countries. It would also have offered opportunities

**89. Vase** patterned in white with human heads and amphoras: Egypt, 5th or 6th century. Ht 5½ in.   **90. Flask** with dimpled body: Syria, 5th or 6th century. Ht 5½ in.   **91. Flask** with spiral thread decoration: Syria, 5th or 6th century. Ht 7 in.

of employment to skilled craftsmen, who probably settled there from far and wide. Thus, it cannot be stated for certain that the pieces found at Samarra were made in or about the city or whether they were brought from afar. What is indisputable is that they show just what was popular and fashionable, and what had been achieved technically and artistically by the end of the 9th century.

Among the Samarra finds are a large number of pieces of

mosaic or millefiori glass of Roman type (Figs 62 and 63, p. 65). While these bear a general resemblance to the earlier Alexandrian material, they are often of a distinctive combination of colours which includes an opaque yellow. Some of the patterns are similar to those popular on pottery of the time, and both share a liking for a series of dotted circles resembling an eye. It has been suggested that this millefiori glass was

**92. Flagon** with trailed ornament: Egypt, 10th century. Ht 5¼ in.
**93. Bottle** of green and amber glass: Syria, 12th century. **94. Bottle** with ribbed body: Islamic (?Iran), 12th century. Ht 7¾ in.

actually of Roman date and had been treasured carefully for seven or eight centuries. While it is not impossible, it is unlikely, and more probably the material was manufactured by immigrant descendants of the original Egyptian makers. Exactly where they worked is another point, but it is thought they had settled in the city of Samarra itself.

One of the more noticeable characteristics of Near Eastern glass dating from the 5th and 6th centuries, and later, is the adoption of un-Classical forms. The drift from the simple

88

Western shapes of the Roman ascendancy is often very marked, but it is equally true that many of the old forms continued in production for hundreds of years after they had been introduced. The pieces in Figs. 90 to 93 are typical of the wares that appealed to customers of the glass-makers of Islam.

Trailed decoration remained much in evidence, either in the

**95. Bottle** moulded with the Cross: Syria, 5th century. Ht 8 in.

form of spiralling 'stripes', almost melted into the body of the article (Fig. 91), or heaped externally as in the flagon in Fig. 92. The sprinkler bottle, used for containing perfumed water, seen in Fig. 93, uses both trailing and colour; the spiral neck banding and the shoulder ornament being tinted green in contrast to the amber of the body of the piece.

The high-shouldered flagon (Fig. 92), which is ascribed to Egypt, finds an echo in the form of a later piece possibly from Iran (Fig. 94). This relies for decoration on the vertical ribbing of the body and the bulb blown at the base of the short neck; the latter being a feature that gives the piece a decidedly un-Western look. Also with moulded ornament is the bottle in Fig. 95, which bears a design incorporating the Cross and is an interesting early example of the use of the Christian symbol on glass. Moulded wares were produced continuously and in many countries. The technique favoured the mass-production of articles that circulated widely and makes identification of their origin little more than guesswork.

A variant of moulding was the result of nipping with patterned tongs the sides of open-mouthed vessels while they remained in the molten state. Bowls and cups decorated in this manner bear formal geometrical patterns (Fig. 97) or, more rarely, designs incorporating animals. The method was employed in the making of impressed discs, which were used in late Roman times as weights. Amongst a quantity of glass medallions in the Victoria and Albert Museum are some early ones of this type, and an example bearing the name of Caliph Mustansir-bi'llah, governor of Egypt from 1036 to 1094.

Other finds at Samarra were of cut glass, in some instances of clear metal coated thinly (*flashed* or *cased*) with a layer of colour. Where the outer skin is pierced by the wheel it results in a doubly decorative effect: the inner and outer colours in contrast as well as the cut design. Some of the patterns on both plain and bi-coloured pieces were simple and geometrical, as in Figs 96 and 98, others embodied birds and animals (Fig. 99). This was usually in conjunction with a background strewn with floral and other motifs in a manner more familiar on rugs and carpets of much later date from the same area.

It has been thought that some of the cut glass, particularly that of a comparatively yellow-toned metal, had a Byzantine origin. Some cups, bowls and other pieces in the Treasury of St Mark's, Venice, belong to this class, but their country of manufacture remains disputed. The bottle in Fig. 96, decorated with circles on the facetted body, is in the Victoria and Albert Museum. Part of the bequest of George Salting, it is catalogued cautiously by W. B. Honey as 'Byzantine or Egyptian; perhaps 7th or 8th century'.

The technique of the glass-cutter is allied very closely to that of the carver of semi-precious stones: the lapidary. It is known that the Persians of the Sassanian dynasty (226–637) were highly-skilled workers in rock crystal, of which magnificent evidence is exhibited in the Louvre, Paris, where there is a medallion carved with a portrait of Kavad I, who ruled the country in 488–97 and 499–531. Taking these facts

**96. Bottle** with cut decoration: perhaps Byzantine, 7th or 8th century. Ht 6½ in. **97. Pincer-moulded bowl:** Egypt, 8/10th century. Diam. 1⅞ in. **98. Bottle** with cut decoration: Islamic, 9/10th century. Ht 3 in.

into account, as well as the marked local feeling of so many of the designs, it has been assumed that at least a proportion of the surviving pieces, unfortunately mostly fragments, was made in Samarra. Equally, it is known that the Egyptians had become carvers of crystal, and from this it is deduced that they would also have decorated glass with cutting. Many specimens have been found in that country and for that reason, also because of their shape and patterning, are presumed to have been made and decorated there.

The most important surviving cut glass of possible Egyptian

origin is the series of beakers known as *Hedwig* glasses. Their name is derived from one of them, now in the Schlesisches Museum, Breslau, which is supposed to have belonged to St Hedwig, Patron Saint of Silesia, who died in 1243. The glasses are made from a tinted heavy metal with walls as much as a quarter of an inch in thickness, and the masterly cutting on them results in patterns in high relief. Some embody heraldic motives that indicate a date not earlier than the 11th century,

**99. Bottle** with cut ornament: Egypt, 10th century. Ht 7¾ in.
**100. Hedwig glass:** Egypt, 10th century. Ht about 6 in.

but their time of production is no less debatable than their place of manufacture.

The half dozen or so surviving Hedwig glasses have remained intact because they were preserved carefully in European Cathedral Treasuries, to which they had been given for use as reliquaries, perhaps by returning crusaders. Apart from agreeing that they came from somewhere in the Near

East, authorities fail to agree on exactly where. While Egypt is the choice favoured at present, it has been argued that they could have been made by craftsmen from that country who had established their workshops elsewhere. Be that as it may, the decoration of the glasses is outstanding; the depth of cutting and the variety of strokes employed resulted in articles that merited the protection they have enjoyed for several hundred years.

The Hedwig glass illustrated (Fig. 100) is in the Rijksmuseum, Amsterdam, and is carved with lions and an eagle. Beneath the foot is inscribed:

> *Alsz diesz Glasz war alt tausent Jahr*
> *Es Pfaltzgraft Ludwig Philipszen*
> *Werehret war.*          1643.

(This glass was presented to the Count Palatine Ludwig Philipsen when it was one thousand years old.   1643.)
Several glasses with similar subjects for decoration are in existence, and one with geometrical patterns is to be seen at Halberstadt in East Germany.

Some painting of glass was done by the Egyptians in Roman times, and revived at a later date. A particular type appears to be in the nature of a stain rather than an enamel, as it sinks level with the surface to which it is applied. The exact materials used and the process employed are uncertain, and the stains often appear on articles in conjunction with irridescent pigments similar in effect to lustre on pottery (Fig. 101). The latter was made in the area of Samarra during the 9th century, but glass of the type, although fragments were found on the site, is assumed to have been imported there from Egypt.

Normal enamelling of glass, with the colour applied to the surface and remaining there visibly although heated to fuse with it, became much improved in technique and more popular from the 12th century. While Alexandria continued as a centre of glass-making, other notable cities where such work might have been done include Aleppo, Damascus, Baghdad and Mossul. Many places acquired fame for their work in the medium, but after five hundred years little remains as evidence of what was produced. This little may or may not be truly representative of the output of the many workshops that must have existed, and in spite of the careful work of archaeologists

**101. Bowl** with lustre-painted decoration: Egypt, 10/11th century. Diam. 4¾ in. **102. Cup** signed ALDREVANDIN ME FECI: Islamic, 13th century. Ht 5 in.

and historians the full story is far from complete yet. The continual interchange of goods and ideas, common throughout the centuries in both East and West, makes it most difficult to interpret such evidence as is available.

Some late 12th-century fragments found at Rakka, near Aleppo, show distinctive decoration with 'a free use of bead-like drops' and may have been made there. The employment of small dots of colour as a background for strapwork and other formal patterns is seen on a famous beaker in the museum at Douai. Another, at Chartres, was once supposed to

94

have been presented by Haroun al-Raschid, hero of the tales in the *Arabian Nights*, to Charlemagne, King of the Franks. As the former died in 809 and the latter five years later and the beaker is not older than the 13th century (if not of 14th-century make), this romantic story is just as apocryphal as are so many others. A third, in the British Museum, was mounted in silver in the 14th century, and is said to have been won at play with a King of France. In the course of time, it appears that the name of the royal personage in question and the nature of the play at which he lost have both been forgotten.

Pieces with more certain Western affiliations include a beaker in the Kunstgewerbe Museum, Frankfurt-am-Main, which is inscribed AV[E] MARIA GR[A]TIA PLEN[A], and two pieces in the British Museum. One of the latter, a tall cup, is painted with a representation of the Virgin and Child, and the words DRIA MATER REGIS ALTISSIMI ORA P PA. The other, half the size of the preceding (Fig. 102), bears a coat of arms and is inscribed MAGISTER ALDREVANDIN ME FECI. The latter was for long accepted as being of Venetian work-manship, but more recently has been supposed to have been made by an Italian craftsman named Aldrevandini employed in a Syrian glass-decorating establishment.

A piece with strong Syrian connections, of typical Syrian shape, is in Fig. 103. This is painted round the body with a band of ornament centring on an oval medallion with a crest believed to be that of Baybars I, Mameluke Sultan of Egypt from 1260 to 1277. Another cup, mounted and in the Waddesdon Bequest at the British Museum, shows a man seated on a low throne and on either side of him stands an attendant holding a sword (Fig. 104).

The European practice of mounting these Oriental glasses in gold and silver, adorned sometimes with precious stones and pearls, shows the veneration in which they were held at the time. It is recorded that a cup given in 1244 to Henry III of England was sent by him to his goldsmith, Edward of Westminster. The latter was ordered to remove the foot of the vessel and replace it with one of silver-gilt, to place a silver band round the piece and to present it to the Queen on behalf of his Majesty. This particular example has disappeared, but others, including those noted above, have survived.

**103. Cup** with arms of Baybars I: Islamic, 13th century. Ht 5¾ in.
**104. Cup** painted with figures: Islamic, 13th century. Ht 5 in.
**105. The 'Luck of Edenhall':** Islamic, 13th century. Ht 6⅜ in.

The Syrian 13th-century beaker known as the 'Luck of Eden Hall' is one of the most interesting surviving examples: interesting not only because it has remained intact for so long, but because it had been in the possession of one family for a succession of centuries. With the longest pedigree of any glass in English history, it was acquired in 1958 by the Victoria and Albert Museum, from the Musgrave family of Eden Hall, near Penrith, Cumberland. It is from their seat that it acquired its name (Fig. 105).

The 'Luck' is enamelled with strapwork in brilliant red, blue and green, and is gilt; the glass itself is of a yellowish tint. An 18th-century traveller wrote of it as follows:

'Antient superstition may have contributed not a little to its preservation; but that it should not, in a more enlightened age, or in moments of conviviality, meet with one gentle rap (and a gentle one would be quite sufficient for an ordinary glass of the same substance), is to me somewhat wonderful. Superstition, however, cannot be entirely eradicated from the mind at once. The late agent of the family had such a reverential regard for this glass, that he would not suffer any person to touch it, and but few to see it. When the family, or other curious people, had a desire to drink out of it, a napkin was held underneath, lest any accident should befall it; and it is still carefully preserved, in a case made on purpose. The case is said to be the second, yet bears the marks of antiquity, and is charged with IHS.

'Tradition, our only guide here, says that a party of fairies were drinking and making merry round a well near the Hall, called St Cuthbert's well; but, being interrupted by the intrusion of some curious people, they were frightened, and made a hasty retreat, and left the cup in question: one of the last screaming out,

> *If this cup should break or fall,*
> *Farewell the Luck of Edenhall.'*

Earlier, in 1729, a long ballad was published describing a drinking-party at Eden Hall, and this opened with the verse:

> *God prosper long from being broke*
> *The Luck of Edenhall;*
> *A doleful drinking-bout I sing,*
> *There lately did befall.*

The leather case, in which the glass has been preserved,
is possibly of French workmanship, and was made about a
hundred years after the 'Luck'. The fact that the cover bears
the Sacred Monogram has led to the suggestion that the
vessel may have been used at some time in the past as a
chalice.

The most famous of the Syrian decorated glasses are the
mosque-lamps or lanterns. Because they were made for, and
hung in, places of worship, a greater proportion of them has
been preserved than of other artistic glass of Islamic origin.
In position, suspended from a roof, they would have been
inaccessible and mainly unnoticed, and their religious significance must also have helped to protect them. Lamps were
mentioned in the Koran, and a verse from the book inscribed
on some examples may be translated as 'God is the light of the
Heavens and the Earth: His light is a niche in which is a
lamp, the lamp in a glass, the glass as it were a glittering star'.

The lamps remained in the mosques for which they had
been made until late in the 19th century, when most of them
were transferred to the Arab Museum in Cairo. There, more
than fifty are to be seen, and about as many again are distributed throughout the rest of the world. The majority of
them are in public collections in the major cities, and only a
very few remain in private hands.

The so-called lamps are in reality outer shades. The oil
was burned in a separate small container within, which has
nearly always been discarded. The burners were probably
held in place loosely by means of wires, and being of glass
must have suffered frequent breakages in use. The complete
lamps were hung before the shrines to which they belonged,
and after they had been removed in the 19th century an
observer recorded that in the mosque of Sultan Hasan the
remaining chains were so numerous that they resembled
falling rain. In some instances, the lamps were suspended from

their three or six chains of bronze or silver, uniting at, or passing through, a decorated glass ball which was itself depending from a roof-member, or from the top of an archway. The ball in Fig. 106 is made of orange-yellow glass richly enamelled in colours and bright gold so it would have glittered in the sunlight or lamplight when hanging aloft in a building.

One of the earliest of the lamps is in the Metropolitan Museum, New York, and was made to commemorate

**106. Glass ball** for suspending above a lamp, 15th century. Diam. 4⅜ in. **107. Detail of painting on a mosque-lamp:** Islamic, 14th century.

Aydakin bīn 'Abdallāh, the Arquebusier, who died in 1286. Others are known with inscriptions on them relating to noble personages dating from the late 13th and early 14th centuries, whose memories have been kept alive far longer than the fragile material could have led their mourners to expect.

It has been noted that all the earlier examples have three small looped handles for suspension, whereas later ones each have six. In London, in the Victoria and Albert Museum, is a

three-loop lamp bearing the name of Sultan al-Muzaffar
Rukn ad-dīn, more familiar under his family name Baybars
II, who ruled Egypt for only a short time before he was exe-
cuted in 1310. The lamp is particularly well painted and bears
a dedication: 'Glory to our Lord the Sultan al-Malik al-
Muzaffar, the Wise and Just, Pillar of the World and the

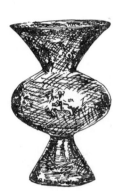 

**108. Lamp** painted with horsemen: Islamic, 13th century. Ht 8¼ in.
**109. Lamp** inscribed to Sultan Hasan: Islamic, 14th century.
Ht 14 in.

Faith. May his victory be great', and some verses from the
Koran: 'Truly the just live in happiness. Thou seest upon
their faces the radiance of happiness. They shall have fiery
sealed wine to drink.'

Also in the Victoria and Albert Museum is the lamp shown
in Fig. 108, which is of the early three-loop pattern. The
decoration is sparse, and on the body are painted figures of
falconers on horseback. The rims at mouth and foot are

bordered with a pattern of curved lines, and, although a few other ornamental details appear upon it, the piece is noticeably lacking in the usual 'busy' work found on most others. For this reason it has been associated with a group having the same characteristic which is supposed to have been made in Damascus, but there has been no real proof forthcoming in support of the statement.

Typical of the cleverly contrived interlaced patterns most commonly seen on the lamps is the detail in Fig. 107, which is picked out in colours of red, blue, white and gold. The same colours appear on the example in Fig. 109. The inscriptions on the neck and body read: 'God is the light of the heavens and the earth. The similitude of His light is a niche in which is a lamp' from the Koran, and 'To our Lord the Sultan, el-Melik en Nāsir, aider of the world and religion, Hasan, son of Muhammad; mighty be his aid rendered'. The Bahri Mameluke Sultan Hasan ruled from 1347 to 1351 and from 1354 to 1361, and was executed in the latter year. He built a magnificent mosque in Cairo between 1356 and 1359, and the lamp is supposed to have come from it by way of 'a Jew at Pola, Istria, who procured it in Cairo'.

Two of the surviving lamps, one in Cairo and one in New York, bear inscriptions stating that they were the handiwork of 'Ali bin Muhammad Amakī (which can be read also as al-Ramakī or al-Zamakī). No others are known with indications of their maker or decorator until the third quarter of the 19th century when a Frenchman, Joseph Brocard, made careful copies of the old pieces. His work was created in response to the demand for such things during the vogue, which was especially strong in Paris, for Moorish and Levantine furnishings. Brocard was sufficiently proud of his craftsmanship, and had perhaps regard for future connoisseurs, to sign his work. At the height of the vogue a genuine lamp might cost anything up to £2,000, so there was a ready market for close copies at a reasonable figure, and the imitations could be made to sell at a profit. Nowadays, they are recognised as minor works of art in their own right, and are bought by those who, like their predecessors in Brocard's day, have no hope of being able to afford a true Islamic specimen.

On account of the unhappy connection of Damascus with oriental soldiery and the consequent possible absorption of

**110. Bottle** with enamelled decoration: Islamic, 13/14th century. Ht 17½ in.  **111. Bottle** with blazon of a State Secretary: Islamic, 14th century. Ht 13⅞ in.

Chinese decorative motifs by the city's artists, a number of pieces of glass are assigned to that place. The ornaments found include lotuses, peonies, cloud-scrolls, dragons and phoenixes; all of which are familiar from their use on ceramics and other articles from the Far East. The bottle in Fig. 110 is painted with medallions each depicting a Chinese phoenix, and around the neck are lotuses and vine-ornament.

It is painted in colours which include a light blue, found only on early pieces and unlike the dark shade used at a later date. Analysis of fragments of the 14th-century dark blue enamel showed that it was free of cobalt, but tinged by the use of powdered lapis lazuli. No explanation has been forthcoming as to why the use of the pale shade ceased and the darker one replaced it.

Chinese phoenixes appear among the decoration on the tall bottle in Fig. 111. This is of a green-tinted glass, and the ornament includes a band painted with dogs chasing a gazelle and other animals. The typically flowery inscription reads: 'His Honourable and High Excellency our Lord, the Royal, the Well-Served Saif ad-dīn Jurjī, Master of the Household of the Noble Porte, Officer, of al-Malik an-Nāsir. May God make his victories glorious and double his power'. In addition, the piece bears medallions showing a writer's pen-box: the blazon of a State Secretary. It may be remarked that other blazons are recorded which, in a similar manner, signify the posts of Court officials: e.g. a napkin for the Master of the Wardrobe.

The foregoing pieces all have translatable inscriptions, but this is not always the case. The beauty of the cursive Cufic writing was such that artists sometimes used it merely as decoration, and the letters were placed in juxtaposition merely for their visual effect. Although they look attractive they have no meaning whatever, and much time has been spent in the past in trying to decipher what is merely gibberish.

In the same style of enamelled decoration as the lamps are a few other surviving pieces: flagons, cups and jugs. Of the flagons, one, in the British Museum, of squat bottle shape with two small handles at the neck, is painted with huntsmen and with medallions. One of the latter (Fig. 112) shows a seated man holding aloft in his right hand a beaker, in the background is another and also a bottle of similar outline to that in Fig. 110. Both beakers resemble those in Figs. 102 to 105.

A similar flagon, but larger in size, is in the Cathedral of St Stephen, Vienna. The decoration on it includes medallions painted with falconers on horseback, and seated musicians playing a tambourine, a triangle and other instruments beneath a tree. The vessel forms a reliquary, is sealed and contains a quantity of earth brought from Bethlehem that is

**112. Detail of decoration on a flagon:** Islamic, 13/14th century.
**113. Jug** painted with polo-players: Islamic, 14th century. Ht 7 in.

supposed to be drenched with the blood of the Innocents. It is inscribed repeatedly with the words 'The Sultan', but as the name of the particular Sultan is not revealed it is impossible to date the piece completely accurately. It is ascribed to the 13th century.

Beakers or drinking-vessels of different patterns from the funnel-shaped ones described and illustrated earlier have also been recorded. One, with a ribbed body and a shaped base, standing almost a foot in height, is decorated with medallions of men on horseback who appear to be playing polo. This piece may perhaps be described more aptly in the past tense: it was in the famous Lanna Collection sold by auction in Prague in 1911. It realised the sum of £2,050, and, in spite of this high figure and the familiarity of experts with it, it seems to have disappeared completely at some unknown date prior to 1930. Another, slightly smaller in size and of different design, is distinguished by having a raised band a short distance down the body from the rim. It is painted with floral medallions, and interlaced Cufic characters which are apparently meaningless, but very decorative.

The jug in Fig. 113 has the feature of a band of projecting tongues of glass round the base of the neck, and is painted with figures of polo-players on horseback and with a bearded servitor carrying a dish of fruit. It is of brown-tinted glass, and like the majority of the other examples with enamelled decoration has lost much of its original gilding, always the least durable portion of the ornament.

While most of the pieces described are of pale green or pale brown metal, there are a few examples surviving of a deep blue shade and others of purple. An unusual lamp which bears the name of the Bahri Mameluke Sultan Malik al-Nāsir (Nāsir al-dīn Muhammad), who reigned for three periods between 1293 and 1341, is in the Victoria and Albert Museum. It is painted with an inner coating of green enamel which gives it a most unusual and unexpected effect when a light is placed inside. A lamp of blue glass is recorded, and this has an inscription referring probably to the Sultan Muzaffar, known as Baybars II, who died in 1310.

It has been observed that the earlier pieces of Islamic glass were painted with much greater care than those of the mid- and late 14th century. In the case of the lamps, perhaps this took place because of a realisation that detailed work was wasted on articles seen only at a distance. From this start, the standard fell generally, and all work was finished in a more casual manner than it had been when the art was introduced. In addition to the use of the dark blue enamel, referred to earlier, the standard of painting is a good guide to the approximate date of the works.

The Syrian glass-decorating industry came to an end abruptly after the sacking of Damascus by Tamerlane in 1400. The conqueror is said to have carried off most of the

**114. Water-sprinkler:** Persia, late 17th century. Ht 14 in.

**115. Bottle:** Persia, late 17th century. Ht 9⅞ in.

skilled craftsmen of the city to Samarkand, but little or none of the work they may have executed after being uprooted so violently has been recognised with certainty.

A small number of mosque-lamps, described as 'of decidedly poor quality', have been recorded. One bears the name of the Burji Mameluke Sultan al-Mu'ayyad Abu-n-Nasir Shaikh, who ruled from 1412–21. This and the other 15th-century examples were perhaps made in Egypt, but it is known that similar ones were supplied from Venice.

The influence of Venice, or at any rate of Western taste, is to be seen in some of the glass made in Persia in the 16th century and later. Under the rule of Shah Abbas I (1587–1628), known deservedly as 'the Great', Persia was raised from a state of anarchy to one of comparative importance. Not only was a considerable amount of building undertaken, but tolerance was shown towards foreigners, and the magnificence of the Court was an encouragement to the arts.

Glass of the period is not without interest, as can be seen from the examples shown in Figs. 114 and 115. The rather

**116. Bowl** with pincered trailing ornament: Persia, 18th century. W. 8½ in.

bizarre forms of the vessels are a cross between East and West, with the predominance of the strong varieties in colouring favoured by the former. An important centre of glass manufacture was at Shiraz, where an Italian is said to have instructed the workmen. This may explain the European influence seen in the design of many pieces, which are versions of the contorted forms then current in Venice. Doubtless the Shah and his entourage welcomed such novelties to satisfy their desire for luxury.

Finally, an early 18th-century bowl (Fig. 116), ornamented with pincered trailing, shows that the tradition lingered. Glass continued to be made in the country and some was given enamel decoration of floral design, but little of good quality appears to have been produced. It has been pointed out that much of the glassware of 18th and 19th century date brought out of Persia in subsequent years did not originate in that country, but had been imported there from Bohemia and elsewhere in Europe.

# CHAPTER VI

# Venetian Glass

The inhabitants of the Venetian Republic were industrious traders, and its situation in Europe made the maritime city of great strategic importance between East and West. The Venetian fleet grew large and well-armed, and came to constitute a formidable force which by 1100 ruled the Adriatic and commanded the route through the Mediterranean to the Holy Land. In due time agreements were concluded for trading, and the Venetian adventurers had buildings reserved for their use in many of the cities of the Levant, including Tyre, Sidon and Acre.

Glass-makers were working in Venice as early as the 11th century, but nothing is known of their productions at that date. Doubtless they were confined to articles of the simpler types made earlier at Rome and Alexandria, and anything more ambitious was brought from the Near East. It is possible, also, that many of the earliest Venetian pieces resemble some of the Syrian so closely that they have remained unrecognised.

The impregnable hold of the Venetians on the trade routes of the world meant that the armies of the Crusaders were dependent on them for passage and for transport. Thus, for the Fourth Crusade of 1202–04, which involved the movement of 9,000 knights, 20,000 foot soldiers, 4,500 horses and provisions for a year, an agreement was made with the Doge that payment should take the form of 85,000 silver marks and one half of all conquests. However, the promised cash was not forthcoming prior to sailing and the force was immobilised until the money could be paid. In the end, it was negotiated

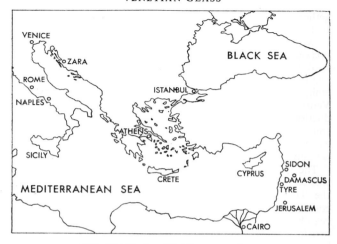

**117. The Eastern Mediterranean Area.**

that to settle (or to postpone) the payment of the debt the Crusaders would act as mercenaries of the Venetians and attack the town of Zara, capital of the nearby seceded country of Dalmatia. This was achieved with success, and finally the entire scheme of the expedition was changed. Instead of attacking their original objective, Egypt, the Crusaders, in company with the Venetians, captured and sacked Constantinople.

It is possible that craftsmen were brought back or migrated to Venice from Byzantium and Syria, and these would then have adapted their native styles to suit western buyers. At the same time, the Venetian workers would have assimilated the more sophisticated styles of the wares brought from the Levant, and had evolved their own variations on them. To-

gether with the Roman-based original inspirations they formed the elements which combined to raise the glass of Venice
to world-wide fame, and to make it one of the notable ex-
pressions of Renaissance art.

Mention should be made here of the rival glass industry
conducted near Genoa at L'Altare, which was founded by
emigrants from Normandy. It developed alongside that of
Venice and in such a closely related manner that the productions of the two places are mainly indistinguishable. In
spite of the fact that contemporary records mention glass
as in the '*façon de Venise*' and the '*façon d'Altare*', they are
no longer to be told apart, except in a very few instances.

The ingredient that led to the success of Venetian glass
was found plentifully in the beds of Italian rivers, especially
the Ticino and the Po. The water-washed white pebbles,
*cogoli*, when combined with alkali from plant ash, formed a
readily-fused metal. From this, the craftsmen fashioned
articles of remarkably light weight, much of it in attractive
tints ranging from the palest yellow to light brown and some
with a slight hint of black.

Much of the metal was of great clarity and purity of colour
(or colourlessness) when compared with the productions
of contemporary and earlier glass-houses. The re-discovery
of manganese as a de-colourising agent enabled this desired
end to be achieved, and the goal of imitating as closely as
possible the magic of natural rock crystal grew nearer.
Although the potentialities of manganese had been found out
probably as much as one hundred years earlier, its use did not
become general until the 16th century. At this time the virtues
of the improved metal became fully appreciated and applied
decoration temporarily became of secondary importance.

Although the industry was commenced in the city of Venice
itself, the ever-present danger of fire led to the removal of
the majority of the workshops to the nearby island of Murano.

There, the authorities wisely reasoned, a mishap would not involve adjoining dwelling-houses, and perhaps even the entire city. From the time of their establishment on Murano in the late 13th century a few of the workshops have remained operating until the present day, manned in some instances by descendants of the workers of the past.

Just prior to the move to the island, the manufacturers in the industry had become sufficiently numerous to form themselves into a guild. Before long this was divided into appropriate sections: *fioleri*, makers of vessels; *verieri*, makers of glass in mass; *cristallai*, makers of glass for spectacles; *specchiai*, makers of looking-glasses; *margaritai* and *perlai*, makers of small and large beads respectively. In addition, there were the dealers in glassware: *venditori*.

The products of the Venetian glass-houses during their active and important life, which endured for several centuries, were so diverse that to deal with them it is most convenient to divide them into separate classifications. This was done by Sir Augustus Wollaston Franks, a prominent collector and British Museum keeper about a century ago, and in spite of the lapse of time the six divisions he proposed cannot be bettered for the purpose. They were as follows:

(1) *Vessels of colourless and transparent glass, or glass of single colours—that is, glass coloured with metallic oxides before being worked into vessels.*

Drinking-glasses are most often of clear glass (Figs 118, 119, 120 and 121), but may be ornamented with additions of colour in the form of trailing. The stems, handles and knobs of covers sometimes take fantastic shapes, such as the dragon with a spitefully curled tail in Fig. 118 and the handles of complex design in Fig. 119. Other articles, such as the table-lamp in the guise of a running horse (Fig. 122), can be little less exotic. These exercises in the bizarre are among the charac-

**118. Cup and cover** with dragon stem: Venice, 16th century. Ht 12 in. **119. Two-handled wine-glass:** Venice early 17th century. Ht 5 in. **120. Wine-glass** with white and blue trailed ornament: Venice, 16th century. Ht 4 in.

**121. Wine-glass:** Venice, 16th century. **122. Table-lamp:** Venice, late 16th/early 17th century.

teristic features of most glass-works, but are particularly suitable to Venetian metal; a material of which the peculiar ductility was exploited fully by men of near-genius. The making and design of such pieces relies entirely on the skill and taste of the craftsman; a combination that never recurs to permit perfect reproduction.

Coloured pieces are in blue, green and purple, with occasional rarities in turquoise blue and opaque white. Except

**123. Cup** of dark blue glass with enamel decoration: Venice, late 15th century.

in the case of the last-named these were used from as early as the 15th century (Figs. 123 and 124), but the employment of them was not confined to Venice alone. There are many formulae for coloured glass in the most famous book on the industry: Antonio Neri's *L'arte vetraria*, published in Florence in 1612, which had a wide circulation.

Opaque white glass (*lattimo*) was in use perhaps as early as 1500 for making vessels, and it was revived in the late 17th century when it was realised that it made a passable rival to porcelain. These later examples were painted in enamel colours in the same manner as chinaware, and can be deceptively like it in appearance.

## (2) *Gilt and enamelled glass*

This technique is the one used by the Islamic workers in the 13th and 14th centuries, but the art would seem to have been forgotten after the fall of Damascus. Its re-invention at Venice is said to have been by a glass-manufacturer named Angelo Beroviero or Barovieri, but this is based only on tradition. The cup in Fig. 123 is supposed to have been made as a wedding present for one of the Beroviero family in the 15th century, but the suggested date, and that of some other similar pieces, has been queried.

The blue glass jug in Fig. 124 is enamelled thickly with

**124. Jug** with coloured enamel decoration: Venice, early 16th century. Ht 8 in. **125. The Fairfax Cup,** of turquoise-blue glass: Venice, late 15th century. Ht $3\frac{5}{8}$ in. **126. Cup** with enamel decoration: Venice, late 15th century. Ht $7\frac{1}{2}$ in.

floral scrolls and tritons and nereids. It may be compared with painted majolica of the same date, the late 15th century, both as regards the shape of the piece and the style of decoration. Of similar date is the 'Fairfax Cup' (Fig. 125), so called because it was in the possession of a Yorkshire family of that name for some three hundred years. It is of an opaque pale turquoise, enamelled in colours with the story of Pyramus and

Thisbe, which is familiar from Shakespeare's use of it in *A Midsummer Night's Dream*.

With the coming of the 16th century, the use of coloured metal as a ground for enamel would seem to have gone out of fashion, and the work was carried out on clear glass. The earlier types of decoration, such as formal floral scrolls, bust portraits and mythological scenes are found to have been

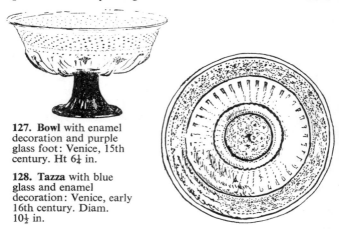

**127. Bowl** with enamel decoration and purple glass foot: Venice, 15th century. Ht 6¼ in.

**128. Tazza** with blue glass and enamel decoration: Venice, early 16th century. Diam. 10½ in.

replaced by simple geometrical patterns. Jewel-like dots and fish-scales are seen also. All these allow the beautiful transparency of the metal itself to play its part in the design, and to emphasise the inimitable delicacy of the article.

The cup in Fig. 126 is patterned with dots in blue glass and is enamelled in white, red and gold. The bowl (Fig. 127) has a foot of purple tint and the body is decorated with enamel dots, while the *tazza* in Fig. 128 (a dish on a low foot) is embellished with blue glass threads and enamelled similarly in colour.

A number of examples are painted with coats of arms which can be an aid to dating them. Typical of these is the *cesendello* (lampshade) in Fig. 129, bearing the arms of the Tiepolo family and made in the late 15th or early 16th century. It is a western version of the earlier Islamic mosque lamp, and similar *cesendelli* appear in the paintings of Carpaccio and Bellini. Some pieces of glass have had such coats of arms added at a

**129. Cesendello** painted with the arms of Tiepolo: Venice 15th/16th century.

**130. Flask** with vertical blue threading and metal neck-band and stopper: Venice, 16th century. Ht 6¼ in.

**131. Ewer** in imitation of chalcedony: Venice, late 15th century. Ht 12 in.

later date; a fact revealed by the quality of their drawing being at variance with that of the rest of the decoration.

Enamelled work passed slowly out of fashion in Venice during the course of the 16th century. This was principally because advances in glass-making resulted in vessels with much thinner walls than had been made hitherto, and they were liable to be distorted if re-heated in the kiln during enamelling. Thus, painting grew noticeably slighter, and more frequently decoration relied on elaborate shaping or on the contrasting colours of trailed and other applied ornament.

In the mid-16th century there was a short-lived vogue for painting executed in unfired oil-paints. Elaborate coloured and gilded scrolling framed pictorial subjects in the manner of Raphael, but such decoration was, of course, easily damaged and very few examples have been preserved in good condition. It is probable that many pieces that were once painted in this way have long ago lost all trace of the work, and their original appearance is now unsuspected.

### (3) *Crackled glass*

This is known sometimes as *ice-glass* because of its resemblance to cracked and broken ice. The method of making it involves the sudden cooling of the vessel followed by reheating; alternatively the heated glass can be placed in contact with some broken fragments which are then partially melted into the surface. Some examples of ice-glass incorporate a portion of this rough-surfaced 'decoration', which must have called for great skill and care on the part of the maker (Fig. 285, p. 245). The technique seems to have evolved and been employed in the 16th century, but was in use intermittently at later dates.

### (4) *Variegated or marbled opaque glass, commonly known by the German word* schmelz

The imitation of precious and semi-precious stones which attracted earlier glass-makers continued to fascinate them and their public in 15th century, and later, Venice.

Onyx, agate and chalcedony were the principal objectives, but jasper and aventurine were not uncommon (Fig. 131). The whole class was known at one time as *calcedonio*, but nowadays is referred to as *schmelzglas*. Aventurine, the gold-speckled reddish-brown stone, is a variety of quartz. The glass it resembles is said to have been discovered by accident in the workshop of a maker named Miotti, when a quantity of copper filings fell into a pot of molten metal. The name comes from the Italian *avventura*, meaning 'chance'.

Examples of some types of *schmelzglas* date back to the 15th century, but others were not invented until later and all were reproduced from time to time.

**132. Ewer** with white thread decoration: Venice, mid-15th century. Ht 6 in. **133. Wine-glass** with white thread decoration: Venice, 16th century. Ht 5⅛ in. **134. Wine-glass** with combed white bowl. Venice, late 17th century. Ht 6 in.

**(5)** *Millefiore or mosaic glass*

As has been described and illustrated earlier (pp. 22 and 65, Figs. 62 and 63) the Romans and the Egyptians knew of this variety of glass. Its use was revived successfully by the Venetians, not only in the same manner as by the Romans, but also with the canes embedded in clear metal.

**(6)** *Reticulated, filigree, or lace glass;* called by the Venetians *vetro filigranato*

This is the most renowned of Venetian methods of decorating glass, and results in the production of fine lace-like patterns within the metal (Figs 132, 133 and 134). When the enclosed threads are of opaque white the glassware is known as *latticino* or *latticinio*. *Vetro filigranato* has been made since the mid-16th century, thereafter having remained continuously in production. Giuseppe Briati, who died in 1772, and later makers specialized in its manufacture, so the dating of specimens can present difficulties. The later examples are frequently much

**135. Diamond-engraved dish**: Venice, 16th century. Diam. 14 in.

more complicated in pattern than the earlier ones, but hard and fast rules cannot be laid down and each piece must be judged on its merits. The work was mostly confined to threads of opaque white, but red, blue, yellow and other colours occur. Each is found alone, in combination or with white.

Decoration achieved by engraving the surface with the point of a diamond may be said to be a sub-division of (1): vessels of colourless or transparent glass (Fig. 135). Some of this work was done in Venice, but it was more popular in other countries on pieces of Venetian pattern. At the German and Netherlandish glass-houses it was especially favoured.

The shapes of the earlier vessels, principally cups or

goblets, bottles, flasks and dishes, show the marked influence of silver design; silhouetted, both would appear to be made from the metal. Alternatively, some of the pieces have a solidity that is associated more accurately with pottery, and this likeness is apparent, as has been pointed out, especially in some of the early enamelled examples. In time, however, changes in taste and a growth of technical skill resulted in glass becoming more individual in pattern, and many of the shapes could be realised in no other medium. When that came about, it could be said with truth that the art of glass was born. It was an event that occurred in the time of the Romans, and one that took place once again in 15th and 16th century Venice.

The popularity of Venetian glass in foreign countries can be gauged from the quantity possessed by the English king, Henry VIII. In an Inventory of his effects taken in 1542 were between three and four hundred glass vessels, which included the following:

'Two bottles or flagons of glass, jasper colour

A basin and a laver [water-jug] of blue glass, partly gilt; the laver having the King's arms upon it

Three bowls of glass, jasper colour, without covers, two of them having feet

Four standing cups [tall goblets] of blue glass with covers to them, painted and gilt

Two little standing cups with covers, chalice fashion, of glass of many colours

Sixteen goblets of glass without covers

Three glasses like pots with two ears [handles] with covers to them

A glass like a pot, tankard fashion with hoops, with a handle and a cover to the same

A cup of glass with two ears, the foot garnished with silver and gilt, with a cover likewise garnished having a knob of silver and gilt, with Queen Anne's [Anne Boleyn's] cipher engraved in it

Four glasses with long small necks and great bellies

One little like [similar] glass rowid [striped] with white

Nine spice plates of green and blue glass, great and small, 4 of them being partly gilt

A low candlestick of glass, jasper colour

Three altar candlesticks of glass

Four spoons, the steels [handles] being glass, the spoons [bowls] being of metal gilt

Two forkes of metal gilt, the steels being glass

64 platters, dishes and saucers of glass.'

Not only does the list record a wide variety of articles, but the colour of the glass from which each was made and the decoration upon it are specified. It may be noticed that most of the goblets were with covers, and it would appear that each of them left the workshop complete with one. The Venetian provenance of all these pieces is virtually certain, because at that date it is very doubtful whether they could have been supplied from anywhere else. The descriptions of 'jasper colour', 'blue', 'rowid with white' and the use of gilding, are all to be recognised readily as features of Murano wares.

The State control of the Venetian glass-makers was extremely strict. Among others, there were penalties to be paid for the exportation of waste glass (cullet), which might be of use to foreign makers who would add it to their product and so improve the latter. Above all, it was enacted that on no account must any of the workmen seek employment abroad. In one instance where this had taken place, it is said that the Doge sent men to follow the glass-makers and murder them. In contrast, the workers at Altare were encouraged to aid expansion of the industry and were loaned for this purpose wherever their services were required. In return, an annual payment was demanded by the Council controlling them. It was the Venetians, however, whose aid and superior skill were in demand, and the courts of Europe vied with each other in bribing absconding workers to set up manufactories for making glass *à la façon de Venise* under their supervision.

The first city in which such a glass-works was established with success was Antwerp, the important trading centre in north Flanders. In 1541 an Italian named Cornachini was given permission to make '*cristallyne en staele spiegels*': glass and steel mirrors. Eight years later, Jean de Lame of Cremona was allowed to manufacture '*verres de cristal à la mode et façon que l'on labeure en la cité de Venise*': crystal glass in the manner practised in the city of Venice. De Lame's concession passed soon to Jacomo Pasquetti of Brescia, who perhaps made the piece recorded in a document of 1569 as '*Une hault verre de cristal d'Anvers*': a tall glass of Antwerp crystal.

By 1569 there was a glass-works operating in Liége, and in 1571 Pasquetti caused two barrels full of glassware from there to be seized in Antwerp. This had been consigned for sale and was looked upon by Pasquetti as poaching on his territory. During the 17th century Liége attained an important position under the ownership of members of the Bonhomme family, who also had establishments at Huy and Maastricht.

Elsewhere, there was activity in Holland, where the Amsterdam workers were resented by those in Antwerp and Cologne. At Middleburg, Godefroid Verhaegen started to make glass in the Venetian fashion. This was in 1581, and it has been stated that he came to the Zeeland town from England, where he had been working. Before long, there were complaints that he was kidnapping workers from Antwerp, and his products were competing with those of the latter city.

Other glass-works are known to have been in existence during the 16th century in Germany, France, and Spain and Portugal. At Hall-in-the-Tyrol one was started in 1534 and eventually came under the patronage of the Archduke Ferdinand. Much of the output there would seem to have been decorated with diamond-engraving, which was employed also at Nuremburg. It has been pointed out that engraved work in a similar style has been found in England and that the same hand might be responsible for them all. Some drinking-glasses with English inscriptions have for long been associated with a French pewter-engraver named Anthony de Lisle (p. 170).

All the continental glass shares the Venetian inspiration in both metal and style and only in a few exceptional instances has it been possible to distinguish the products of one factory from those of another. In addition, it cannot often be said with any certainty that a piece was not made in Venice itself, and this further complicates the position. Some of the surviving specimens have been identified as to their origins on grounds of traditions that do not bear overmuch investigation.

The introduction of Venetian-style glass-making in England took place, as in other countries, during the 16th century, and is dealt with more conveniently in the chapter on that country (p. 165). More appropriate here will be a mention of the glass ordered to be made by Allesio Morelli in Venice and sent by him to London. The English dealers who placed the orders, John Greene and Michael Measey, were working in partnership and gave their address as The Kings Arms, Poultry (in Cheapside, near the Mansion House, in the City of London). By the greatest of good fortune the original 'office copies' of some of their letters have been preserved and are in the British Museum. The correspondence, which is illustrated with sketches (Figs 136 to 141) of the goods required, runs from 1667 to 1672, and the first letter is as follows:

' London, December the 12th, 1667. S$^r$ Yours of the 4$^{th}$ November last was received, and we thank you for your ready care (you express) to observe and perform our last order: and S$^r$ we desire you to take the same

**136–138. Sketches of glasses** and other vessels ordered from Venice by John Greene and Michael Measey, about 1670.

care to get us a few more glasses made (and added to our former order and sent with them) according to the number and forms herein expressed: and also to pack up with them 4 dozen speckled enameld beer glasses and 6 dozen ditto for wine: the

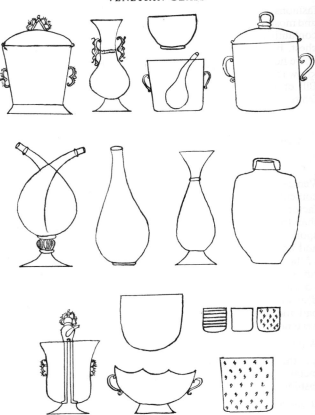

**139-141. More sketches of vessels** ordered from Venice by John Greene and Michael Measey.

fashions of these we leave to you, only let them be all with feet and most with ears and of good fashions, we suppose this order containing 90 dozen of glasses may be packed in one large chest, but if not let the remainder be packt in a small chest. S$^r$ we hope we need not to say any more to you, but to let you know that we shall credit ourselves so much as to honour your Bill or Bills with punctual payment: which is all at present from

your humble servants
M.M. & J.G.'

A later communication carried complaints:

'August 28th, 1668

'. . . we have received the five chests and one small box of Venice glasses that you consigned unto us and as to the contents thereof, they were right for number according to the factory [invoice], but the beer glasses were something smaller than the patterns and as to the chest No. 5 it was almost quite spoiled; it had received much wet which had rotted the glasses, and we suggest it was wet before it was shipped for the Master of the ship and all his men do affirm that it did receive no wet since it came into their custody, and therefore we could get no satisfaction from them; the box of enamld glasses were dear and the worst that ever we had, the colours were very bad and were laid too thick and rough, and pray let these we have now writ for be better . . .'

A postscript added firmly:

'. . . the drinking glasses [to] be made of very clear white sound metal and exact according to the patterns both for size, fashion and number of no other sorts or fashions.'

It concluded by listing the following requirements:

'1 dozen of speckled enameld covered beer glasses
  1 dozen ditto uncovered

127

1 dozen clouded calsedonia covered beer glasses
1 dozen ditto uncovered
2 dozen enameld covered claret glasses
1 dozen clouded calsedonia covered claret glasses
2 dozen enameld covered sack glasses
1 dozen calsedonia sack glasses
4 dozen speckled enameld claret glasses
2 dozen clouded calsedonia claret glasses
4 dozen speckled enameld sack glasses'

A final note added:

'I have not drawn patterns for these. But let them be made with feet and ears of good handsome fashions and packed by themselves in a small box or case and marked as in the margin.'

In the following year a further order was sent, together with a mention that water had again caused damage to part of a previous consignment:

'London, September 17, 1669.

S$^r$—Our respects presented unto you, we have here enclosed you our patterns for a parcel of drinking glasses and a few false pearl necklaces, which we desire you may be sent us with all convenient speed upon the first good free ship that presents, and that special care be taken in the providing them according to our directions under written and to the well packing them up, for the last we received from you out of the *John & Thomas* and *African* many of the chests were very ill-conditioned; for there was above forty dozen broken and some of the chests had taken water which does stain and rot the glasses, and we could not see how they could take wet after they were shipped for both the ships were in a very good condition, so that we suppose your servants let the chests stand out in the rain after they were packed, and therefore we hope you will freely make us some satisfaction for the damage we received thereby, and order more care to be taken for the future (and therefore S$^r$ we desire you exactly to observe our directions under written in all respects) that we may have no cause to complain. There is of all sorts 600 dozen of drinking glasses, but if you cannot procure the whole parcel ready to send by the first good free ship, then send us 2 or 3 chests or what you can get ready and let the plain glasses (as in the Margin) be first made in readiness, for them we want most especially . . . . . Thus not doubting of your uttermost care and kind usage, we take our leaves and rest your friends and servants.'

The order was not a small one, and it can be seen that Greene and Measey were most particular to obtain exactly what they required for their customers. The 600 dozen comprised the following:

| | |
|---|---|
| Beer | 300 |
| Claret | 120 |
| Sack | 80 |
| Tumblers of all sorts | 80 |
| Toys, etc. | 20 |

It is obvious that beer was the national beverage, followed by French claret and Spanish or Canary Islands sack; the latter a strong and dry white wine usually taken with sugar. 'Toys' were not necessarily playthings, for the word was used also to describe ornamental trifles.

A final letter of 30th November, 1672, stresses the favoured qualities of Venetian glass and gives a further order:

'S$^r$ My respects presented unto you not hearing from you in answer to mine of the — — —. I have now sent you my patterns for a small parcel of drinking glasses &c., which I will pray you to order to be made with all convenient speed, and shipped upon the first good sure ship for England that

VENETIAN GLASS

I may have them here in March or April next if possible: but
as for those additional patterns which I sent last May, which
came too late to be performed with the last glasses you sent
me, I would now have you let them alone and not send them:
but only give order for these that I now send for and that
they be made as exact as may be to the pattern both for
quality and quantity and of very good clear white sound
metal; for truly the last you sent me the metal was indifferent
good and clear, but not so sound and strong as they should
have been made; for therein lies the excellency of your Venice
glasses that they are generally stronger than ours made here,
and so not so soon broken. Therefore S$^r$ I pray take such
care that these be made of very good sound metal and thicker
and stronger than the last, that I may gain credit by them
though not so much profit: here is 120 dozen beer glasses, 90
dozen French wines and 20 dozen cruets for oil and vinegar,
which makes up 230 dozen . . . and S$^r$ when you have shipped
these goods you may please to draw a bill upon me for the
value, and it shall be punctually paid. So committing you to
the protection of the Almighty, I rest

Yo$^r$ real friend and servant<br>John Greene.'

The letters give a clear and interesting picture of the trials
of an importer of the period—the worries about damage and
breakages and the pleas for speedy delivery; trials that are
unchanged today. From the designs sent to Venice by Greene
and Measey it is possible to learn what were the fashionable
and saleable shapes in London at the time of writing. Unfortunately, no glasses have been found that can be identified
with certainty as having formed part of the consignments, but
a few are known that bear a close resemblance to some in the
sketches.

During the five years covered by the correspondence the

importations totalled nearly 2,000 dozen glasses, and these two men were by no means the sole importers of them. In the course of the letters there is a mention of three others, Sadler, Allen and van Mildert, and surely there were more. The total annual trade in glasses between Venice and London must have been very large and, while it lasted, was no doubt a profitable one. Although according to the letter of 30th November, 1672, the Venetian glasses were 'generally stronger than ours made here', it is hardly surprising that they have proved unable to withstand the wear and tear of nearly three hundred years.

Venice, however, shortly lost its long-held monopoly. A visitor to the city in 1688 wrote:

'Formerly the Glass call'd *Venice-Crystal* was the finest in *Europe*; but at present it does not merit that title. Not that 'tis courser than before, but because they have found the Secret in other places . . . And one of my Friends assured me, that a few Years ago, having carry'd a Vial of the finest crystal of *Murano* to *London*, the workmen were so far from looking upon it as extraordinary or inimitable, that they said they cou'd and sometimes did, make finer Work. The Skill they have acquired in other Countries, and the Manufactures they have erected, have almost ruin'd the Trade of *Murano*.'

The productions from this time onward often prove a worry to collectors, for a proportion of the output was devoted to copies of earlier pieces. The most successful innovations in the 18th century were chandeliers (Fig. 142) and looking-glass frames, both exhibiting a welter of floral ornament in tinted glass. Of this, a pale opaque pink is most noticeable amid the riot of glittering shapes. As an alternative to flowers, it was not unusual to have fruit which was shaped with realism, but sometimes coloured indiscriminately.

Prominent among the glass-makers of the period was Giuseppe Briati, whose clever imitations of earlier *latticino* pieces are deceptively like their originals. The metal he used was clearer and more brilliant than that of the 15th and 16th centuries, but his manipulative skill rivalled that of his forerunners in the art. Realising that his glass was not competing successfully with the Bohemian material, and that the Venetian was unsuitable for decorating with the newly-popular cutting, he is said to have disguised himself as a

142. **Chandelier** with flowers of coloured glass: Venice, about 1750. Ht *about* 6 ft.   **143. Oil-lamp:** Venice, 18th century. Ht 15½ in.   **144. Stand** for oil and vinegar bottles, with salt-cellars: Venice, about 1750. Ht *about* 15 in.

workman in order to obtain employment in a Bohemian glass-house. He stayed there for three years, and put his knowledge to good use on his return. In 1736 he was granted a patent to make glass in the Bohemian manner, and in 1739 transferred his premises from Murano to the city of Venice. He died in 1772.

Other productions of Briati and his contemporaries included exotic ornaments for dining-tables, dishes and other ornamental domestic wares of all kinds, and panels of looking-glass decorated with engraving; some of the latter made especially for embellishing furniture. Apart from direct copies of earlier patterns or pieces inspired by the past, much of the 18th century output was of original design (Figs. 143 and 144). It represents a fragment of the final flowering of Venetian artistic talent; a talent seen in painting in the work of Guardi, Tiepolo and others, who caught on canvas the spirit of the city in the evening of its long-lived prosperity.

The industry and importance of Venice declined continually during the course of the century. Following the discovery of the route to the Orient by way of the Cape of Good Hope, the use of the Mediterranean rapidly lessened. Maritime supremacy passed to the Dutch and Portuguese, and a series of wars waged between the Republic and the Turks proved a constant drain on resources. Finally, in 1797 a bloodless victory by Napoleon resulted in the city passing under Austrian rule.

Towards the end of the eighteen-thirties there was a revival of glass-making, started by a man named Bussolin, who investigated and revived many of the ancient and near-forgotten processes. His work was carried on by Pietro Bigaglia, to whom goes the honour of having made the first of the well-known paperweights of which the French quickly became the foremost makers. Some of Bigaglia's have been preserved, and include in their patterns his initials and the date when they were made and first exhibited in Vienna in 1845.

During the second half of the 19th century the work of Antonio Salviati was concentrated on the earliest styles, which were once more executed with great skill. Again it was the *latticino* that proved so widely popular, and more than one Victorian example has changed hands in the mistaken belief that it was genuinely of the Renaissance. In such instances,

133

the price charged is often that of the antique, so the unfortunate buyer may find himself cheated both chronologically and financially.

The great chandeliers and looking-glass frames with their extravagant floral and other ornament were also copied during the 19th century, and specimens are not uncommon today. Careful consideration of the styling of these later examples usually dates them, but dust-laden and hanging at a height in an ill-lit room they can ensnare all but the most expert. In a hundred years the freedom and exuberance of one period was replaced subtly by the comparative stiffness and changed colour-sense of another, but such points are far from obvious.

In just the same way *latticino*, however carefully reproduced in the 17th, 18th or 19th centuries, is never precisely the same as the original. The metal itself, the whiteness of the filigree the intricate curving and cross-curving of the innumerable fine threads, are all just a little different. Singly, each of these details is of small account, but cumulatively they condemn a piece to an experienced and sensitive eye.

# CHAPTER VII

# German and Bohemian Glass

The glass made in medieval times in the well-wooded area of the Rhine continued to be made, and was in production while the more sophisticated Venetian industry was coming into operation. The green, yellow or brown tinted material, known often as *Waldglas* (forest glass), had already been formed into the *Rüsselbecher* during the 5th century, and the applied blobs of molten metal, coaxed into 'claws' or other shapes, remained an effective part of the German glass-maker's repertoire. The use of *prunts* (or *nuppen* Fig. 14, p. 23), in profusion was practised by them and resulted in the creation of an enduring series of vessels.

One of the earlier types was the *Maigelein*, a short thick-walled drinking glass with a distinctive pointed boss rising from the bottom (Fig. 145). For a vessel to stand evenly the mark left after the pontil was removed had to be depressed, forming a hollow known as a *kick*, leaving a flat rim on which the vessel would rest. The term *Maigelein* also refers to comparable articles made of metal.

The custom of burying relics of one kind or another in parts of important buildings has been responsible for the preservation of a few glass vessels of early date. These had been used for holding sacred relics and were incorporated in the altars of churches by their builders. Carefully sealed with wax, they remained undisturbed for some hundreds of years until excavation revealed their presence.

One of them, of a bluish-green metal ornamented with prunts, was found in these circumstances in the altar of a

Tyrolean church in 1891 (Fig. 146). The mouth is filled with wax and bears the seal of an ecclesiastic, inside can be seen 'the linen wrapping of the relics', and round them a strip of parchment with an inscription in Latin. A similar find in Würtemburg two years earlier was of a Roman-type vessel containing a document in Latin dated 1282 (Fig. 147). In it were also some bone and wood fragments wrapped in red silk, but it has been pointed out that paradoxically these once-revered relics are perhaps of slight value when compared with that of the glass that can be dated with tolerable accuracy.

**145. Maigelein:** Germany, late 15th century. Ht 3¼ in. **146. Beaker** decorated with prunts, found in the altar of a church in the Tyrol in 1891: Germany, 15th century. Ht 3½ in. **147. Beaker** with trailed ornament, found in a church in Würtemburg in 1889: Germany, 13th century. Ht 3 in. **148. Dwarf Krautstrunk:** Germany, 16th century. Ht 3 in.

The prunt received several different types of treatment. The drop of metal might be left as a raised boss; it could be drawn out to a point and then curved over; such a drawn spike could be sheared and left flattened; the spike could be curled over to form a loop to receive a metal ring; or the molten prunt could be stamped with an engraved tool to make a pattern on it. Any of these might be re-heated briefly to smooth and fire-polish the finished article.

One type of glass with prunt decoration is referred to as a *Krautstrunk*: literally, cabbage-stalk (Fig. 148). Its taller brother, although resembling the stripped vegetable much more closely in appearance, is known as a *Stangenglas*: pole or rod glass (Fig. 149).

In time, the shape of some of the drinking-glasses changed until the spreading mouth and raised ornament led to the evolution of the well-known *Roemer*; a vessel of which the use grew with the appreciation of Rhenish wines (Fig. 150). It

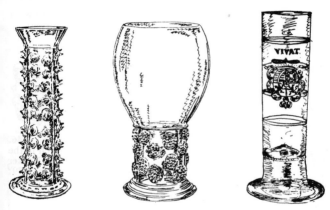

**149. Tall Stangenglas:** Germany, 15th/16th century. Ht 10½ in.
**150. Roemer:** Germany, 16th century. Ht 7½ in. **151. Passglas** enamelled with the arms of Saxony: Germany, late 17th century. Ht. 12¾ in.

continued to be manufactured in tinted metal long after the discovery of the means of de-colourizing it, and it was made in other countries as well as in Germany. The glass was at the height of its popularity during the 17th century, and is frequently seen beside piles of fruit, fish and much else in Dutch 17th-century still-life paintings. W. B. Honey wrote of Roemers that 'their often noble proportions entitle them to rank among the best of all glass vessels made in Europe'.

The fully-developed Roemer has a globular bowl and straight-sided lower part decorated with rows of prunts, the domed foot formed from a skilfully manipulated series of coils of glass thread. This was made on a wood or metal core which was then removed, but later a blown shape provided the base on which the thread was wound. Modern versions imitate this feature with a moulded stepped pattern.

Other glasses which were made alongside the Roemer include the *Passglas*; a tall straight-sided vessel with two or

**152. Kuttrolf:** Germany, 16th/17th century. Ht ?7½ in.

three bands of trailing at intervals down the body (Fig. 151). They were made for offering drinks to favoured guests, who were required by custom to drink down to one of the lines. Failure entailed drinking on until the next was reached, so bad judgement or lack of a thirst were duly penalised. The *Willkomm* (sometimes incorrectly called a *Wiederkom*) was offered, filled, to greet guests, and became known in the 17th century as a *Humpen*. It was a glass of indeterminate pattern, and often of gigantic size.

One other vessel may be mentioned: the *Kuttrolf*, which has a small mouth and was presumably used for slow pouring or as a sprinkler (Fig. 152). There was also a large variety of trick glasses for use at festivities, and for this purpose animal and human forms were adapted. The results are usually clumsy, but doubtless adequate for the occasion.

Although the Roemer, Kuttrolf and other vessels were peculiar to Germany, it is probable that many were made in Venice for export and it is certain that quantities of them came from the glass-houses in other Northern European countries. In most instances these latter cannot be distinguished from the native product.

The most typical and plentiful of German glass is that decorated with enamel-painting. The earliest specimens date from the late 16th century and carry on the style of work that had earlier been fashionable in Venice. When this was executed on *façon de Venise* pieces it is, again, usually very difficult to decide its origin. Not only can the glass have been made in Venice for export, but it is possible that the painting can have been done either there or in Germany and on Venetian metal or German.

It has been suggested that enamelling was first practised extensively in Germany in the well-wooded Fichtelgebirge region of Bavaria, to the east of Bayreuth, where there were numerous glass-houses. Thence, the art spread elsewhere, until in the late 16th and early 17th centuries it was centred in Bohemia. In that country, the Riesengebirge district was the most active area, and much of the work was carried out at glass-works near Falkenau and Krebitz, and at Wilhelmsberg, near Gratzen in the south.

One of the most imposing of the decorations used on the larger drinking-glasses shows the Imperial double-headed eagle, the *Reichsadler*, depicted with the names and arms of a supposed heirarchy of the Holy Roman Empire on its wings. The earliest of these *Reichsadlerhumpen*, dated 1571, is in the British Museum, and a rather later one of 1663 is shown in Fig. 153. The design would appear to have been taken from a woodcut issued in 1511, but it had appeared in other versions in prints from as early as 1493.

A similar type of glass known as a *Kurfürstenhumpen* is

painted with figures of the Emperor and the Seven Electors: the Archbishops of Mainz, Cologne and Trier, the Palatine of the Rhine, the Duke of Saxony, the Margrave of Brandenburg and the King of Bohemia. Others depict religious figures (*Apostelhumpen*), and workers at their trades. Some of these last were doubtless made to order for presentation to Guilds

**153. Reichsadlerhumpen,** dated 1663: Germany. Ht 10½ in. **154. Enamelled blue glass tankard,** dated 1601: Bohemia. **155. Enamelled flask** dated 1676: Saxony. Ht 7¾ in.

for ceremonial use, as was done also with vessels of silver and pewter.

Towards the end of the 16th century the earlier Venetian fashion for enamelling on coloured glass, especially a deep blue, was popular. Roughly-painted jugs and beakers are among the survivors of this short-lived activity, which is ascribed mainly to Bohemia (Fig. 154).

In addition to those mentioned above, subjects used by the enamel-painters include landscapes and portraits, processions of guild members, and satirical and allegorical scenes 'with inscriptions usually illiterate and sometimes obscene'. Coats of arms, with or without names, mottoes or dates, occur on many pieces, and occasionally can aid identification (Fig. 155).

As the standard of craftsmanship is often too undistinguished to claim serious attention, it is seldom possible to be certain where much of the work originated. Certain of the districts are said to have produced metal that is recognisable by a particular tint or tints, and that of Hesse shows a pale green or a golden-yellow. The harsh colours and summary drawing that are common to so many of the existing specimens give them a charm comparable to that of folk art. While it must be admitted that so many of the pieces are of indifferent quality and unworthy of a deep interest, they have an undeniable attraction.

Enamelling very similar in style to that of Bohemia was done in other glass-houses in various parts of the country; at Altenburg in Thuringia, at Gross Almerode in Hesse, and in Saxony. In the latter there were several manufactories, from one or more of which came glasses for the use of the Court. They bear on them an inscription denoting the fact that they belonged to the *Hofkeller* (Royal Cellars), and usually also the arms of the Elector (Figs. 156 and 157). Sometimes they have in addition a series of initial letters such as F.A.R.P.E.S. or F.A.H.Z.S.I.C.B.E.U.W.C., for Frederick Augustus the Strong (1670–1733); the latter a reminder that he ruled not only Saxony and Poland, but the Duchies of Julich, Cleve and Berg.

The specimen in Fig. 158 is inscribed *Kellerey Lofnitz* 1655, bears the arms of Prince Johann Georg III of Anhalt-Dessau and his initials J.G.D.H.Z.S.J.C.U.B.C.: Johann Georg Der Herzog Zu Sachsen Julich Cleve Und Berg Churfurst. With the help of a Venetian, Bernardo Marinetti, the Prince set up a glass-house at Dessau in 1679. It was a short-lived enterprise, terminating in 1686.

The 18th century saw the continued use of coloured enamel decoration (Fig. 159). The Bohemian houses made large quantities of small hexagonal bottles, usually fitted with a threaded pewter neck and domed cover, painted with flowers,

**156. Humpen** enamelled 'Hofkellerey Dresden' and dated 1697: Saxony. Ht 7½ in. **157. Enamelled glass**, dated 1623: Saxony. Ht 6¼ in. **158. Humpen,** enamelled and dated 1655: perhaps Saxony. Ht 9¾ in.

birds and figures in colours. These were exported widely, together with beakers and other useful articles. Along with them came cups and saucers, often decorated sketchily with flowers, more or less resembling tulips, in approximately natural colours, and with slight use of dull gilding. Most of the cups and saucers and a proportion of the other pieces were made from an almost opaque whitish metal, doubtless in attempted imitation of porcelain. Occasional examples are decorated carefully and need a second glance to decide that they are not made of china.

Sometimes opaque metal was combined with that of other colours and worked into wares with a 'combed' or 'marbled' appearance. The flask in Fig. 160 is an example of this process, and in this instance the white ground is relieved with streaks of red and blue.

**159. Bottle** enamelled with a coat of arms: Silesia, about 1745. Ht 9¼ in. **160. Marbled flask:** South Germany, about 1700. Ht 8¼ in. **161. Ruby glass flask:** Potsdam, about 1700. Ht 5¾ in.

As in Venice, and elsewhere, a certain amount of decorating was carried out in unfired oil paints, but very few examples survive. The glass-house at Hall-in-the-Tyrol, founded in 1534, is known to have done work in this transient medium. It is likely that many specimens that are now completely devoid of ornament were once oil-painted, but all traces of the colours have vanished and we can only guess at how popular such ornament may have been.

The 17th-century chemist, Johann Kunckel, was responsible for developing some metals of fine and distinctive colours. Under the patronage of Friedrich Wilhelm, Elector of Brandenburg, he worked in a glass-house opened at Potsdam in 1679, the year in which his book, *Ars Vitraria Experimentalis*, was published. Kunckel left Potsdam in about 1690, and died in 1703, but many of the examples attributed to his few years in Potsdam were certainly made elsewhere. The factory was transferred eventually to Zechlin, and continued under State ownership until 1890.

Kunckel's ruby glass was particularly successful, and is much sought after today (Fig. 161). It is of a 'redcurrant or red-ink' tint, and not to be confused with the later commonplace ruby glass from 19th-century Bohemia. It was made by the use of gold chloride, and although the secret of this is supposed to have remained in the possession of the Potsdam works and their successors, there is little doubt that it was soon discovered and put to use elsewhere. During its first years the Potsdam metal was very liable to decay (or crisselling, see p. 180), and in some instances this led to the complete disintegration of specimens. By 1689 the formula had been changed to correct the fault.

As well as employing colour as an attractive form of decoration, enamelling, and the addition of trailing in clear and tinted glass, the Germans became exceptionally adept at the revived art of cutting. This, they rescued from the neglect it had suffered in the West since Roman times, when it had been used to produce such masterpieces as the Portland Vase (Fig. 64, p. 66). They made full use of both the wheel and the diamond point, although the former was more suited to heavy rock crystal than to the comparatively thin available glass. The delicate material demanded the highest degree of skill, as the slightest error was quickly apparent and could not be disguised.

The first European since medieval days to use the wheel of the lapidary for glass-decorating was Caspar Lehmann, born about 1570 in the north of the country, at Ülzen near Lüneburg, who died in 1622. He was appointed '*Hofdiener und Kammeredelsteinschneider*' (Court Lapidary) to the Emperor Rudolf II at Prague, and it is thought that he was in Dresden in about the years 1606–8.

His productions are extremely scarce, and only one signed piece is known. It is an armorial beaker inscribed *C. Lemann F. 1605*, but three fine panels in the Victoria and Albert Museum, although without signature, are undoubtedly his work. One depicts Perseus flying through the air on his charger to save Andromeda, standing apparently unconcerned at the entrance to a cave, from the attentions of an approaching sea-dragon. On the plaque are two shields with crowned initials: those of the Elector Christian II of Saxony and of his wife, Hedwig of Denmark. They were married in 1602 and the former died in 1611, so the work must have been executed between those dates. Lehmann did his engraving solely upon the wheel, and made no use of the diamond point which was employed additionally by later craftsmen.

Work of comparable quality to that of Lehmann was executed by his pupil, Georg Schwanhardt of Nuremberg (1601–67). He further ornamented his accomplished wheel-engraving with diamond-point, and a number of signed pieces by him have been preserved. His sons, Georg the Younger, Heinrich, and three of his daughters, followed in the footsteps of their father. Nuremberg was a centre for such work, and goblets with tall hollow-knopped stems, as in Fig. 162, were particularly popular for ornamentation and are therefore usually ascribed to the city's craftsmen (a knop is a hollow or solid protuberance in the stem of a glass). Among other 17th-century artists who worked alongside the Schwanhardts were Hermann Schwinger and Friedrich Killinger, both of whom are represented in the Victoria and Albert Museum.

At about the same time, *c.* 1680, when George Ravenscroft was working in England to make a glass that would compete with the Venetian, comparable experiments were afoot elsewhere. Some success was achieved in Bohemia, perhaps in the north of the country, and before long the secrets of an improved material had been learned and were in general use.

**162. Goblet** with green glass bowl and clear stem, with engraved decoration. Nuremburg, 17th century. Ht 15½ in.

Potash was employed in place of soda and a large proportion of chalk was added, to produce a metal having an acceptable similarity to rock crystal in both appearance and working qualities.

The appreciation of this natural stone goes back far in history, and the Romans brought the carving of it to a high pitch of perfection. In the early Renaissance period the Italians and Germans vied in producing works from it, and the ultimate aim of their glass-makers in the late 17th century, as of all glass-makers before them, was to reproduce the beauty of the semi-precious product of Nature. When their skill as lapidaries was allied with the newly-devised metal they achieved this with success.

The comparatively thin-walled vessels of the earlier material could only be cut to a slight depth or engraved, with great effect, in diamond-point, but the new metal was usable in heavier masses. This enabled the craftsman to carve it in the same manner as he would have dóne had it been the stone it simulated. No longer was he limited by the size of pieces won from Nature, nor was he forced to build together a large article by means of metal mounts to link the component parts. The glass could be formed into a complete vessel; thus, a glass cup would be in a single piece, whereas its crystal counterpart would be made as a bowl, a stem and a foot, all three joined by an internal metal rod and with the junctions masked by bands of gold or silver.

Glass-making experiments were not confined to any one district, and typical of the spirit of inquiry of the time was the career of the Saxon nobleman, Ehrenfried Walthers von Tschirnhausen (1651–1708). A student of mathematics and physics at Leyden University, he is remembered principally as the man who recommended the Elector of Saxony to employ the services of a then-unknown young alchemist, Johann Friedrich Böttger, whose researches duly led to the making of porcelain at Meissen, near Dresden. Tschirnhausen was as concerned at combating the importation of glass from outside the realm as he was at the entry of porcelain from the Far East; because of the currency sent out of his country for the latter he is said to have named China 'the bleeding-bowl of Saxony'.

He was involved foremost in obtaining the necessary heat for melting metals, and to do this he employed burning-glasses of various kinds, including mirrors of polished copper and iron. Then he turned to glass for the purpose, and made lenses that were known everywhere in Europe. He had workshops for glass-cutting, but although nothing can be ascribed with certainty to him it is sometimes accepted that a few surviving specimens of glass resembling semi-precious stones may have come from his furnaces. More certain is the fact that his lapidaries were employed in cutting and polishing Böttger's earliest red stoneware; the attractive hard red material that preceded the long-sought white porcelain.

Much glass-decorating was carried out in various parts of the country by men who worked on their own accounts and unfortunately most of them have remained anonymous; it is doubtful whether the names of more than a few will ever be known. On the other hand, those employed in the workshops set up by the various Courts have usually been recorded. Much of their work was also unsigned, but it has been possible in many instances to attribute specimens to particular men or workshops on strong stylistic grounds or because of the use of recognisable insignia in the decoration.

In 1687 Count Christoph Leopold von Schaffgotsch granted Friedrich Winter a privilege 'for the engraving of glass in the manner of crystal', which he proceeded to do at Petersdorf. There, the Silesian mountain streams provided ample power for a water-mill, without which the arduous and complicated work would have been impossible to accomplish. Some of Winter's pieces bear among much other ornament the device of the Schaffgotsch family: a fir tree and cones. To him, or to a craftsman under his supervision, is ascribed the covered goblet in Fig. 163.

This magnificent piece shows clearly the manner in which the solidity of rock crystal was imitated. It has resulted in an article that appears to have been hewn from a solid chunk of the transparent stone, instead of having been made roughly to shape by assembling the semi-molten component parts. Only its great size and absolute flawlessness (it stands almost a foot in height and lacks completely the natural imperfections found in crystal) and the fact that goblet and cover are each in a single piece make it instantly recognisable as glass. The foot is engraved on the underside with a flower head, the knop above the short plain column shows a pair of horns

**163. Covered goblet** made at the Schaffgotsch glass-works: Silesia, about 1700. Ht 11 in.

and foliage, and the cornucopia-shaped bowl is carved with a bird of prey perched on curled leaves which emerge from a horn terminating in a fox's head. A strange assortment of elements, perhaps, but they form a decorative composition, and the use of game-birds and animals as motifs has always been acceptable to those who combine wealth and position with a love of hunting and shooting.

In the same year as the Schaffgotsch glass-works was opened, a workshop for engraving was started in Berlin. It was directed by a brother of Friedrich Winter, Martin

Winter, and was under the patronage of Friedrich Wilhelm, Elector of Brandenburg. Martin Winter taught his nephew, Gottfried Spiller, who became his partner in due course and whose skill was such that he eventually outstripped his teacher. He specialised in designs which depict naked children at various pursuits: examples in the Victoria and Albert Museum show *putti* gathering grapes and playing with goats.

**164. Ruby glass beaker** carved with a Bacchanalian scene: Potsdam or Nuremburg, late 17th century. Ht 4 in.   **165. Beaker** engraved with figures in a park: Silesian, about 1760. Ht 4⅞ in.   **166. Sweetmeat dish** with engraved decoration: Silesia, about 1760. Ht 4¼ in.

As elsewhere, two types of engraving were practised with the aid of water-power at Berlin. *Hochschnitt* (literally, high-cut) with the decoration standing out in relief, and *Tiefschnitt* (deep-cut) with the ornament cut into the surface in intaglio. The glass used at the establishment was supplied from Potsdam, and rare examples were executed there and elsewhere on the ruby metal made to Kunckel's formula (Fig. 164). Many of the pieces show signs of the decay which was a common fault with the metal in the early days of the glass-house.

The Landgrave Carl of Hesse-Cassel named as *'fürstliche Glasschneider'* one of the most eminent of all the talented German glass-engravers, Franz Gondelach, who was born in

1663. He sometimes used Potsdam glass for his work, on which he employed *Hochschnitt* and *Tiefschnitt* techniques, singly or in combination. The latter appears on one of his two known signed works, a covered goblet engraved with classical figure-subjects. Other pieces attributed to him include 'a portrait of the Landgrave Carl himself, shields of arms, *putti* bacchantes, and the like, on goblets on which the stems and feet and knobs of covers are superbly carved in shell forms or with acanthus and other foliage and even with openwork monograms'.

From the last years of the 17th century glass-engraving grew to an important industry, with numerous centres throughout Silesia and Bohemia. Most of the earlier inspiration would appear to have had a common derivation in the work done at Nuremberg by Georg Schwanhardt and his followers, which has been mentioned earlier (p. 145). Very few of the surviving examples can be identified positively as having come from a particular area or town; equally, only in very exceptional instances has it proved possible to identify an artist responsible for what was often work of high quality (Figs. 165 to 169). Much of it, however, was designed and finished less thoughtfully, and as the 18th century proceeded these less important pieces formed a growing proportion of the output.

Apart from engraving on the wheel or with the aid of a diamond, there was one other decorative process that achieved a lasting success. This was the variety of *verre églomisé* known as *Zwischengoldglas* (between-glass-gold), of which the process of manufacture has been detailed earlier (p. 35). Beakers and goblets with the work in gold, silver and colours were made somewhere in Bohemia in about 1730. Most of the examples depict scenes of the chase, but others are decorated with ecclesiastical coats of arms or figures of saints. The two latter have led to a suggestion being put forward that they were all made in a workshop attached to a monastery. It cannot be denied that the unknown artist (or artists) who executed them in an unlocated place was extremely skilful and has left for posterity a number of very charming mementoes (Fig. 170).

A further type of double-walled glass has a space between the inner and outer sections filled with carefully composed scenes made from glass, coloured paper, straw and other suitable materials. Only three examples of this most unusual

**167. Engraved covered goblet:** Bohemia, about 1700. Ht 12½ in.
**168. Engraved covered goblet:** Bohemia, mid-18th century. Ht 9½ in. **169. Engraved covered goblet:** Silesia, mid-18th century. Ht 9 in.

decoration have been recorded, and it is suggested they were made at the Bakhoeteff Glass Works in Nikolskoy, south-eastern Russia, or at an unspecified workshop 'in Bohemia', in the last decade of the 18th century.

In the course of the second half of the century the newly-introduced neo-Classical style with its simple straight lines prevailed over the curvaceous excesses of the baroque and rococo. In all aspects of art the change became noticeable:

glassware, no less than furniture, silver and ceramics, showed the influence of the mode in changed forms, fresh decorative motifs and new combinations of colours. Straight-sided goblets and tumblers replaced the tall glasses with shaped bowls and elaborately-knopped stems; in many instances the latter atrophying into heavily-facetted feet (Fig. 171).

An encouragement to the German glass-makers was provided by the outburst of travelling that followed the end of the

**170. Beaker** with *Zwischengoldglas* decoration: Bohemia, about 1730. Ht 3 in.   **171. Beaker** painted with flowers and butterflies: Vienna, about 1840. Ht 4½ in.   **172. Beaker** painted with a view of the Cathedral in Vienna, by Anton Kothgasser: Vienna, about 1830. Ht 4¼ in.

Napoleonic Wars. Although the wealthy and the adventurous had not had their peregrinations greatly interrupted, the more prudent had remained within the frontiers of their native lands for more than a decade. Once they became free to move about, they swarmed over the Channel and along all the roads leading to the continental capitals. Equally, it may be remarked, the continentals visited London, and the great and the inquisitive who had attended the Congress of Vienna in 1814–15 were welcomed in turn by the subjects of George III. All this coming and going demanded souvenirs, and what better to take in one's baggage than a small and exquisitely-painted piece of glass; preferably with a view of a foreign building or landscape, or the portrait of a royal personage?

Johann Joseph Mildner (1763–1808) was one of the earliest of a group of highly accomplished men who provided beautifully decorated pieces to suit the neo-Classical taste, but he catered for local purchasers rather than for tourists. He worked at Gutenbrunn, Lower Austria, and some of his pieces, which are usually signed and dated on the reverse of the decoration, bear inscriptions in German such as 'Completed at Gutenbrunn at the great Weinsberg forest in Furnberg'. Much of his work was executed in the *Zwischengoldglas* technique, but, unlike the earlier Bohemian examples which were completely double-walled, his had only shaped panels and borders. The body of the vessel was cut carefully to receive the additional parts and, as with the other specimens, the joints are invisible to the unsuspecting eye. The medallion panels set into the sides of tumblers were particularly well made, as they had to follow the exact shaping of the outside of the piece and make a perfect fit when finally fixed in place with an adhesive. Occasionally he used miniatures painted on parchment, which were then sealed between the wall of the vessel and the covering glass.

Mildner's subjects range from portraits of saints to head-and-shoulders studies of ladies and gentlemen who had their likenesses perpetuated in this pleasing manner. Other tumblers bear medallions, which record names and messages of devotion and friendship written in a copper-plate hand embellished with curlicues.

Among the other artists responsible for some outstanding pieces in the early years of the 19th century are the two Mohns and Kothgasser. Samuel Mohn (1762–1815) and his son Gottlob Samuel Mohn (1789–1825) prepared and used colours that were transparent, whereas their forerunners had been confined to an opaque palette. The elder of the men lived in Dresden from 1809, and his son established himself at Vienna two years later. They painted views, silhouettes and figure-subjects. The father had been a decorator of porcelain and the younger painted stained glass for the Emperor of Austria's Castle at Laxenburg.

Anton Kothgasser (1769–1851), a decorator at the Vienna porcelain manufactory, made the acquaintance of Gottlob Samuel Mohn and they worked together on stained glass. He, too, painted drinking-glasses and made use of the transparent colours developed by his colleague, in particular a fine yellow stain which was much employed in window work. Kothgasser's tumblers bear varied subjects: children, animals, flowers, playing-cards, and views; the latter often of the Cathedral of St Stephen in Vienna (Fig. 172). His work is usually signed, and rare examples give his address: '*Der Mahler "wohnt" auf den Spanischen Spitalberg. N. 227 in Wien*', where he was from about 1810 to 1820.

Similar tumblers, often with the bases cut with indentations and described aptly as 'cogwheel bases', were signed with initials 'C. v S' for Carl von Scheidt of Berlin, and in full by Hoffmeister of Vienna. The Mohns and Kothgasser had numerous imitators and pupils, some of whom did not sign their work and others who marked it with initials which remain unidentified.

In Bohemia there came about in the 1820's and 1830's a revival of glass-making and engraving, with an emphasis on the use of colour as opposed to clear metal. Researches resulted in the introduction of many new shades. These included an opalescent greenish-yellow and a yellowish-green which were produced in the Isergebirge glass-houses of Josef Reidel, and which he named in honour of his wife Anna: '*Annagelb*' and '*Annagrün*'. Examples of these were decorated with cutting and with painting in colours and gilding.

A group of factories situated near Gratzen in southern Bohemia, owned by Georg Franz August Longueval, Graf von Buquoy, made articles from a glass named *Hyalith*. This is an opaque agate-like material in a sealing-wax red or black, which was decorated in silver and gold with motifs found on Oriental lacquer, or was made into articles reminiscent in shape and decoration of Wedgwood's black hard pottery *basaltes*. The latter also inspired a black glass, first made in the early years of the 19th century, at Zechlin.

**173. Beaker** of light and dark green Lithyalin glass: Blottendorf, Bohemia, about 1830. Ht 4½ in.

Even more closely resembling agate and other stones was *Lithyalin*. This was a marbled near-opaque glass produced from about 1828 by Friedrich Egermann (1777–1864) at Blottendorf near Haida. Jugs, tumblers and other pieces were made, and their decoration was confined principally to cutting and slight gilding. Rare examples have added shaped panels in glass of a contrasting colour, but most rely on geometrical faceting and bands of heavy bosses (Fig. 173). The attraction of such pieces rests in the colour rather than the shaping, and cutting has been used to give flat surfaces by which this is seen to the best advantage.

From this time date the highly-popular pieces with thin (*flashed*) layers of contrasting colours, which were cut through to show, say, a clear glass body with the sloping cut revealing an inner coating of white under an overlay of blue, red, green or yellow flashing (Fig. 174). Any combination of these colours was used, and the 'windows' finally revealed were often painted in enamels and gilded. Such articles, which ranged from tumblers to very large vases, were made over a long period, in varying qualities, and their manufacture was not confined to any one workshop or even to Bohemia.

**174. Coloured and overlay glass** shown at the Great Exhibition, London 1851.

Of distinguished quality was the delicate engraving of Dominik Bimann (1800–57), who spent his time working at Prague with intervals during the visitors' season at the resort of Franzensbad. His portraits are often signed in full with his initial and name, or with the letter 'B', and a few examples are dated. Equally talented was August Böhm (1812–90) whose wanderings took him farther afield and included visits to America.

Tumblers and goblets, the latter often of large size, flashed with a ruby-red, stain were made in quantity at many glassworks from about 1850. They were decorated with cutting that is frequently of hunting scenes. Excellent work in this manner, in blue- as well as red-flashed glass, was executed by A. H. Pfeiffer of Carlsbad and Karl Pfohl of Steinschönau, but most of it is anonymous and it is sometimes difficult to be certain of its country of origin (Figs 175 and 176). A fashion

**175. Beaker** with blue overlay, engraved with a portrait by A. H. Pfeiffer: Carlsbad, about 1850. Ht 4¾ in.

**176. Beaker** with red overlay, engraved by Karl Pfohl: Steinschönau, about 1855. Ht 4¾ in.

for cutting articles with facets to resemble the skin of a pineapple was current at about the same date. The group of pieces in Fig. 174, shown at the Great Exhibition, held in London in 1851, is representative of Bohemian wares of the day, and it may be noticed that in addition to overlay vases there was a liking for pieces with glass snakes wound around them in a realistic manner.

Exhibitors included Franz Pallme König of Steinschönau, Graf Buquoy of Schwarzthal and Silberberg, Ignatz Pelikan of Meisterdorf, Wilhelm Hofmann of Prague (who had an agent in Old Jewry, London), and Meyr's Nephews of Adolf and Leonorehain. All these were in Bohemia. The principal German exhibitor was 'The Glassworks of the Count of Schaffgotsch', at Josephinenhütte, near Warmbrunn, whence came articles of similar pattern to those from Bohemia.

As the century progressed interest in glass of earlier periods increased; genuine examples had become scarce and were costly in the money of the time. Predictably, copies began to appear on the market and for a while deceived buyers. Many varieties of old glasses were reproduced and the forgers even attempted *Zwischengoldgläser*, but the 19th century pieces cannot withstand comparison with their prototypes.

Large quantities of inexpensive glassware enamelled with figures of playing children were made in Bohemia at the end of the 19th century, and later. The painting is usually roughly executed on jugs, decanters and other articles of tinted or clear metal. Occasional examples are inscribed in gold 'A Present from . . .', with the name of a town or watering-place. Pieces

**177. 'Mary Gregory' child** painted in opaque white enamel.

of this type are attributed in error to the grossly-overworked brush of a lady named Mary Gregory, an American decorator employed at the Boston and Sandwich glass-works, in Massachusetts, and whose name is thus immortalised (Fig. 177).

At about the same date the sombre colours and flower-inspired shapes becoming popular elsewhere, grew fashionable and were made in Germany. There, the vogue was known as the *Jugendstil*.

# CHAPTER VIII

# English Glass: I — To 1670

The Romans must assuredly have set up glass-houses in England during their occupation of the country. Although surviving examples datable to the period are of types common to Europe there is no proof that they were all made there; equally, they can have been manufactured locally. In the story of glass it arises continually that there is so often little, if any, discernible difference between the wares of one land and another: a popular design was quickly copied wherever it was introduced. With comparatively few specimens to study and an interval of some 1,500 years to bridge, it is not unexpected that opinions should differ on the origin of pieces. It may be hoped that the present archaeological fervour will result in fresh and positive evidence coming to light.

However, it does appear certain that whatever may have been the state of affairs earlier, the industry had lapsed sadly by the end of the 7th century, A.D. The evidence for this lies in a passage written in 731 by the Venerable Bede, the historian and theologian. Recording the building of the church and monastery at Wearmouth, Co. Durham, in the year 675, he noted in his *Ecclesiastical History of the English Nation:*

'When the work was drawing to completion, he [Abbot Benedict, the founder] sent messengers to Gaul to fetch makers of glass, more properly artificers, who were at this time unknown in Britain, that they might glaze the windows of his church, with the cloisters and refectory. This was done and they came, and they not only finished the work required, but also taught the English people their handicraft, which was well adapted for enclosing the lanterns of churches and for the vessels required for various uses.'

Whatever may have been made by these men and their followers disappeared long ago, and it is probable that it was of simple pattern and poor metal. A greenish glass, like bottle-glass, would have been used for making small window-panes and simple vessels. In both instances the principal requirement was that the finished article should be water-tight; functionalism was paramount, and the addition of artistic ornament did not enter into consideration.

It is not until the year 1226, or thereabouts, that the story of glass-making in England really begins. At that date, one Laurence, described at the time in Latin as a *Vitrearius* (maker of glass), established himself with a furnace at Dyers Cross, close to Chiddingfold. The latter is a hamlet not far from the busy town of Guildford, actually in Surrey, but close to the border with Sussex. The spot lay at a cross-road by the western edge of what was a great forest; a situation suitable because there would be ample supplies of wood available for fuel and for the making of potash.

The choice of such a place for the settlement of this French emigrant could not have been entirely haphazard, and it is probable that glass-making had been carried out there, or elsewhere in the vicinity, for some unspecified time in the past. Certainly, Laurence achieved success, for in 1240 he was supplying plain and coloured glass to be used in the part of the Abbey at Westminster then being built by Henry III.

The principal use of the material was then for ecclesiastical purposes, and the French were the foremost (and the nearest-placed to England) in the making, staining and painting of glass for the great windows in such buildings. Laurence may well have come across the Channel expressly to furnish the windows for the Abbey, but we have no evidence to show if this was the case. Nor, unfortunately, do we know if he or his fellow-workers made vessels.

Laurence was followed by his son, William, and we have records of other families who lived and worked in the neighbourhood. A man known as John le Alemayne is supposed to have been a dealer as well as a glass-maker, and to have been one of those who supplied itinerant hawkers with 'urynells, bottles, bowles, cuppis to drinck and such lyke'. From soon after 1340 John Schurterre appears in records as owner of both a house and a furnace in the district. A century later the family of Peytowe (Peto; probably indicating that the members came originally from Poitou in France) were active for several decades.

All these men, and others, successively built or bought glass-houses and made window-glass and vessels that have now vanished. Fragments have been found in the area in sufficient quantity to corroborate the written evidence that the industry was an active one, but such fragments give us the minimum of information. They do not convey the high degree of skill apparently reached in the 16th century, when a poet of 1557 noted:

> *As for glassmakers, they be scant in the land*
> *But one there is as I do understand*
> *And in Sussex is now his habitacion,*
> *At Chiddingfold he works of his occupacion.*
> *To go to him it is necessary and meete,*
> *Or send a servante that is discreete,*
> *And desire him in most humbly wise*
> *To blow thee a glasse after thy devise:*
> *It were worth many an Arme or a Legge,*
> *He would shape it like to an Egge;*
> *To open and close as a haire,*
> *If thou have such a one thou needst not feare.*

Shortly after, in 1584–5, no fewer than eleven glass-houses in the area were shut down by Parliament. The glass-makers were competing with the local iron-smelters for the essential and valuable fuel, and the makers of iron were the more important in the eyes of the government. In addition, the vital industry of ship-building relied on timber, and the great nautical activities of Elizabeth's reign had made serious inroads into stocks of English oak. The Spanish Armada of 1588, although unsuccessful, was not only a shock to the islanders, but it justified the actions taken to conserve the better qualities of wood for defence purposes.

In addition to the men in Surrey, some were working at glass-making in other parts of the country. During the building of St Stephen's Chapel, Westminster, between 1349 and 1356, instructions were given for suitable window-glass to be sought at Oxford, Colchester, York, Gloucester and elsewhere. No doubt these places were then centres of activity where such material might be obtained, but little information about them has endured the passage of time. Perhaps, too, drinking vessels and other useful articles were made at one or more of them, but this can be no more than conjecture.

While it is probable that other continental glass-makers came and went over the years, few of them left any record of their stay. It is known that in 1549 there were eight Venetians who set up a glass-house in London. They had been brought from Antwerp at the behest of Edward VI, but within three years all but one had returned to their native city and eventually this last man crossed the Channel to work in Liége. From these middle years of the 16th century came the beginnings of more modern glass-making in England: the end of the small old-fashioned workers in Surrey and elsewhere, and the arrival of men with new ideas of manufacturing, both as regards methods and materials, which owed their origin to the highly successful and long-envied workers in Murano.

The first of the new arrivals were some window-glass makers from Lorraine. Descendants of these families remained connected with the industry for many generations and their names, after numerous minor changes in spelling, still endure in various districts. They include the families of Hennezel (Henzey, Ensell), Thisac (Tyzack), Thiétry (Tittery) and Houx (Hoe, Howe, How).

These men started in Surrey, but the stringent regulations concerning the use of wood soon affected them, and with the long-established Norman glass-makers from the area they began to spread elsewhere in England where there were suitable forests. Hampshire, Gloucestershire and north Staffordshire saw settlements of the wanderers, and eventually they centred on Newcastle upon Tyne and Stourbridge. At these latter places they were able eventually to draw on convenient local supplies of coal for fuel, and both grew to become important glass-making districts.

Excavations at some of these provincial sites have resulted in the recovery of fragments of thickish green-coloured glass, many of which are the remains of small bottles, and others are of beaker-type drinking-glasses. A few examples of goblets raised on tall stems ornamented with knops have been found also. They demonstrate that Venetian influence had begun to spread far to the north of Murano.

Towards the end of 1564 a man named Cornelius de Lannoy was brought by the government from the Continent to teach the Venetian way of glass-making as it was practised in the Netherlands. He was unsuccessful at the task, and blamed not only the materials with which he was provided, but the English craftsmen who were his students. In a letter written to William Cecil, Secretary of State, it was noted: 'All our glasse makers can not facyon him one glasse tho' he stoode by them to teach them. So as he is now forced to send to Antwerp and into Hesse for new provisyons of glasses [materials for glass-making], his old being spent. The potters cannot make him one pot to content him. They know not howe to seasson their stuff to make the same to susteyne the force of his great fyers.' De Lannoy apparently persevered for some three years, but without achieving worthwhile results and modern writers have decided he was little more than an impostor. Perhaps he was, or perhaps he was unlucky; we may never know.

Then, in 1567 Jean Carré, of Arras and Antwerp, who had a knowledge of the industry, came to England and within a few years had set up two furnaces for making window glass and a third for Venetian-type vessels. The first were situated near Alfold, Surrey, and were manned by craftsmen brought from Normandy and Lorraine. They spent much of their time quarrelling with one another, with the result that before long the former had 'departed owt of the realme and made no further meadle in the sayd works'. The third of the glasshouses was in London in a former monastery, the Crutched Friars, just north of the Tower of London, the workers coming from Carré's homeland, Flanders. By mid-1571, however, they had been replaced by Italians, and in the following year Carré died.

Certainly there was demand for the type of glass Carré set out to imitate, and a fortune awaited the attainment of success. A good picture of habits at the time was written by William Harrison between about 1577 and 1586, and shows that some men then esteemed Venetian glass even above gold and silver; the latter more readily obtainable than ever before owing to the Spanish conquests in South America. The glistening and fragile productions of Murano were a prize for which the wealthiest competed, and the desires they aroused are described clearly by Harrison in the following extract:

'As for drink, it is usually filled in pots, goblets, jugs, bowls of silver, in noblemen's houses; also, in fine Venice glasses of all forms. . . . It is a world to see in our days, wherein gold and silver most aboundeth, how that our gentility, as loathing those metals (because of the plenty) do now generally choose the Venice glasses, both for our wine and beer, than any of those metals or stone wherein beforetime we have been accustomed to drink; but such is the nature of man generally that it most covets things difficult to be attained; and such is the estimation of this stuff that many become rich only with their new trade into Murano (a town near to Venice, situate on the Adriatic Sea), from whence the very best are daily to be had. ... And as this is seen in the gentility, so in the wealthy communalty the like desire of glass is not neglected, whereby the gain gotten by their purchase is yet much more increased to the benefit of the merchant. The poorest also will have glass if they may; but, sith the Venetian is somewhat too dear for them, they content themselves with such as are made at home of fern and burned stone; but in fine all go one way—that is, to shards at the last.'

He goes on to point out the unfortunate wastefulness and worthlessness of the material once it is shattered, and wishes something might be found to add strength to it. In his own words:

'It would induce such a metallical toughness thereunto that a fall should nothing hurt it in such manner; yet it might peradventure bunch or batter it; nevertheless that inconvenience were quickly redressed by the hammer.'

Like the philosopher's stone, which would turn lead to gold, this unbreakable glass continues to elude discovery.

Among the men brought to London by Carré was his manager, a Venetian named Jacopo Verzelini (1522–1606) (Fig. 178). He took over the direction of the new factory on its owner's death and all was flourishing until one morning two years later, in 1575, in the words of the contemporary chronicler Raphael Holinshed:

'The fourth of September being Sundaie about seven of the

clocke in the morning a certain glasshouse which sometime has been the crossed friars hall neere to the Tower of London burst out in a terrible fire: whereunto the Lord Mayor, aldermen and shiriffes with all expedition repaired and practised there all means possible by water buckets, hookes and otherwise to have quenched it. All which notwithstanding, whereas the same house a small time before had consumed great quantitie of wood by making of fine drinking glasses, now itself having within it neere fortie thousand billets of wood was all consumed to the stone walls, which walls

**178.** Jacopo Verzelini (1522–1606), from his memorial brass at Downe, Kent.

greatlie defended the fire from spreading further and dooing anie more harme.'

It would seem that Verzelini did not waver at this tragedy. Not only did he recommence operations by opening a new glass-house in Broad Street, but he probably rebuilt the damaged one, and he applied to Elizabeth I for a Patent. On the 15th December, 1575 it was granted to him for a period of twenty-one years, 'for the makinge of drinkinge glasses suche as be accustomably made in the towne of Murano and [he] hathe undertaken to teache and bringe uppe in the said Arte and knowledge of makinge the said drinking Glasses our natural Subjects'. In other words, he was allowed to do

167

as he wished provided he taught the art to the Queen's 'natural' (i.e. native-born) subjects. In addition it was stated that the glasses made would be 'as good cheape or rather better cheape than the drinking Glasses commonly broughte from the cittie of Murano or other parts beyond the Seas'.

Also, by the terms of the Patent, importation of glass was prohibited for as long as he was able and willing to sell his wares at prices no greater than those charged for foreign ones. Objections to the monopoly were raised by a group of the merchants who imported or dealt in Venetian and other glass, but their protests went unheeded. However, the laws of the time were not always put into action as literally as may be imagined from reading them; no doubt Venice glass continued to arrive and the dealers continued grumbling, but carried on trading.

Less than a year after all this had taken place, Verzelini took out naturalisation papers, and settled down to the English way of life with his wife, Elizabeth, and their children. There can be no doubt that he prospered, and he bought a number of properties in Kent where, at Downe, he died at the age of eighty-four in 1606. A monument, erected according to his instructions at a cost of twenty pounds, remains in the church to this day. The plain marble slab bears effigies in brass of himself and his wife, each with their respective coat of arms at the head, and of his children, the husbands of his daughters and his eldest grandchild. At the foot of the slab is the coat of arms of Verzelini impaling Vanburen and Mace, and the inscription reads:

'Here lyeth buried Jacob Verzelini Esquire borne in the citie of Venice and Elizabeth his wife borne in Antwerpe of the ancient houses of Vanburen and Mace who haveing lived together in holyestate of Matrimonie fortienyne yeares and fower months departed this mortall lyfe. The said Jacob the twentye day of Januerye Ano. Dnii. 1606 aged LXXXIIII yeares and the said Elizabeth the XXVI daye of October Ano. Dnii. 1607 aged LXIII yeares. And rest in hope of resurrection to lyfe eternall.'

A small number of surviving drinking-glasses have been attributed to Verzelini, and although it is very tempting to assert that they came definitely from his glass-house there is insufficient evidence to do this. The attribution is based on

**179. Goblet** dated 1580, formerly belonging to Horace Walpole (died 1797). Ht 5⅛ in.

the metal and form of the pieces, both of which can be paralleled by wares made in the Netherlands and possibly elsewhere, and on the facts that some of them bear inscriptions in English and dates that tally with the years when Verzelini enjoyed his monopoly. This might be taken as proof that they were engraved in England, but it cannot be a guarantee that the actual metal is of that origin, and the whole question will doubtless continue to be argued for many years to come. In the meantime, whoever may have been their maker, they enjoy a cautious acceptance of having been made by Verzelini and his men.

The 'Verzelini' goblets are all engraved in diamond-point and most of them bear dates in addition to other ornament (Fig. 179). The earliest is dated 1577 and is in the Corning

**180. Goblet** inscribed IN GOD IS AL MI TRVST and dated 1586. Ht 5¾ in.

Glass Museum, New York, which is the fortunate possessor of a second example of ten years later inscribed IN GOD IS AL MI TRVST. The same legend is on a goblet in the British Museum (Fig. 180), with the date 1586 and the initials G.S. A glass of similar type, now in the Musée de Cluny, Paris, was

**181. Engraving on a goblet** dated 1578.

found in Poitiers, and is engraved with the fleur-de-lis, a group of initials, and the date 1578 (Fig. 181).

The engraving of all these glasses has been attributed to a Frenchman named Anthony de Lisle (or de Lysle), who came to England from France and took out papers of denization in 1582. Three years later he was noted as working in the district of St Martin-le-Grand, an area of the City of London that enjoyed privileges of sanctuary and freedom from ecclesiastical and civil jurisdiction. There, he worked as an engraver who 'useth his trade without licence from the Pewterers Company'.

A connection between the engraving of two such dissimilar materials as pewter and glass and the linking with them of de Lisle's name, is the fact that 'In God is all my Trust' is the motto of the Pewterers' Company. If the Musée de Cluny goblet is by the same hand as the others, it suggests that he, or another Frenchman, may have been responsible for the entire group. The hypothesis that de Lisle engraved the glasses has not been accepted by all authorities, and rests mainly on the negative evidence that he was the only man to have been recorded as an engraver at the relevant time. Thus, both the glasses themselves and the ornament on them remain of problematical provenance and it can only be hoped that eventually the mystery will be solved.

None of Verzelini's sons would seem to have shown an interest in their father's business. Indeed, two of them must have caused him considerable disappointment, for he left them annuities of £40 apiece, but only on condition that they did not 'vex, sue or molest or rouse or assent to suing, rousing or molesting of the said Elizabeth, their natural mother' ... or 'molest or trouble any of the tenants or occupiers'. In spite of these injunctions an obviously deep-seated love of litigation eventually came to the surface, and the two brothers, Jacob and Francis, spent the years from 1620 to 1652 bitterly fighting one another in court.

In 1592, when the monopoly had four further years to run before it was due to expire, the remainder was bought by Sir Jerome Bowes. Sir Jerome had been a soldier, but deserted warlike arts for the lucrative position of a company-promoter. He was the first of a series of men, of similar calibre to himself, who were concerned with the glass industry as a money-making business rather than as an art, and all sought the means of manufacture with the aid of coal as fuel in place of the diminishing stocks of timber.

It was found that to burn coal a greater draught was essential and that smoke affected the clarity of the metal. Many experiments were made to devise a suitable furnace with covered pots, and success was eventually achieved. In 1613 a patent was applied for and a committee appointed to investigate the situation. In a report presented to the king, James I, it was stated that:

'They have repaired to the glass-house lately erected at Lambeth, by virtue of his letters patent to Sir Edward Zouch and Mr Louis Thelwall. By judgement of divers glaziers of the city of London, etc., perceived the glass for the metal to be clear and good, but in some places uneven, and full of spots, by reason of the negligence of the workmen. The glaziers affirm to have sundry times bought glass as good and cheap there as any other of the same size. The fuel used is Scotch coal, and not fuel made of wood.'

In 1615 a retired admiral, Sir Robert Mansell, formed yet another company to acquire the much-coveted Patent and in that year a royal proclamation absolutely forbade the use of wood fuel for glass-making. Soon, Sir Robert bought out his partners and in 1623 he was granted a Patent permitting him alone to make 'all manner of drinking glasses, broad glasses, window glasses, looking glasses and all other kinds of glasses, bugles [beads], bottles, vials or vessels whatsoever'. He managed this wide monopoly for the following thirty years, and remained in absolute control of the entire English glass-manufacturing industry until his death in or about 1656.

Mansell's principal glass-house was that started by Verzelini in Broad Street, but he owned others in various parts of the country. One of his managers was, like himself, a Welshman, James Howell, who wrote from the Continent to his father in 1618:

'The main of my employment is from that gallant Knight, Sir Robert Mansell, who, with my Lord of Pembroke, and divers others of the prime Lords of the Court have got the sole Patent of making all sorts of Glass with pit-coal only, to save those huge proportions of Wood which were consumed formerly in the Glass-furnaces; and this Business being of that nature, that the Workmen are to be had from Italy, and the chief Materials from Spain, France, and other Foreign Countries, there is need of an Agent abroad for this use; (and better than I have offered their service in this kind) so that I believe I shall have employments in all these Countries before I return.'

A year later, he wrote from Middleburg to the manager at Broad Street, introducing a Signor Miotti:

'. . . who was Master of a Crystal-glass-furnace here a long time, and as I have it by good intelligence, he is one of the ablest and most knowing men for the guidance of a Glass-work in Christendom; therefore according to my Instructions I sent him over, and hope to have done Sir Robert good service thereby.'

In May, 1621 Howell communicated with Sir Robert himself:

'The two Italians who are the Bearers hereof, by report here, are the best Gentlemen-Workmen that ever blew Crystal, one is allied to Antonio Miotti, the other is cousin to Mazalao . . . I was, since I came hither, in Murano, a little Island, about the distance of Lambeth from London, where Crystal-Glass is made, and 'tis a rare sight to see a whole Street, where on the one side there are twenty Furnaces together at work; they say here, that although one should transplant a Glass-furnace from Murano to Venice itself, or to any of the little assembly of Islands about her, or to any other part of the Earth besides, and use the same Materials, the same Workmen, the same Fuel, the selfsame Ingredients every way, yet they cannot make Crystal-glass in that perfection, for beauty and lustre, as in Murano . . .'

The king is said to have wondered that having had an honourable career on the water, the ex-admiral should then 'tamper with fire, which are two contrary elements'. In spite of this Royal doubt of his capacity, it is clear that Mansell proved

**182. Glass** inscribed BARBARA POTTERS and dated 1602. Ht 8⅛ in.

a clever and determined businessman. He skilfully and firmly organised and controlled the glass industry in England, and left his successors a sure foundation on which to build.

Although there is a reasonable amount of information about Verzelini's numerous followers, there is a sad absence of examples of their various manufactures. Entries of glassware in inventories and accounts of the first fifty years of the 17th century are not infrequent, but most of them are brief and uninformative. A well-known drinking-glass inscribed BARBARA POTTERS and dated 1602, in the Victoria and Albert Museum, has been attributed to some Italians working at a glass-house started at Blackfriars in about 1600 (Fig. 182). It is engraved in diamond-point in the same style as the earlier pieces ascribed to Verzelini, but it must be borne in mind that a date on an article does not mean invariably that it was made in that year. Often such numerals indicate an anniversary, or refer to some event that had taken place many years before.

Antonio Miotti, born a Venetian, was sent to work in London from previous employment at Middleburg in the Netherlands. Could his work be expected to show any particular national characteristic? More probably, glasses which were made in England by Miotti and his fellows are masquerading today as having come from any country but the correct one, and their true origin is quite unrecognised. Not only was there an interchange of craftsmen between one land and another, but there was an equally continuous circulation of styles and any new fashion, as today, was quickly available in every sophisticated city of Europe.

Mansell was the first man in England to make looking-glasses on a commercial scale, and it is probable that the Broad process, as used in Venice, was employed. Here, again, there are no surviving examples as evidence of what was achieved. Perhaps Sir Robert's petition to the King in 1621 was somewhat optimistic, but such documents are seldom otherwise in tone. This one stated:

'And as concerning Looking glasses Sir Robert Mansell hathe brought to such perfection, That he hathe Chused our Natives to be so fully instructed and taught therein, That the said glasses are now here made w$^{ch}$ was never wont to be in England beforetyme, So that thereby we hope in tyme to sett many hundreds in work wch many as those doo import have never done here, but beyond the Seas.'

The charges made by Mansell for his drinking-glasses, at wholesale rates, do not seem to have been excessive. In fact, he claimed that they had been reduced progressively in spite of the payment of higher wages to his men 'than is paid in any other part of Christendom'. Ordinary glasses for beer were sold at four shillings a dozen; for wine at 2/6d a dozen; Venetian-type covered beer-glasses at ten shillings a dozen, or a shilling more if they were of 'extraordinary fashions'; and crystal glasses for beer, 'made by me (which never were before in this Kingdom) and of all fashions that are desired and bespoken', nine shillings a dozen.

One mid-century event should be noticed: the imposition on 24th November, 1645 by Oliver Cromwell of a Duty on glass. The Protector 'ordered that an Excize of Twelve pence shall be laid upon every Twenty Shillings value of Glasse and Glasses of all sorts made within the Kingdom, to be paid by the Maker'. This was exacted in order that the industry, like others, should pay its share towards the cost of government; a doubtful honour that probably went unappreciated. There is little otherwise to relate concerning the period when Cromwell ruled: artistic endeavour of every kind remained at a standstill and men's lives and thoughts were occupied with larger issues than the mere comforts of the home.

With the Restoration of the monarchy in 1660, came one last monopolist, George Villiers, Duke of Buckingham, lampooned as 'chymist, fiddler, statesman and buffoon'. He managed to obtain a patent for a temporary monopoly for making looking-glass plate, and established a glass-house at Vauxhall for its manufacture. If for no other reason, he may be remembered as the instigator of 'Vauxhall glasses', few or none of which survive, but of which the name is given proudly today to any stained and dull looking-glass of old appearance. Like Mansell, the Duke's craftsmen employed the 'broad' process introduced from Murano. John Evelyn, the diarist, paid a visit to Vauxhall on 19th September, 1676, and recorded in his Diary that he saw there '. . . looking-glasses far larger and better than any that come from Venice.'

For the years between 1667 and 1672 we have a reliable guide to the fashions in glassware that were current in London. These are exemplified clearly in the designs sent with their orders to Venice by the dealers John Greene and Michael Measey (Figs. 136 to 141, pp. 125 and 126). It is a reasonable assumption that English makers were using very similar patterns; not only would the designs be indistinguishable, but also the metal in which they were executed. As occurred earlier, it is now well-nigh impossible to be certain whether particular specimens were made on one side of the Channel or the other. In fact, it is not improbable that examples labelled proudly as rare Venetian are in reality far rarer English.

# CHAPTER IX

# English Glass: II—1670–1760

The Restoration of the Monarchy in 1660 was followed by great changes in many aspects of life. The lengthy strife of the Civil War and the ensuing years of puritan ascendancy led to an outburst of keen scientific inquiry which, among much else, gave rise to the founding of the Royal Society in 1662. There was also a move towards gaining independence from costly imported goods by replacing them, or improving on them, with British-made products. Not least, the glass industry was concerned in these activities and in 1664 a Royal Charter was granted to the Glass-Sellers' Company of London, which enabled them to control 'the art, trade or mystery of grinding, polishing, casing, foyling, and finishing of looking glasses and in selling of glasses and looking glasses' both within the boundaries of the City and for seven miles around. A special clause exempted the looking-glass enterprise of the Duke of Buckingham from the supervision of the Company.

It is thought that a group of the men who later formed the Company persuaded Dr Christopher Merret (1614–96) to make the first translation into English of an important Italian book on glass-making. This was Antonio Neri's *L'Arte Vetraria*, which had been published in Florence in 1612, and in 1662, exactly fifty years later, made an appearance in London as *The Art of Glass*. According to the translator's Preface: 'an eminent Workman, now a Master, told me most of the skill he had gained was from this true and excellent book'.

Of equal or greater importance was the engagement of George Ravenscroft (1618–81) as official glass-maker to the Company at their experimental glass-house at Henley-on-

Thames. He is known to have been operating a glass-house in the Savoy, by the Strand in London, in 1673. In that year he petitioned the King for a Patent for 'a particular sort of Christalline Glass resembling Rock Crystall, not formerly exercised or used in this our Kingdome', and a month after this he laid before the members of the Company samples of the metal. As a result he was given the position at Henley, and the sale of the whole of his output was guaranteed, provided it was made in shapes specified by the Company's Clerk.

Little is known of the details of Ravenscroft's work, although it was noted at the time that he had an Italian assistant named Da Costa. Probably he tried replacing the pebbles used in Murano with flints of English origin, which he calcined by burning them in a closed container and then grinding them to a fine powder. They would have proved difficult to fuse, in contrast to the imported pebbles, and it has been suggested that in order to counteract this difficulty he experimented with the addition of oxide of lead.

Only a few years earlier, Christopher Merret had written on the subject in *The Art of Glass*: 'Glass of Lead is a brilliant thing unpracticed by our Furnaces and the reason is, because of the excessive brittleness thereof ... And could this Glass be made as tough as that of Crystalline 'twould surpass it in the glory and beauty of it's colours, of which no man can be ignorant, that hath any experience of this Metall.' He was writing of the occasional use by the Venetians of a lead oxide (such as Red Lead) as an ingredient in making certain types of glass, and it may be wondered whether he realised the truly great potential of his words. Whatever may have been Ravenscroft's inspiration, or his reason for using it, the lead oxide led eventually to success. Known variously as 'glass of lead' or as 'flint glass', the new material gave English wares an individuality that pleased the public and quickly halted foreign imports. It may be mentioned that the use of flints was soon dropped, and in spite of their replacement by sand as a source of silica the term 'flint' remained current as a description of the metal.

At first the new glass gave trouble by partially decaying and exhibiting 'crisselling': the appearance on it of a network of very fine cracks, somewhat like a spider's web. In 1676, once this defect in the formula had been overcome, it was

**183. Roemer** bearing the seal of Ravenscroft. Ht 6½ in. **184. Raven's head seal** of George Ravenscroft. **185. Silver-mounted beer tankard** with Ravenscroft's seal on the handle. Ht 3½ in.

agreed that Ravenscroft should mark his pieces by placing on each of them during manufacture a small glass seal. It took the appropriate form of a raven's head, and the whole medallion is little greater than a quarter of an inch in diameter (Fig. 184). Because they must have been re-heated after they were first stamped, it is often difficult to distinguish the pattern on them and it is not at all surprising that sometimes they should have been overlooked.

Albert Hartshorne, the first man to make a study of English glass, knew of the sealed examples only from a 17th century document, and wrote in 1897 that none had then been found. Since that time, about thirty examples have been brought to light, and they include such things as bowls, ewers, posset-pots (small pots with spouts for taking a drink made from milk curdled with ale or wine, see Fig. 186), as well as drinking-vessels (Figs 184 and 185), and a decanter (Fig. 247, p. 216). There is always a possibility that more will appear in due

**186. Posset-pot** with a seal on the spout. Ht 3 in.

course, but it cannot be expected that very many remain undiscovered after the lapse of some three hundred years.

A complete goblet, a posset-pot, and the stem of a wine-glass are known bearing a seal with the letter 'S' on it. This is ascribed to a glass-house known to have been operating in or about 1680 in Salisbury Court, to the south of Fleet Street, but the attribution remains unconfirmed for the present. Another wine-glass stem, this one in Northampton Museum, and a posset-pot in the British Museum (Fig. 186) have each a seal showing a female figure shooting with a bow. It is thought to be the 'mark' of John Bowles and William Lillington, owners of a glass-house at Ratcliff, in Southwark, London. The metal of both of the latter pieces is not lead-glass, and shows that trade-marking of this kind, which was in use for only a few years, was not confined to the newly-devised metal.

181

In 1676 a change occurred at Henley and the glass-house came under the control of Hawley Bishop, a man who also took over the Savoy glass-house on the death of Ravenscroft five years later. From then onwards, glass-of-lead increased in popularity to such a degree that by 1700 it was being made all over the country.

The month of May, 1695, saw the government passing an Act authorising a duty of twenty per cent on flint glass and glass plate and one shilling a dozen on common glass bottles. The imposition was for a definite period of five years in order to raise much-needed money with which to finance the war being fought against the French. However, the temporary nature of the Act was soon dispensed with, and a year later it was made permanent. Immediately there was a great outcry from members of the industry, who pointed to the immediate and certain threat of bankruptcy and unemployment to all concerned. In spite of considerable, and predictable, overstatement of the case, it was agreed that there was a substance of truth in the allegations, and in 1698 the duty was halved. A year later it was abolished. The fact that it apparently realised a total sum to the Exchequer of under £10,000 a year during the time it was in force indicates that it caused more annoyance than it gave benefit.

An interesting statement as to the number and location of English glass-houses at the end of the 17th century was published in 1696. It listed them as shown opposite:

The list was prepared by John Houghton, a reputable Fellow of the Royal Society, who issued it in one of a series of printed letters which he compiled 'for the improvement of commerce and trade'. Allowing for the difficulties of gathering such information and for the inevitable gaps that must be expected under the circumstances, the table is probably a reliable picture of the industry at the time. Houghton's use of the term 'flint glass' refers to Ravenscroft's glass-of-lead, as

| An Account of all the Glass Houses in England & Wales | The several Counties they are in | The Number of Houses | And the Sort of Glass each House makes |
|---|---|---|---|
| In and about London & Southwark | | { 9 2 4 9 | For bottles Looking glass plates Crown glass & plates Flint glass & ordinary |
| Woolwich | Kent | { 1 1 | Crown glass & plates Flint glass & ordinary |
| Isle of Wight | Hampshire | 1 | Flint glass & ordinary |
| Topsham, nr Exeter | Devonshire | 1 | Bottles |
| Odd Down, nr Bath Chellwood | Somersetshire | { 1 1 | Bottles Window glass |
| In and about Bristol | | { 5 1 3 | Bottles Bottles & window glass Flint glass & ordinary |
| Gloucester Newnham | Gloucestershire | { 3 2 | Bottles Bottle Houses |
| Swansea in Wales | Glamorgan | 1 | Bottles |
| Oaken Gate | Shropshire | 1 | Bottles & window glass |
| Worcester | Worcestershire | 1 | Flint, green & ordinary |
| Coventry | Warwickshire | 1 | Flint, green & ordinary |
| Stourbridge | Worcestershire | { 7 5 5 | Window glass Bottles Flint, green & ordinary |
| Near Liverpool Warrington | Lancashire | { 1 1 | Flint, green & ordinary Window glass |
| Nottingham Awsworth Custom More Nr Awsworth | Nottingham | { 1 1 1 1 | Bottles Flint, green & ordinary Bottles Flint, green & ordinary |
| Nr Silkstone Nr Ferrybridge | Yorkshire | { 1 1 1 | Bottles Bottles Flint, green & ordinary |
| King's Lynn Yarmouth | | { 1 1 1 | Bottles Flint, green & ordinary Bottles |
| Newcastle-upon-Tyne | Northumberland | { 6 4 1 | Window glass Bottles Flint, green & ordinary |
| | Total | 88 | |

opposed to the older type of metal which he calls 'ordinary'.

The frequent references in the list to the making of bottles shows the importance of that branch of the glass trade. Out of a total of eighty-eight glass-houses, no fewer than thirty-seven devoted their output exclusively to them, and another couple combined this with the manufacture of window glass. Bottles had been made for many centuries and in many lands, but the English wine-bottle, which remains a familiar object today, was born in the 17th century when the nation's glass-houses were controlled by Sir Robert Mansell.

Whereas they had been used in the past for innumerable purposes, for the holding of oils, medicines and holy water among much else, the employment of bottles for wines and beer was a novelty. Their introduction for the purpose was said in 1662 to have been the idea of Sir Kenelm Digby (1603–65), who was an author and diplomat and had been, like Mansell, in the Navy. His strong beliefs in astrology and alchemy were not shared by all his contemporaries, but some of his strangely-compounded panaceas would have needed sturdy bottles for their retention and may well have led to his demand for such things. There is no record surviving of any-one else who may have instigated these most useful articles, which like other everyday conveniences, can equally well have developed by a series of accidents.

The wine-bottle has always been made from a dark green or brown glass, partly because of the cheapness of these impure coloured metals and partly to keep daylight from harming the contents. It was also important that they should not be expensive because they were, and in the main still are, expend-able items. The study of their development has been simplified by a fashion for applying to many of them a glass seal, similar to those that had been used in Roman times, as on the 2nd-century flask in Fig. 73 (p. 74).

The seals bear on them a variety of designs: names or marks

of the men for whom they were made; their coats of arms or crests; the names or insignia of inns (Figs. 187 to 190), and, above all, often they show a date. It is from the latter that it has proved possible to trace the sequence of styles in which the bottles were made. In few other branches of glassmaking has it been feasible with such simplicity and certainty to classify the successive forms in which an article was made (Figs. 191 to 194).

In his exhaustive work on English and Irish glass, published

**187. Wine-bottle seal** with the owner's name and date. **188. Wine-bottle seal** with a merchant's mark. **189. Wine-bottle seal** with the arms of Chadwick and date. **190. Wine-bottle seal** with the initials and insignia of Anthony Hall of the Mermaid inn at Oxford, 1682.

in 1929, Mr W. A. Thorpe suggested some appropriate names for the principal varieties of bottle. They are as follows:

1. *'The Shaft and Globe'*—in use about 1650. The distinctive tall neck of the bottle is topped by a ring of glass about a quarter of an inch below the orifice. This formed a rim beneath which could be tied a string to keep in place a cover of parchment, or even paper. During the next century this *string-course* or *string-rim* was modified and more bands were added, usually having the top one level with the bottle-top, as in present-day practice.

2. *'The Onion'*—in use about 1690. In spite of the pleasing 'antique look of these bottles, the short neck and squat, heavy body makes them difficult to grip and to pour from.

**Wine-bottles**

**191.** 1650 to 1700.

**192.** 1714, 1721, 1733.

**193.** 1746, 1756, 1765.

**194.** 1774, 1784, 1793.

186

3. '*The Slope-and-Shoulder*'—in use about 1715–50. Both parts of the bottle, body and neck, grew taller until they were approximately equal. The outline of the present-day article can be recognised, but as each was hand-blown there are countless minor variations of pattern.

4. '*The Cylinder*'—from about 1750. The shape owes its introduction to the habit of storing wine in bottles laid on their sides, so that the liquid kept the corks expanded and air-tight. Binning followed slowly on the importation of Port wine following the Methuen Treaty with Portugal, concluded in 1703.

Bottles gradually became slighter in circumference during the following two decades, and they began to be made in moulds, which resulted in a standardisation of design. While this would undoubtedly have pleased the original buyers by providing a safeguard against short measure, the modern collector is less contented with their appearance.

The *kick* or *kick-up* beneath the base of wine-bottles owes its origin to an effort at making the first examples stand upright. The rough mark remaining when the pontil was broken away left an uneven surface, so while the metal was still molten it was a simple matter to press the centre of the base slightly inwards. The pontil-mark was thus raised to the top of a cone and kept clear of the standing surface. As in the case of the once-important string-rim, this feature survives on many modern bottles which are made by machine and show no sign of anything resembling a pontil-mark. Its original purpose now long forgotten, it is sometimes the innocent target of dark hints from the uninformed that it exists solely to enable the vintner to cheat his clients.

On October 23rd, 1663, Samuel Pepys recorded: 'Went to Mr Rawlinson's and saw some of my new bottles, made with my crest upon them, filled with wine, about five or six dozen'. Two years later, John Evelyn recorded in his diary how he had visited a Mr Povey and admired his house, 'but, above all his pretty cellar and ranging of his wine-bottles'. Whether they were sealed or not he does not state, but as with silver and so much else it was quite usual for a gentleman to have his mark of ownership, whether a coat of arms, crest or mere initials, placed upon all his possessions.

The earliest surviving dated bottle is one of 1657 in the museum at Northampton, but there is a seal of 1652 in the London Museum. It is not unusual for seals to be found intact

**195. Wine-bottle seal** found in Colonial Williamsburg, Virginia.

while the bottles to which they were once attached have been smashed to fragments. Many have been brought to light in the course of excavations at Jamestown and Williamsburg in the United States of America, and have revealed interesting facets of the history of those early and important settlements in Virginia. The more prosperous members of the communities ordered their wine-bottles from across the Atlantic, and within the last few years at Jamestown alone 20,000 fragments of 17th century date have been unearthed. Of these, 104 were seals, and many of them have had their original ownership traced by skilful research (Fig. 195).

In some instances it is quite clear from the pattern of bottle that the date on it does not imply the year of manufacture, and must refer to some other event. An illustration of this is to be found on some bottles sealed *W. Leman Chard 1771*, with the legend *H. Ricketts & Co. Glass Works* in raised letters under the base. The latter marking did not come into use until about 1820, and the explanation of the discrepancy is probably that Mr Leman of Chard was a wine-merchant who founded his business in the year 1771. Equally of doubtful genuineness are a number of bottles bearing a crowned *N*, apparently having a direct connection with the illustrious Emperor Napoleon. Many of these 'historic relics' were made long after Napoleon died in 1821.

Judging by the number of drinking-glasses and other pieces that have survived from the last two or three decades of the 17th century, the output of the time must have been large in comparison with that of earlier years. This is explained by the renaissance of the arts under Charles II; when the pendulum of fashion swung away from the rigours of Puritanism, and most of those who could afford it indulged in a degree of good-living unknown for half a century. Furniture and silver, as well as glass, played their share in the rediscovery of comforts and luxuries, many of which were of continental origin and were introduced by immigrant craftsmen. The new articles and their designs were brought into being by the demands of the public, but the public in turn was further stimulated by their novelty and the output of all kinds of chattels increased rapidly.

While the dating of specimens of antique glass relies much on the style of the piece under consideration, the newly-introduced glass-of-lead can be detected with certainty. Its weight, when compared with that of comparable soda or potash glass specimens, is noticeably greater, and the appearance of the metal, both in colour and brilliance of surface, is superior. Above all, the presence of lead can be checked with finality by means of simple chemical tests. Thus, in a great majority of instances the glass made in England after Ravenscroft's successful experiments of 1673 ceases to present a problem regarding its country of origin.

Not only was the new type of glass of an incomparably better appearance than the old, but it had different working qualities. It was difficult to blow as thinly as the Venetian as it was less fluid when molten, and in vessels with thick walls an unequalled interior luminosity was revealed. These factors led, or forced, the English craftsman to design shapes that were suitable to the metal rather than continue slavishly

**196. Wine-glass** with stem containing a tear, about 1705. Ht 6¾ in.
**197. Goblet and cover,** about 1690. Ht 13 in.   **198. Candlestick,**
about 1725. Ht about 7 in.

imitating the Venetian models he had been content to follow in the past.

While a proportion of George Ravenscroft's output bore his seal, it is assumed that much of it did not and specimens resembling closely those with seals are, not unreasonably, assumed to have come from his glass-house. Once his Patent had expired in 1681, the use of the new metal rapidly became wide-spread. This fact is made clear in the list given by John Houghton, where he records makers of 'flint' glass in 1696 in the counties of London, Kent, Hampshire, Bristol, Worcestershire, Warwickshire, Lancashire, Nottinghamshire, Yorkshire, Norfolk and Northumberland.

The output of the time varied from simple wine-glasses to large and elaborate covered bowls and goblets that must have been intended more for display than for use (Figs. 196 and 197). Some of the earliest of the pieces made by his followers show signs of the crisselling that beset Ravenscroft in his first experimental wares, but by the last decade of the century it was very rarely to be seen. Possibly it was once much more common than is now suspected and the majority of affected pieces have been destroyed long ago, but the matter can be judged now only from surviving specimens.

Whereas the glasses were made at first with hollow knopped stems like those of former years, these soon became solid and their shapes conformed with the baluster columns of silver candlesticks and the turned work of the furniture maker. Some of the larger examples were made with a silver coin enclosed in one of the knops, and these can provide a terminal date: i.e. the glass can be as old as the date on the coin, but it must be remembered that the latter was not necessarily put there in that year or even in the one following. The use of coins in this way was popular for making glasses to commemorate coronations, and 20th century ones have continued to be the occasion for the making of souvenirs in the same manner.

As the 18th century progressed, more and more articles were added to the repertory of the glass-maker. Candlesticks (Fig. 198); tapersticks, miniatures of the foregoing (Fig. 199); salt-cellars (Fig. 200); custard or jelly, and sweetmeat glasses (Figs. 201 and 202); oil-lamps (Fig. 203); cream or milk jugs for the tea table (Fig. 204); and much else including such in-

**199. Taperstick,** about 1700. Ht 5¾ in.   **200. Salt cellar** of a pattern made in silver, about 1740.   **201. Jelly glass,** about 1730. Ht 4½ in.

**202. Sweetmeat glass,** about 1740. Ht about 7 in.   **203. Early 18th-century oil-lamp.** Ht about 6 in.   **204. Cream jug** of silver pattern, about 1740. Ht about 4 in.

congruities as teapots and fruit baskets. The latter were 'woven' in close imitation of wickerwork, and many of the others were based closely on the forms of contemporaneous silverware that provide a useful check in dating them.

The most popular and useful of articles made from glass

was undoubtedly the wine-glass in one of its innumerable shapes. These varied with changes in fashion during the course of time, and the sequence of the most important of their stems between the years 1680 and 1730 has been classified as follows:

| | |
|---|---|
| Inverted Baluster | 1682 to 1710 |
| Drop Knop | 1690 to 1710 |
| Angular Knop | 1695 to 1715 |
| Ball Knop | 1695 to 1715 |
| Annulated or Triple-ring Knop | 1695 to 1725 |
| Multiple Knops | 1700 to 1720 |
| True Baluster | 1710 to 1730 |
| Acorn Knop | 1710 to 1715 |
| Mushroom Knop | 1710 to 1715 |
| Silesian Stem | 1715 to 1730 |

Whereas most of the stems were straightforward developments of Venetian originals, the Silesian stem reached England by way of Germany. From there it came close on the heels of the Elector of Hanover when he sailed to the country to ascend the throne as King George I, and following his death its use declined rapidly. Some of the types enumerated above are illustrated in Figs. 205 and 206, but it will be found in practice that there are numerous variations which will not fit comfortably into any category. Herein lies much of the charm of these pieces; pieces that proclaim the individuality of the craftsman who made each of them with his own hands, and state the fact with pride.

As much as the stems varied in design, so did the bowls of the glasses; not only in size, which was to suit wines, cordials, ales and so forth, but also in shape. A number of the shapes are shown in Fig. 207. One further feature should be mentioned: the foot. In most of the glasses up to about 1750 it was given a folded edge by turning the rim under the base during the making (Fig. 208). This made a stronger finish that

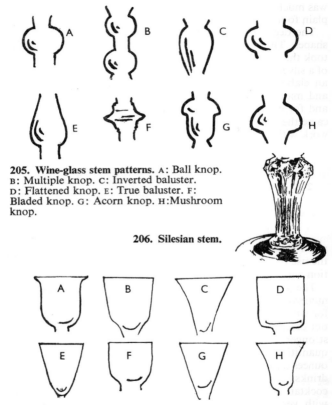

**205. Wine-glass stem patterns.** A: Ball knop.
B: Multiple knop. C: Inverted baluster.
D: Flattened knop. E: True baluster. F:
Bladed knop. G: Acorn knop. H: Mushroom
knop.

**206. Silesian stem.**

**207. Wine-glass bowl patterns.** A: Flanged or lipped. B: Ogee. C:
Trumpet. D: Bucket. E: Round Funnel. F: Cup or Ovoid. G: Conical.
H: Bell.

194

was much less prone to get chipped than the smaller diameter plain foot which followed.

The decoration of wine-glasses was just as varied as their shapes. The first part to receive any was the stem, where it took the form of a trapped bubble of air with the appearance of a silvery tear-drop (Fig. 196). By about 1730 there appeared an elaboration of this, in which the bubble was elongated and manipulated so that it extended the length of the stem and formed the so-called *air twist*. Fifteen or so years later came the opaque white twist made in the manner of Venetian work with clear and white glass. Finally, between about 1760

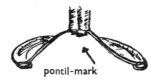

208. Folded foot in section.

pontil-mark

and 1780 there was a fashion for a variation on the preceding: the use of twists of one or more colours, usually in combination with white and including red, green, blue and yellow.

The glasses were in sizes and shapes to accommodate the numerous drinks popular from time to time. The normal ones for wine stood about 6¾ inches in height (Fig. 209). Beer was not drunk invariably from a tankard, but as much of it was stronger than the present-day brew it was taken in small quantities. The ale-glass had a capacity of three or four ounces and was usually of the shape shown in Fig. 210. Strong drinks, of a type that have been compared with the modern cocktail, were known as cordials, and were served in glasses with very small bowls (Fig. 211). Of these potent liquors John Bunyan wrote in 1682: 'I have a cordial of Mr Forget-Good's making, the which, Sir, if you will take a dram of,

**209. Wine-glass with bell bowl,** inverted baluster stem and folded foot. **210. Ale glass** of about 3 ounce capacity. Ht about 6¾ in. **211. Cordial glass.** Ht about 5¼ in.

may make you bonny and blithe'. A particular variety of cordial, known as Ratafia and flavoured with almond kernels, was taken in a glass of tall and narrow shape which was known sometimes as a flute glass (Fig. 212).

The taxation imposed in 1645 and 1695 did not have any effect on glass that is discernible today, whereas the Excise Act of 1745 certainly did. It laid a tax of 9s 4d per hundred-weight (112 lbs) on the materials used and not, as might be expected, on the finished articles. In order to keep prices stable, it became necessary to get the maximum number of objects from each pot of metal and to achieve this each was made of lighter weight. In the case of the wine-glass, the folded foot ceased to be made, the stem grew simpler and as a compensation the bowl was decorated with cutting or engraving.

The emergence of decoration was not due entirely to the

tax, but it happened that there were in the country at the time a number of German craftsmen who excelled in the work. The demand was stimulated, without doubt, by the Hanoverian followers of the Georges and the fashion spread from the Court outwards. Both cutting and engraving remained in the repertoire of glass-makers for the rest of the century and for long afterwards. Much recognition has been accorded to

**212. Ratafia glass** on air-twist stem. Ht about 7½ in.

**213. Newcastle glass** with portrait of 'The Young Pretender' and motto 'Audentior Ibo'. Ht about 6 in.

them from their employment on glasses with Jacobite emblems (Fig. 213, and Fig. 249, p. 218), which have intrigued several generations of collectors.

The term Jacobite is applied to one who held the view that the descendants of James II instead of those of William of Orange should have reigned in England. James's son, by Mary of Modena, James Francis Edward Stuart, was proclaimed 'king' on his father's death in 1701, but following an abortive attempt to claim his kingdom he retired to Rome and the protection of the Pope. He is known as 'The Old Pretender', and his son, Charles Edward, 'The Young Pretender', born in 1720, similarly attempted to assert his royal rights and then retreated to Rome. Both men behaved in such a way that they alienated their followers, whose numbers they seem to have over-estimated, and when each in turn arrived in the British Isles to overthrow the regime, he found a dearth of organised helpers and had to leave in disorder.

The considerable number of surviving glasses with Jacobite emblems on them were not necessarily all possessed by ardent followers of the Pretenders. Many of them were made for those who enjoyed the thrill of belonging to semi-secret clubs, and

**214 and 215. Jacobite emblems** engraved on wine-glass bowls.

to toast in a furtive manner the cause of the King over the Water; a cause that was high treason, and was fairly obviously a hopeless one. The whole movement was fostered for its nuisance value by the Pope and Louis XIV, and was identified with the other suspect activities of the Catholics of the time.

Various explanations have been put forward as to the meanings of the different emblems that represent the protagonists (Figs. 214 and 215). The principal feature is a large rose, with or without one or two buds; the latter representing the Pretenders, and the flower the Crown of England. Some glasses, known as Amen glasses, are engraved with emblems and with hymn verses that conclude with the word 'Amen'. Another variety bears the word 'Fiat' and is supposed to have been made for members of the Cycle Club founded by Sir Watkin Williams-Wynn, and others again were made for the kindred societies that drank to:

> . . . the King
> Who hath blest right to Reign
> It is the only thing
> Can save the Nation.

The glasses made between about 1745 and 1765 with Jacobite emblems have been sought by collectors more eagerly than those of any other variety, and much time has been given to the deciphering of their decoration. Many of them have realised high prices, and in consequence have been the subject of keen attention by the unscrupulous. Forgeries, good and bad, have been manufactured in modern times, and some of the superior ones are very deceptive.

Opponents of the Jacobites favoured mementoes bearing portraits of William III. These exist with or without references to the battle of the Boyne, where he defeated the forces of James II on 1st July, 1690. Few were made, or have survived the intervening years, but the scarcity of genuine examples has been eased by the addition of good and bad fakes.

Convivial gatherings of men were commonplace throughout society, and clubs both large and small flourished to promote various practical or impractical projects—or just in order to have a good time. A feature of many of them was the use of the *firing-glass*: a squat wine-glass with a very thick and heavy foot (Fig. 216). They were banged on the table as an accompaniment to toasts and to applaud speakers, and it is supposed they acquired their name from the likeness of the noise to musketry-fire.

While London was the most important centre in the country

for the production of glassware, the provincial towns listed by Houghton were not inactive during the 18th century. Newcastle upon Tyne had two 'flint' glass-houses that owed their origins to a bottle-making establishment started by an Italian family named Dagnia. In due course, the Hensells and the Tyzacks became prominent (Fig. 217), and all of them contributed to the trade of the port which sent glass down the

**216. Firing glass**, about 1740. Ht about 4 in. **217. Newcastle tankard** engraved 'G. Tyzack Glass-Maker'. **218. Newcastle wine-glass**, about 1725.

coast to London and across the North Sea to Scandinavia and Holland.

A group of wine-glasses has been ascribed to Newcastle, and is to be distinguished by the light elegance of the stem designs (Figs. 213 and 218–20). The three-piece (or *stuck shank*) construction was favoured: bowl, stem and foot being made separately and then put together. The alternative two-piece (*straw stem*) was made with the stem and bowl in a single piece, the one drawn out from the other, and was popular in London and elsewhere. While other items were made in Newcastle, the bulk of the output was of window glass made by the Crown process (p. 37). In a book written in 1703 it is noted that the sheets (called *tables*) were packed in straw in light wooden frames, from 35 to 45 in a case: 'these cases are brought to London in the coal-ships, they being set on end in the coles more than half its depth, by which means they are kept steady from falling, and being broke by the motion and rowling of the ship.'

Another member of the Dagnia family was responsible for starting the first recorded glass-house in Bristol. The articles

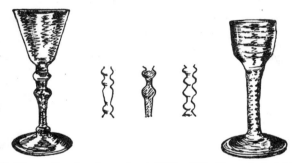

**219.** Newcastle wine-glass, about 1725. **220.** Three typical New-castle stem patterns. **221.** Lynn type wine-glass with horizontally-ribbed bowl.

made in the 'flint' houses of the city prior to 1750 or so have not been identified, and much of the output comprised wine-bottles of common metal. The surviving numbers of them with west-country names and places on their seals are a testimony to the importance of that branch of the trade, as it seems probable they would have been produced adjacent to where they were required. Many were sent out to be filled by the buyers, but others were sold containing health-giving waters from the local Hotwells.

One other provincial centre making 'flint' glass deserves a mention: King's Lynn. The Norfolk port is noted by Houghton as having a bottle-making glass-house, but three years prior to John Houghton's mention a London journal advertised: 'To be sold all sorts of the best and finest Drinking-Glasses and curious Glasses for Ornament, and likewise all sorts of Glass Bottles, by Francis Jackson and John Straw . . . at their Glass-Houses near the Falcon in Southwark, and at Lynn in Norfolk'. A further announcement appeared in the *Ipswich Journal* during 1747. It is thought that the tax of 1745 seriously affected the establishment and that it did not last for very long after the latter notice.

A particular type of wine-glass with a horizontally-ribbed bowl has been ascribed to King's Lynn (Fig. 221). Albert Hartshorne, who made the attribution, gave as his reason for making it: 'all the examples that have been noticed come out of Norfolk'. In spite of the rather weak evidence, or perhaps because nothing better has been put forward, this theory of their origin has persisted.

# CHAPTER X

# English Glass: III—1760-1820

It was in the middle years of the century that Bristol, in the west of the country and a leading seaport, became prominent as a centre of glass-making. The three 'flint glass and ordinary' manufactories noted in 1696 by John Houghton had grown in number as the years went on, and an increased trade both at home and overseas kept them busy. In modern times the term *Bristol glass* is applied to almost any of a blue colour, and often to pieces in opaque white, purple, green and red. While it is quite certain that some wares in these colours were made there, it is accepted also that they were manufactured in other parts of the country. In addition, a large proportion of the Bristol output was in clear metal, and this was made into wares that are generally indistinguishable from those made elsewhere.

Among the distinctive Bristol blue articles are decanters. These were usually of pint size or under for spirits and cordials, and smaller for sauces. Each has its stopper ground to fit, and often with an initial in gold to match the word on the label painted on the body (Figs. 222 and 223). They were made in sets of three or more and the names found on them include most of the liquors and condiments current in the late 18th and early 19th centuries. Examples of similar shape and pattern are found also in green metal.

The making of coloured wares cannot be claimed exclusively for the Bristol glass-houses. Green, especially, is known to have been used for drinking glasses in fashionable styles from at least as early as Queen Anne's reign. In 1751 a traveller in the Midlands noticed that coloured glass was being made at Stourbridge, 'famous for its glass manufactures, especially for its coloured glass, with which they make painted windows, which is here coloured in the liquid, of all the

**222. Blue glass decanter** with gilt 'label': about 1780. Ht 9½ in.

**223. Blue glass sauce bottle**, labelled 'ANCHOVY': about 1770. Ht 5½ in.

capital colours in their several shades.' There is little doubt that public demand stimulated production in many places, and it is likely that such wares were made also at London, Newcastle and elsewhere in the north of the country.

**224. Signature (gilt) of I. Jacobs, Bristol.**

**225. Blue wine-glass cooler** with gilt decoration, signed by Jacobs. Ht 3⅞ in.

A few surviving specimens of blue glass can be claimed unequivocally for Bristol: those with a signature in gold *I. Jacobs Bristol* (Fig. 224). Only a handful of such pieces has been recorded. They include wine-glass coolers, lipped small bowls for holding cold water in which wine-glasses could rest for cooling before use at the table (Fig. 225), dishes with shaped and cut edges, and decanters. Lazarus Jacobs and his son had a glass-house in Temple Street, Bristol, where the son was duly appointed 'Glass Manufacturer to His Majesty' (George III). In 1806 he advertised that he had 'Specimens of the Dessert set, which I. Jacobs had the honour of sending to her Majesty, in burnished Gold upon Royal purple coloured Glass, to be seen at his Manufactory, where several Dessert sets of the same kind are now completed from Fifteen Guineas per set to any amount'.

Michael Edkins, a man who began his career by decorating Bristol pottery, is known to have worked also at painting and gilding glass made in the city. His business ledger, which is preserved in Bristol City Museum, shows that he was employed at the task at least between the years 1762 and 1787. His grandson, William Edkins, formed a collection of pottery, porcelain and glass, and stated that amongst the latter were some specimens decorated by his ancestor. One of them is the tea-caddy shown in Fig. 226 (now in the Victoria and Albert Museum, London), and another is the bottle, one of a pair, in Fig. 227. Both are decorated in colours on opaque white glass.

When they were sold in London in 1874, these latter pieces, and others of the same type, were catalogued under the heading:

### BRISTOL ENAMELLED GLASS

*Manufactured by Little and Longman, and Successors, on Redcliffe-back, Bristol, from 1750 to 1770; painted and enamelled by Michael Edkins.*

Many similar pieces have been attributed subsequently to Edkins, but it is now considered doubtful whether he executed more than a very small proportion of them. The surviving records of payments he received for his work show that he was paid surprisingly little for what he did. For instance, in 1762:

Jan 19   To 1 Sett of Jars and Beakers
              5 in a sett                                              2. 6.
July 26   To 1 Pint Blue can ornamented
              with Gold and Letters                            0. 8.

From this evidence, it seems possible that these and other pieces may have been painted with ordinary unfired paints, or gold leaf on size, of which all traces have now vanished.

**226. Opaque white tea caddy** painted in colours: about 1760. Ht 5¼ in. **227. Opaque white bottle** with coloured decoration: about 1760. Ht 4⅝ in. **228. Opaque white scent-bottle** with coloured decoration: about 1770. Ht 2½ in. **229. Blue glass scent-bottle** with painted and gilt decoration: about 1770. Ht 3 in.

In view of this and other facts it is now considered that neither Edkins nor Bristol had a connexion with surviving examples of the work. It is known that similar metal was also in use elsewhere (e.g. at Warrington and Newcastle), so the pieces can have been made at one or more of several places. The painting was not necessarily done at the manufactory, but could be the work of anyone who cared to buy the undecorated wares and finish them in the manner of the porcelain 'outside decorators'. At present, in view of a likeness to styles of painting seen on enamelled copper, long thought to be from Battersea, but now known to have come from the Midlands, the white glass is referred to as 'South Staffordshire'.

18th-century scent phials, bodkin cases and other small-sized containers, in clear, coloured or opaque white glass were at one time attributed indiscriminately to Bristol. This was probably because of the vogue for 'Bristol Blue' as a name for anything in that colour, and from that it was easy to attribute articles of a similar type, but different colour to the same source. It is realised now that many or all of them may have come from London workshops where comparable painting was done on watch-cases and other small pieces. The two examples illustrated (Figs. 228 and 229) are typical of these pleasing and rare trifles which were made in the last half of the century, although their precise source awaits discovery.

Some eight miles north-by-west from Bristol is Nailsea, where a Bristol bottle-maker, John Robert Lucas, set up a glass-house in 1788. Use was made of local coal, and among the wares made were articles from the green metal normally used only for bottles, taxed at about one fifth the rate of clear glass. Several varieties of the material would seem to have been made, but the particular favourite with which the name of the place is associated most strongly is of green flecked with white and other colours. It is known that it was made also at Wrockwardine, in Shropshire. Doubtless, because imitation quickly follows success it was produced in many other places, but the name of Nailsea is used commonly for all wares of the type (Fig. 230).

Early in the second half of the 19th century some French and Belgian glass-makers came to the place, and it has been suggested that these men were responsible for the introduction to the glass-house of latticino work in the Venetian manner (Figs. 231 and 232).

Harry J. Powell, a practical glass-maker, wrote rather scathingly in 1923 of the various decorative pieces ascribed to the factory:

'The great Nailsea works were famous for the fine quality of their crown window-glass, but are unworthily commemorated in museums and private collections by the rude

**230. Colour-splashed green jug:** about 1800. Ht 9½ in.    **231. Green and white striped jug:** early 19th century. Ht 5 in.    **232. Red, white and blue flask** with pewter cap: early 19th century. L 8 in.

vases, flasks, jugs, candlesticks and rolling-pins originally made by the glass-blowers in their spare time. They are colourless or coloured, and many are marked, spotted, streaked or roughly threaded with opaque white enamel or crude-coloured glasses. Similar objects known colloquially as "friggers" may be seen as chimney-piece ornaments in glass-blowers' homes in every glass-making district. In the Bristol district these by-products were exploited by dealers and became for a time staple products. They were widely distributed, and copies are still made in many districts and sold as antiques. Even the originals, with very few exceptions, are entirely devoid of artistic, technical or historic interest.'

They are strong words of condemnation with which not everybody will now agree, but Powell is correct in pointing out that whatever their source and age *friggers* are described invariably as Nailsea. Most commonly to be seen are the rolling-pins (Fig. 233), which are painted, often in unfired oil-colours, with inscriptions and scenes. The suggested uses

**233. White rolling-pin** with painted decoration: 19th century. L 13¾ in.

for which they were intended are varied: as love-tokens to be hung in the kitchen while Jack was at sea; as clandestine containers for rum or tea smuggled to avoid duty; as convenient containers for sugar or salt; or simply as rolling-pins.

A more elaborate frigger is shown in Fig. 234; an ornament that must have been the pride of the home when it was first made. Comparable display pieces were in the form of fully-rigged ships that are sometimes complete with crew, and fox-hunting scenes with the hounds in full cry. Less flamboyant were walking sticks, long-stemmed pipes, hats and yards-of-ale (Figs. 235, 236 and 237). The sticks are clear or coloured, plain or ribbed, and some very late ones are hollow and filled with 'hundreds and thousands'.

The yard-of-ale is a glass holding an indeterminate amount of liquid, but measuring some three feet in length. It can have either a normal foot, or terminate in a hollow bulb which makes it into a trick glass. Because of the bulb it cannot be stood during use, and once started the drinker must continue to the end. The trick about the glass is apparent when

**234. Group of birds at a fountain:** 19th century. Ht 17 in. **235. Glass hats.** A: Bowler. B: Topper: 19th century. **236. Red glass pipe:** 19th century. Ht about 24 in.

the contents are almost all consumed. After the vessel is raised above the horizontal in order to drain it, the air trapped in the bulb suddenly forces the remaining liquid into the face of the unsuspecting user.

Friggers go back in time, and a report in a newspaper of 1738 mentioned a visit of the Prince and Princess of Wales to Bristol, where they took part in a ceremonial parade. The paragraph concluded:

'The Companies of the City made a magnificent appearance in their formalities, marching two by two, preceding the Corporation and the Royal Guests. The Company of Glassmen went first dressed in white Holland shirts, on horseback, some with swords, others with crowns and sceptres in their hands, made of glass.'

210

Equally for display purposes were 'set pieces' like those used in the Guildhall of the City of London on important occasions. When Queen Victoria attended banquets there the decorations included 'a superb crystal star, and a Prince of Wales's plume in spun glass, nine feet high'.

A group of other articles attributed to Nailsea, although made elsewhere as well, includes hand-bells. They are to be found in glass of all colours, and all or partly latticino

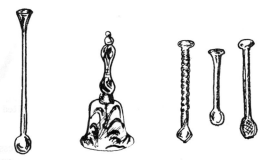

**237. Yard-of-Ale:** 19th century.   **238. Bell** with latticino handle: 19th century. Ht about 11 in.   **239. Sugar crushers** or stirrers: 19th century. L 4–5 in.

(Fig. 238). Most of them date from late in the 19th century, but many are of more recent manufacture. It may be wondered why there should have been, and still is, a sizeable demand for such things made from a completely inappropriate breakable material. Equally doomed to a short life in use were bugles and coaching-horns, which survive in small numbers.

A note in a Newcastle newspaper almost a century after the Bristol one noted above refers to hand-bells in use, and doubtless other noise-producing glassware featured on similar occasions. Members of the Guild of Glassmakers paraded in the streets of their city, and the contemporary description runs:

'Each wore a hat decorated with a glass feather, a glass star sparkled at their breast suspended from a chain or collar formed of drops of cut glass in variegated colours hung round the neck. Each man carried a staff, a cross piece at the top displaying a specimen of his art: decanters, goblets, drinking glasses, jugs, bowls, dishes. Some carried a Glass Bell which he rang lustily.'

More practical was the application of tuned glasses to music of the concert-hall. It is thought to have been devised in the 17th century, but nonetheless the composer Gluck announced in the London press in 1746:

'A Concerto upon Twenty-six Drinking-Glasses, tuned with Spring-Water, accompanied with the whole Band, being a new Instrument of his own Invention.'

The sounds were produced by the friction of wet fingers on the rims of carefully-selected wine-glasses, but some performers used small hammers. Benjamin Franklin mechanised the whole proceeding by fixing a series of tuned convex glass basins along a rod, which was made to revolve in a trough of water by means of a pedal. The name Harmonica was given to the instrument, which was played with the fingers of both hands rubbing the edges of the bowls. Later, German inventors modified Franklin's instrument by adding a keyboard so that it could be performed upon in the same manner as a harpsichord or a pianoforte.

In the same category as all the preceding, made perhaps at Nailsea and certainly in other places, are sugar-crushers or stirrers, and doorstops. The former are purely functional articles, of slight artistic appeal and usually quite roughly made. Some have patterns impressed in their flattened spade-like ends, and others are with ribbed stems (Fig. 239). The doorstops, known sometimes as *dumps*, are egg-shaped with a flat base, and stand about six inches high. The green clear metal encloses a fountain or a spray of flowers defined in silvery bubbles.

From 1760 the use of cutting for decoration increased, and in the case of the wine-glass often resulted in a faceted stem which tended to be shorter as the years progressed (Fig. 240). The thinness of the bowl generally precluded any use of the

**240. Glasses** with faceted stems. A: Double-ogee bowl and straight stem. B: the stem with a knop. C: Engraved ogee bowl and straight stem: about 1780.

wheel, and such ornament was therefore confined to the base. In spite of successive rises in the Excise Duty in 1777, 1781 and 1787, heavier glasses began to be made at the turn of the century and the cutters were then able to employ a wider range of motifs. At the same time, they gave no less attention to the bowl of a glass than they had given formerly to the stem.

In addition to the increased use of cutting, wine-glasses were embellished with other types of decoration. One of the most attractive and scarce is that of enamelling, either in white or in colours. The name most associated with the art is that of Beilby: two brothers and a sister, William (1740–1819), Ralph (1743–1817) and Mary (1749–97). Their surviving output is small and dates from about 1762, and as the family lived and worked in Newcastle upon Tyne it is not surprising to find that they decorated pieces made in the local glass-houses. While some bear scenes (Fig. 241) or inscriptions, others have the coats of arms of Northumbrians, and a few very splendid specimens show the arms of George III with crest, supporters and motto within elaborate rococo mantling. Some examples of the family's work are signed with the sur-

**241. A landscape in colours** by one of the Beilby family of Newcastle: about 1765.

name only, and one has the inscription 'W. Beilby Junr Ncastle inv$^t$ & pinx$^t$'.

The *rummer*, a large-bowled goblet on a short stem, became favoured for many kinds of drink from about 1760. It remained popular for the next seventy years or so, and during that period underwent a few changes of form. Bowls were either rounded or bucket-shaped, and the latter were often ornamented with a series of broad shallow cuts. A square foot was not uncommon, but rarely before 1790 (Figs. 242–4).

As the century progressed, the feet of nearly all wine-glasses shrank in comparison with the diameter of the bowl; the earlier examples show a foot about as large as (or larger than) the bowl, but as the years passed it became customary for the foot to be somewhat smaller in proportion. From

**242. Goblet** with bucket bowl and square foot: early 19th century.
Ht about 5 in.   **243. Goblet** with square foot: early 19th century.
Ht about 5 in.   **244. Goblet** with cup-topped bucket bowl and
round foot: early 19th century. Ht about 5 in.

about 1780 it was usual to remove traces of where an article
had been affixed to the pontil during manufacture. While
there are exceptions to this, it will be found that most bases
from then onwards have been ground smooth. It may be
remarked that the presence of a pontil-mark does not mean

**245. Two toddy-lifters** with cut
ornament: about 1800.

inevitably that a piece is genuinely old. Like so many other
signs of old workmanship, it can be imitated sufficiently well
to deceive the unwary.

Toddy, a mixed drink, became fashionable during the 18th
century. It was served from a bowl, and occasionally use was
made of a glass device known as a *toddy-lifter* (Fig. 245). This

215

looks like a small-sized decanter, without a stopper and pierced through the base. It works on the principle of the pipette: the wide end is immersed in the toddy, and when it is lifted with a finger or thumb over the hole in the stem it retains its contents by vacuum. As soon as the hole is uncovered, air enters the stem and the contents are released.

**246. Decanter-jug:** about 1685. Ht 11¼ in.   **247. Decanter** with 'nipt diamond waies' decoration and Ravenscroft's seal: 1677–78. Ht 8 in.   **248. Decanter** with engraved decoration: about 1760. Ht 11¼ in.

The decanter made an appearance in the Ravenscroft period, but examples dating from before 1760 are now very rare. Some of the early ones were given handles, and a few still retain their original loose-fitting stoppers. In most instances these have been lost and the decanters are described as 'jugs', but their comparatively narrow necks differentiate them from the latter. They were given trailed ornament of various patterns (Fig. 246), and some were covered partly or completely in the trellis design known at the time as 'nipt diamond waies'. An example of the latter, bearing the seal of George Ravenscroft, is in the British Museum (Fig. 247), and two others of similar pattern but in purple glass and without a seal have been preserved. They are in the Victoria and Albert Museum, London, and the Ashmolean Museum, Oxford.

The decanter really came into its own when engraving, cutting and enamelling were fashionable. As with wine-glasses, these various types of ornamentation came and went in popularity, and style succeeded style. Engraved and enamelled examples include some with 'labels' on them, which take the form of a wine-name surrounded by a border and with a simulated chain for suspension exactly like the current silver labels (Fig. 248). Names that have been recorded range from the familiar PORT and CLARET to such forgotten ones as MOUNTAIN (a white wine from the Malaga district). A few examples are known of decanters engraved with Jacobite emblems and mottoes (Fig. 249), and a very few others exist with the likeness of William III. One of these latter is in the fine collection belonging to the Grocers' Company, London.

Cutting on decanters began to appear in about 1760, at the same date as this form of decoration was first used on wine-glasses. It usually took the form of an all-over pattern of shallow facets, but examples are very scarce nowadays (Fig. 250). Stoppers, which varied in shape over the years, were often cut and polished, and were ground into the neck to ensure a perfectly tight fit. A variant of the normal decanter was the one made for use at sea, and known as a *Ship's Decanter*, which was given a heavy large-sized base so that it would remain upright and stable during rough weather (Fig. 251).

Just as much sought after as the foregoing are decanters with handles, sometimes termed decanter-jugs, which came and went in popularity from about the year 1670 (Fig. 246).

**249. Decanter** (lacking stopper) engraved with a portrait of the Young Pretender and the motto 'Audentior Ibo': about 1760. Ht 9¼ in. **250. Facet-cut decanter:** about 1760. Ht 12 in. **251. Ship's decanter:** about 1790. Ht 9½ in.

Less rare examples with heavy cut ornament, dating from the 1820s, were intended for the serving of claret. Today, they have a fresh lease of life dispensing cocktails (Fig. 267, p. 230).

**252. Examples of cutting.** A: Diamond. B: Strawberry diamond. C: Horizontal prisms.

The first years of the 19th century saw a much greater employment of cutting on all forms of glassware, not excepting the decanter. All the many ingenious variations of angle and surface were used in combination, and the glittering finished work was rivalled only by a cut and polished gemstone. Some of the different patterns are shown in Fig. 252, but no illustration, either in line or half-tone, can do justice to the actual effect produced either in natural or artificial light. This form of craftsmanship has had its critics, and not least amongst them was John Ruskin, the arbiter of mid-Victorian taste. Living at a time when every surface of glass and other materials was subjected to the maximum of lively ornament, he stated sweepingly that 'all cut-glass is barbarous'. It seems a pity that his words should be taken too literally

**253. Champagne glass** with folded rim to the bowl: about 1750. Ht about 5 in.

and applied retrospectively to work of the years prior to 1800; after that, when the cutter so often tended to let his wheels run riot, there is much to justify Ruskin's condemnation.

Champagne, which had come into the wine list gradually during the course of the 18th century, was taken perhaps from the tall-stemmed, wide-bowled glasses that are liable to be confused with sweetmeats (Fig. 253). However, the edges of the latter were usually decorated with trailing or cutting so that drinking from them would be hazardous or impossible. Decanters for champagne were made and are now very rare. They were fitted with a pocket formed in the body so that ice could be inserted to cool the wine. Other decanters, of

normal 1760–70 pattern, are found engraved with the word
CHAMPAIGN.

Ale-glasses, mentioned briefly on p. 195, were sold not only
plain and relying for embellishment on a twist-patterned stem,
but with engraved bowls. The engraving usually took the
form of sprays of hops and barley, which were arranged to
cover the tall tapering surface. The patterns vary, but unlike
the series of Jacobite emblems they were not, so far as is
known, endowed with any hidden meanings. Probably, they
are no more than the results of random selection by makers
and dealers, and they can be appreciated as purely decorative.
The variations have been classified according to the number
of leaves to each stalk of barley, whether the stalks are crossed
or not, or whether the barley stalks also bear hop fruits—this
latter understandably classified as 'very rare'. At least nine
distinct patterns have been noted, and the most common of
the glasses shows two separate ears of barley, each with a leaf
and with the stalks crossed, and on the reverse side a hop
fruit with two leaves (Fig. 254).

Tumblers of all ages are now hard to find, which may be
because they have had hard and continual usage and suffered
breakage. Equally, they may have been less popular in the
past than they are today, and were not made in large numbers.
The early 19th-century examples are heavy-based with thick
walls and of large capacity, but in time became smaller and
were decorated with cutting. Both tumblers and tankards
sometimes bear commemorative inscriptions.

Condiment containers were decorated with cutting, and are
often datable by means of the silver mounts at the necks
(Fig. 255). Many of them are very well finished, and are
occasionally found complete in their original stand, or *War-
wick*, of silver, Sheffield plate or wood.

Other articles made in the 18th century and seen occasionally nowadays include the salver: a flat circular dish

on a central round foot which was often used in the form of a 'pyramid' on the dining-table. One was placed on top of another and on each of them were glasses of jellies or some other dessert; the whole forming a striking centre-piece. A few examples of old pestles and mortars have survived the stresses of the laboratory, and the sugar-bowl accompanied by one or two tea-canisters found in tea-caddies from about 1760 was generally of cut glass. One unusual drinking-glass seen from time to time is in the form of a jack-boot (Fig. 256). It is

**254. Hop fruit** with two leaves. **255. Caster and vinegar-bottle** with cut ornament: late 18th century. Ht 5 in. **256. Drinking-glass** in the shape of a jack-boot: late 18th century.

supposed to have been made at a time when the third Earl of Bute (1713–1792) was very notorious because of his intrigues with the Princess of Wales, and this rather weak pun (Bute: boot) is said to commemorate him.

Decoration by means of cutting on the wheel meant that articles had to be made with thicker walls than would have been necessary for enamelling or engraving. The rising fashion for the work coincided with the increases of Duty imposed in 1777, 1781 and 1787, and manufacturers strove to find ways of offsetting the higher costs involved. As early as the sixties of the century, a number of English makers had set up glass-houses in Ireland, where glass was untaxed, and in the following decades the numbers increased. The majority went there following the grant of full freedom of trade to the island in 1780, before which all manufactures had been restricted in sale to the small home market.

The principal glass-making centres during the years between 1760 and 1830 were the undermentioned:

**Belfast.** The most important manufacturer was Benjamin Edwards, who came from Bristol to Drumrea, Co. Tyrone, in 1771 and moved to Belfast a few years later. He employed English workmen who had been trained at Bristol. Edwards was succeeded by his son, also named Benjamin, but the business did not long survive the effects of a Duty on glass imposed in 1825. Although this was only about one-third of the prevailing English tax, it halted expansion of the industry in Ireland.

**Cork.** Some local men with English employees opened a glass-house in 1783 and styled themselves, through many vicissitudes, the Cork Glass Company. It seems to have closed in 1818. The Waterloo Company was established in 1815 by a man named Daniel Foley. On Christmas Eve of the year following, the *Cork Overseer* stated:

'Foley's workmen are well selected, from whose superior skill the most beautiful glass will shortly make its appearance to dazzle the eyes of the public, and to outshine those of any other competitor. He is to treat his men at Christmas with a whole roasted ox and everything adequate. They have a new band of music with glass instruments with bassoon serpents, horns, trumpets, etc., and they have a glass pleasure boat, a cot and a glass set which when seen will astonish the world.'

From this promising beginning the business prospered until the retirement of Foley in 1830, and a decline into bankruptcy five years later.

**Dublin.** *The Dublin Society for Improving Husbandry, Manufactures, and other Useful Arts,* founded in 1731, offered financial rewards to those who might establish suitable enterprises in the country. Some members of a Welsh family named Williams gained a premium of £1,600, and with this they started a glass-house in or about 1764. It endured until 1827.

The glass-house of Charles Mulvaney was opened in 1785, competed with that of the Williams's and outlasted it by eight years.

Soon after 1780 John Dedereck Ayckbowm went to Dublin from London and set up as a glass retailer. It is thought he may have had a workshop for cutting articles bought from the makers, and his name is found occasionally on pieces.

**Waterford.** A factory here was mentioned in a newspaper in 1783: 'Waterford Glass House. George and William Penrose have established an extensive glass manufacture in this city; their friends and the public may be supplied with all kinds of plain and flint glass, useful and ornamental.' A number of craftsmen from Stourbridge, led by John Hill, stated to be 'a great manufacturer' from that town, were responsible for the output, but Hill does not appear to have stayed for more than three years. His place was taken by Jonathan Gatchell, also an Englishman, who eventually became owner of the business. He died in 1825, but the factory remained in operation until 1851.

Much has been talked and written about old Irish glass, and Waterford in particular, but with a few exceptions it is not possible to state with any certainty whether a particular piece was made there or not. It has become almost a tradition

257. Irish decanters. A: B. EDWARDS BELFAST. B: CORK GLASS CO. C: PENROSE WATERFORD: early 19th century.

to label as 'Waterford' any article decorated with deep cutting and made of a greyish-tinted metal. In fact, this colour was not peculiar to any single glass-house, and arose probably because of a fault in the mixing of the ingredients.

Pieces that are undoubtedly of Irish origin are those which bear the names of their makers (Fig. 257). Decanters, finger-bowls and jugs show in a circle beneath their bases in slightly raised letters, which are often illegible or go unnoticed, any of the following:

B. EDWARDS   BELFAST
CORK GLASS CO.
WATERLOO CO. CORK
J. D. AYCKBOWM   DUBLIN
C. M. & CO. (Charles Mulvaney, Dublin)
FRANCIS COLLINS   DUBLIN
MARY CARTER & SON   80 GRAFTON STREET DUBLIN
PENROSE   WATERFORD

Marked pieces have been reproduced, and will be found to be much heavier in weight and with clearer lettering than genuine examples.

Many bowls, dishes, jugs and other articles adorned with cutting are thought to be of Irish origin without any positive proof of the fact. As most of the output of such pieces in Ireland was intended for the English market they followed the styles favoured by their potential customers, and they would have been as close as possible to those in use in English glass-houses. Certain types of cutting are suggested sometimes to be peculiar to craftsmen who worked in Ireland, but it is very

**258. Candlesticks** hung with faceted drops: late 18th/early 19th century.

doubtful whether any particular cutter or workshop on either side of the Irish Sea showed a discernible originality. On the whole, designs were confined to the severely geometrical, which left very little scope at all for the display of individual characteristics.

The use of cutting, both in England and Ireland, was in no instance employed more effectively than when it was applied to lighting appliances, candlesticks, candelabra and chandeliers, so that it reflected the wavering light of candles from innumerable polished points. The earlier candlesticks which had had moulded stems (Fig. 198, p. 190) were given facets at first, and appeared later with widened tops hung with glittering drops and with every surface cut (Fig. 258). The glass drops ranged from simple circular buttons and pears with shallow facets to elongated many-sided 'icicles', and

**259. Two-light table candelabrum** (one of a pair): about 1780.
Ht 26 in. **260. Chandelier:** about 1740.

**261. Chandelier:** about 1775. Ht 42 in. **262. Chandelier:** about 1820.

finally to prisms sometimes as much as six inches in length.

Table candelabra appeared early in the 18th century, but most surviving examples are at least fifty or sixty years later in date. Much ingenuity was expended in their design, and equal thought was given to the manner in which the many parts were assembled so that any constructional details were hidden. Examples of both rococo and neo-classical design were made, and some of the latter stand on bases of marble, coloured glass or Wedgwood jasperware set in gilt-metal mounts. Most of them were hung with festoons of cut drops, like the example in Fig. 259. Wall-lights of similar design were made in pairs and sets, but are now scarce.

The chandelier is one of the most splendid of glass-making achievements. Anyone who has seen one of the more important examples, especially when illuminated, must agree that they are supreme examples of design and craftsmanship. Certainly, they make the most of the natural properties of George Ravenscroft's 'glass of lead', and the latent fire in that material is given the fullest play.

The first examples followed the simple lines of early 18th-century brass chandeliers, with curved arms and a central shaft built up from spheres of different sizes (Fig. 260). Later in the century, the patterns grew more complex, with faceted pinnacles, canopies and traces of the rococo details found in contemporary decoration (Fig. 261). During the Regency, the central shaft and the sinuous arms were replaced by a great cascade of hanging drops, which formed a cloak to conceal the central shaft supporting a gilt-metal ring set with short candle-holders (Fig. 262). A famous one of the type, dating from about 1815, is in the Victoria and Albert Museum, and is recorded as being composed of no fewer than 4,500 separate pieces.

# CHAPTER XI

# English Glass: IV—1820-1900

The glass of the first decades of the 19th century continued in the styles set for it in earlier years. The complexity of cut patterns increased, and it must have been to specimens of this time that Ruskin referred when he used the term 'barbarous'. Justification for his comment may be found literally on the many pieces finished with jagged teeth at the edges,

**263. Boat-shaped fruit bowl** with cut decoration: late 18th century. W. 12 in. **264. Celery vase** with fan-cut rim: early 19th century. Ht about 10 in.

and on which every surface was made to bristle with sharp diamonds (Figs. 263–5). The effect is an unequalled glitter; well-suited to a time that saw the costliest of coronation ceremonies and the exotic extravagance of the Royal Pavilion at Brighton.

Production of coloured and multi-coloured novelties **and**

useful wares continued at various centres as before, but the fashionable world favoured clear metal. In part this was due to the high degree of skill reached by the cutters in England and Ireland, and equally the tight grip of the excise officer on glass-houses made experiment on such things as colouring almost impossible. Such innovations as occurred were in connection with applied decoration and did not actually affect the composition of the metal.

One of the new processes was patented in 1806 by John Davenport, better known as a maker of pottery and porcelain. Powdered glass was spread on an article, a pattern was then drawn on it and fused to the main body; a matter requiring careful control of the heat. Some decorated goblets with the word 'Patent' under the base have been recorded as survivors of the method, but it is often unrecognised for what it really is and described wrongly as 'acid-engraving'; a process that was not employed until considerably later in the century (p. 32).

A French innovation of embedding in clear glass small models made from a special material was adopted by Apsley Pellatt, owner of the old-established Falcon glass-house in Southwark, London. The portrait heads and other objects were made from a white ceramic paste that would not form gas when heated and would also expand and contract at much the same rate as glass. Failure on these points would have fractured the covering. Pellatt called his productions *Crystallo-Ceramies*, but they are known also as *Sulphides* and *Cameo Incrustations*.

Pellatt's sulphides date from about 1820, and surviving specimens showing the head of George IV were perhaps made to celebrate his coronation in the following year, or at least during his reign, which lasted until 1830. Similar pieces were made at about the same date in France, and it is not always possible to be sure about the origin of some examples.

It is probable that pieces with portraits of Englishmen and Englishwomen were produced here. Sulphides were used in articles like tankards and paperweights, and even in table candelabra, where their shining silvery-white forms are matched by the glitter of the cutting with which the surrounding glass is usually decorated (Fig. 266). Apsley Pellatt's firm continued to make sulphides until at least the middle years of the century, and others were using the process later still.

**265. Decanter:** about 1820. Ht 9¾ in. **266. Scent-bottle** inset with a sulphide portrait bust of Princess Charlotte, (1796–1817): about 1820. **267. Decanter-jug:** early 19th century.

Engraving on the wheel was used frequently and effectively for commemorative inscriptions and designs on goblets and other articles. Many of these have survived the years, which is probably because they combine both a decorative and a historical appeal and therefore have had more careful handling than purely functional objects. The variety of subjects is a wide one and includes sporting scenes, military and marine subjects, and important national events. Caution is needed when examining engraved glasses, especially those with popular interest like the battle of Trafalgar, as they have been reproduced over a period of many years.

Between 1800 and 1820 cutting was lavish, but by about 1830 a noticeable simplicity of design became apparent. Articles were made as heavily as hitherto, but instead of the mass of cutting which had been so long current there were patches of flat or concave surface with no criss-crossing channels on them. The decanter-jug in Fig. 267 is a typical example of the time; the external form has not altered greatly, the weight of metal is little different, but the decoration comprises simple bands of horizontal fluting and broad upright facets.

Apart from the work which continued to be done in Ireland up to the time of the Excise Duty levied there (1825), the 19th century saw a change in the industry which, with a few notable exceptions, ceased to be based on London. The clay of Stourbridge in the Midlands, which was eminently suitable for making glass-house pots, and the nearby Staffordshire coal, had long before attracted makers to the district. They gradually increased in number until it became the centre of English glass-making, and by about 1850 it occupied the pre-eminent position which it retains to this day.

The Excise Duty of 1745, and its successive rises, bore on the trade very heavily. Evidence to this effect was given by a manufacturer before the Commissioners of Excise in 1833, who stated:

'Our business and premises are placed under the arbitrary control of a class of men to whose will and caprice it is most irksome to have to submit and this under a system of regulations most ungraciously inquisitorial. We cannot enter into parts of our own premises without their permission; we can do no one single act in the conduct of our business without having previously notified our intention to the officers placed over us. We have in the course of the week's operations to serve some sixty or seventy notices on these, our masters, and this under heavy penalties of from £200 to £500 for every separate neglect.'

Many years after the duty had been withdrawn, Harry J. Powell wrote of it as it had affected the glass-house of his forbears at Whitefriars:

'The sites only remain of the sentry-boxes in which the "officers of excise" spent such part of their time in sleep as was not occupied in harrying the works' managers or being harried by the glass-house boys. Two, at least, of these officers were quartered in every glass-works, and as the duty was payable partly on the worked and partly on the unworked glass, it was their business to register the total weight of glass melted and to prevent the removal of any piece of manufactured glass which had not been weighed.'

In order that the full and correct amount of duty was levied, it was necessary for the internal dimensions of every pot to be registered and every annealing oven had to be 'rectangular in form, with only one entrance, and with a sufficient iron grating affixed thereto, together with proper locks and other fastenings for securing the same'. The officers had to be given written notification every time a pot was heated or filled, and whenever a leer was heated or closed or when goods were taken from it. In addition to the duty there was an annual licence charge for each glass-house.

Although there was, inevitably, an unrecorded number of illicit glass-houses which worked on a small scale, the majority of those in the industry conformed to the law. It was so strict, however, that even the Commissioners themselves agreed 'that the regulations presented a great impediment and in many cases a complete bar in the way of those experimental researches that are necessary'. They announced that fact in 1833, but it was twelve years before action was taken. In 1845 the Excise Duty was removed at last, and the manufacturers were free from interference for the first time since 1745.

It is untrue to say that there was no experiment whatsoever before 1845, but there was certainly only a fraction in comparison with what followed the advent of that year. The withdrawal of the hated duty was one stimulus and the other came a few years later: the Great Exhibition of 1851. This mighty display, its full title was 'The Great Exhibition of the Works of Industry of All Nations', resulted in a comprehensive showing of every type of manufactured article from the various parts of the world. Not least among them was glass, which was shown by exactly one hundred British firms and a greater number of foreign ones.

Although the Exhibition certainly had the effect of spreading continental ideas among English makers, it must not be thought that they had been completely idle prior to the opening day. This is exemplified in the range of pieces that were then seen, and which must have been prepared considerably earlier after some years of trial and error. In addition to much cut clear glass there was a wide choice of coloured pieces with and without added ornament of various kinds. They included the following, which comprised a small part of the exhibit of a Stourbridge firm:

'A great variety of vases, jars, and scent-jars for holding flowers, &c., in the Egyptian, Etruscan and Grecian styles; many of them cut, coated, gilt, painted in enamel colours, after the antique, with figures, ornaments, flowers, landscapes, and marine views, of the following colours, viz., ruby, oriental blue, chrysoprase, turquoise, black, rose colour, opal-coated blue, cornelian, opal frosted, pearl opal, mazareen blue, &c.' There was no lack of choice, and the colours rival in range and name those of a modern motor-car manufacturer. 'Chrysoprase' is a green stone; 'rose colour' can, of course, be anything from pink to yellow; 'mazareen blue' is a dark navy colour, and 'oriental blue' might be that of blue-painted Nankin porcelain, cobalt.

Not only were purchasers offered single colours, but 'overlay', or layered, pieces were made and cut so that the tint of the body metal showed through the design in the outer coating (Fig. 268). As well as this process, there was a less expensive variant that involved firing a stain into the surface and then cutting lightly through the thin skin of colour to produce a somewhat similar effect. At first this was done with

**268. Two overlay goblets** shown at the Great Exhibition in 1851, by G. Bacchus and Sons of Birmingham. **269. Butter-dish,** cover and stand in white and green opaline: about 1850. **270. White opaline vase** painted with roses on a gilt ground: about 1855. Ht 10½ in.

a red of much the same tint as the familiar Bohemian ruby colour, and later a brownish-yellow was used in the same manner. Both were often applied to tall decanters, of which a large proportion were engraved with a running pattern of vine-leaves and grapes.

Most popular of all the mid-century types of glass was *opal* or *opaline*; the latter being the name by which the French variety was known in France. It was made in colours including white and apple-green, often used in conjunction, and ornamented with gilding, but only slight cutting. A common embellishment was a realistically coiled snake, also in glass, with gilt scales on its body (Fig. 269). Some examples were given a matt surface and this, together with its lack of transparency, results in a distinctly lifeless appearance in contrast to most other types of glassware. With justice, it has been described as resembling blancmange.

Vases of many shapes and sizes were made in the white opal material, and some of the larger and more imposing examples were painted in a masterly manner. Flowers in natural colours were much in demand, and studies of birds would seem to have been a second choice. The gilding used on most of these pieces was applied very thinly and has often worn away, wholly or partly, as a result of successive washings and dryings and the friction of careful dusting.

The dwarf candlestick with a hanging fringe of cut-glass drops, which was so popular earlier in the century, took on a new form after about 1850. Somewhat larger in size and with bigger pendants, it lost its original purpose and became an ornamental vase. In pairs, one at either end of a mantlepiece, they were to be seen in the majority of Victorian parlours. Few homes did not boast at least one pair of these 'lustres', of which the body was made cheaply from coloured opal glass or more expensively in red or green overlay (Fig. 271).

Colour is seen also in the mid-century imitations of French *millefiore* paperweights. They were made in Birmingham, and while some of the examples compare favourably with their originals, most are paler in tint and lacking in ingenuity of design. Also, they differ in shape: the English ones usually being larger in diameter and taller. It appears they were being made by 1848, but it is uncertain how long production continued. As the English paperweights are comparatively rare, it is probable that attempts to compete with the French in this particular field had a short life.

Engraving was much used throughout the century, and a development was the use of acid as an alternative. The effect is freer than that obtained on the wheel, but it lacks the great delicacy of the diamond-point. While experiments with it had been made in the forties, it was not in use to any degree until some thirty years later.

At about the latter time, there was a revival of interest in the Roman technique of cameo-cutting. Not only was the

**271. White opaline lustre** with painted and gilt ornament and clear drops: about 1860. **272. Cameo-glass scent-bottle** in the form of a duck's head. About 6 in. long.

famous Portland Vase copied more than once, but a number of important pieces of original design were made in the same manner. Within a few years firms in Stourbridge were producing vases, scent-bottles and other objects ornamented with suitable patterns (Fig. 272). Most of them show the design in white on a pale-coloured ground; the latter including yellow, pink and turquoise, and the surface was often given a matt finish. Many of the pieces of later date show only cursory craftsmanship, which is to be expected when attempts were made to do such work on a commercial scale. The more important commissioned pieces, whether for the homes of millionaires or for one of the many international exhibitions, were usually given a meticulously careful finish that vied with that of the Roman work they emulated. The foremost men at cameo-cutting were John Northwood and his pupils, Thomas and George Woodall, all of whom worked at Stourbridge. Their careers have been studied in recent years, and their productions are esteemed on both sides of the Atlantic.

The withdrawal of the Excise Duty in 1845 meant a freedom for the glass-makers to experiment with new types of materials and processes to compete with those developed on the Continent. While much of the effort was directed towards manufacturing wares that were frankly direct copies of the imported ones, there began at the same time a movement to produce original designs. These attempted to find satisfactory combinations of both shape and decoration, and the search, then as now, is an interesting undercurrent to the mainstream of commercial work.

The first of the efforts to essay the creation of something better was that of Henry Cole (1808–82), later Sir Henry and a prominent Government official throughout his life, who founded an enterprise called 'Summerly's Art Manufactures'. The firm commissioned work in pottery and porcelain as well as in glass, and their best-known in the latter are some sets of drinking-glasses and carafes enamelled in colours with a pattern of aquatic plants: an appropriate theme, if perhaps a laboured one.

The water-plants design was registered in 1847, but it was not until the emergence of William Morris (1834–96) that the home-inspired product made its next important impact. Morris in 1859 caused the architect, Philip Webb, to design for him wine-glasses and tumblers, which were made at James Powell's Whitefriars Glassworks in London (Fig. 273). This firm, among a few others, continued making articles in a comparable style, relying more on the beauty of the material itself and the pleasing shapes into which it could be formed, than on the types of decoration popularly admired. Powell's removed their manufactory from London to Wealdstone, Middlesex, in 1922, and continue to this day to make articles that are, in the words of W. B. Honey, 'worked in such a way, by variations of mass and waving of surface, as to engage that

**273. Drinking-glass** designed by Philip Webb: about 1860. Ht 5 in.
**274. Blue slag glass cream jug** made by Davidson, Gateshead (*See* fig. 278): about 1880. Ht 4½ in.    **275. Purple slag glass candlestick,** the base moulded with three dolphins: about 1880. Ht 8¼ in.

interior play of light which is so essential a part of the beauty of glass'.

The process of press-moulding (p. 27) was developed commercially in America, and introduced into England in about 1830. The mass-production of wares that resembled, more or less, expensive handmade cut-glass became possible, and for the first time every family could afford to own and use one or more pieces of decorated glassware. Pressed work was not confined to clear metal, but ranged over the spectrum for effects that nowadays may not always be considered

238

attractive. The search for novelty resulted in a greenish-yellow material known today as *Vaseline glass*, resembling in colour the patented product of that name, and *Slag glass*, which is an opaque streaked glass resembling no other known substance. One maker, Sowerby, was aware of the fact and gave his product the name of *vitro porcelain* (Figs. 274 and 275).

Most surviving pressed glass articles date from the end of the 19th century. Often a design remained in use for many years, not only because there was demand for the particular item, but because the mould had been so costly to make in the first place. The Patent Office Registry Marks (Fig. 276), on

**276. Patent Office Registry mark** used between 1842 and 1883: a key to the letters is to be found in many books of china marks.

such pieces that bear them, indicate the date when the pattern was registered there, but do not give the actual year of manufacture. The marks do indicate, however, when a pattern may have begun to be popular, and are in that way a useful guide to successive styles.

The opaque white dish in Fig. 277 bears the mark of a peacock's head used by Sowerby of Gateshead; together with marks of other makers in the Newcastle area it is shown in Fig. 278. The marks are all of small size, raised slightly above the surface and moulded during manufacture.

Pressed goods filled the big demand for cheap, useful and decorative glassware, and the more costly market was supplied with a variety of goods that relied on skilful hand craftsmanship for their making. While clear metal was employed for many articles, it was the clever use of colour to produce a number of unusual effects that represents the output of the last quarter of the 19th century.

It has been pointed out that much of the work shows the

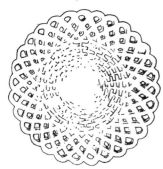

**277. Opaque white plate** made by Sowerby of Gateshead: about 1880. Diam. 8¾ in.

influence of the imported productions of Antonio Salviati, and while there were few direct copies there was a wide use of palely-tinted metal and trailed ornament. Great ingenuity was shown in the design and making of elaborate

**278. Marks used on pressed glass:** (left to right) by Sowerby, Gateshead; by Greener, Sunderland; by Davidson, Gateshead.

centre-pieces for the table, some of them in the complex tradition of 18th-century chandeliers. They were hung with numbers of removable little baskets, fitted with candle-holders, and mounted with glittering pointed spikes and twisted curlicues, like the example in Fig. 280. Such pieces first became fashionable in the sixties, and continued in use for some forty or more years afterwards.

The Stourbridge glass-makers made numbers of vases and other articles in a variety of techniques. Much use was made of semi-opaque tinted metal with a matt (or *satin*) surface, and sometimes finished ingeniously with an interior patterning of elongated air-bubbles (Fig. 279). In 1886, Webbs brought out their famed Queen's Burmese glass, in near-opaque pink shading to yellow, and followed it with several other novelties

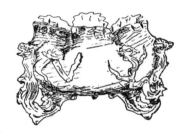

**279. Bowl of pink and white glass** with internal air-twist ornament and satin finish: about 1885. Ht 5½ in.

which were copied quickly by rivals. Indeed, plagiarism was rampant in spite of the law of copyright, and the Burmese was itself an imitation of an American product.

Glass with an iridescent surface was developed in the late seventies. It was produced first in Austria and Bohemia, and by 1878 Webbs of Stourbridge, along with other firms, were making it. Various methods were devised for producing the desired effects: subjecting the heated articles to chemical fumes in an enclosed chamber; boiling them in acid under high pressure, or exposing them to the fumes of what were termed mysteriously 'pink salts'. This aping of metalwork (one type was called by Webbs 'Bronze') became very fashionable for a period, but such an uncharacteristic form of the

241

material could not be expected to endure for long. It has been remarked that 'iridescent glass became almost as much a trade-mark of the Art Nouveau as the whiplash curve'.

Shaded and tinted clear glass was used for many pieces in the eighties and nineties (Fig. 281). Most of them show the current taste for shapes with crimped edges or with a resemblance to gnarled tree-trunks. Others are hung with realistic

**280. Ruby and clear glass stand for flowers:** about 1905. Ht 22½ in.
**281. Ruby and clear glass cream jug:** about 1890. Ht about 4½ in.
**282. Vase with rock crystal engraving:** about 1880. Ht 9¼ in.

glass cherries with stalks and leaves, and all are in imitation of the work being done at the time at Murano. A large proportion of the surviving examples show far more originality than taste, and not a few defy description in everyday words.

In spite of Ruskin's earlier strictures on glass-cutting, there was a revival of it in the eighties. A number of Central European craftsmen came to England at about that time, and produced work in what is termed the *rock crystal* style: deeply engraved in thick-walled pieces, and with the incisions polished to match the uncut portions (Fig. 282). Slightly earlier, designs were made by etching, but the principal employment of hydrofluoric acid was in producing the satin surface that fashionably robbed glass of so much of its beauty.

**283. William Hamilton's 'egg' bottle** patented in 1809.

**284. Hiram Codd's bottle** first patented in 1870. Lth 9 in.

The discovery of carbonic acid gas and its use in making imitations of natural mineral waters led to a big demand for bottles. To prevent the gas escaping a bottle had to be laid on its side to keep the cork moist; when stood upright the cork began to shrink and was no longer an airtight fit. Two bottles of the many designed for the purpose became widely popular: those invented by William Hamilton of Dublin and Hiram Codd of Camberwell. Hamilton's, patented in 1809, was given a pointed end so that it could not be stood upright, and therefore the cork remained wet (Fig. 283). Codd's, first patented in 1870, had a constriction at the base of the neck and above this was a loose glass ball (Fig. 284). Pressure of the gas in the liquid pressed the ball up against a rubber washer to make a perfect seal, and when the ball was forced down the contents could be poured out.

# CHAPTER XII

# Netherlandish Glass

The countries known today as Holland and Belgium were referred to in the past as the Netherlands or the Low Countires. The glass-making practised in the area owed its inception to Venetian craftsmen, who set up their furnaces in Antwerp, Liége, Amsterdam and elsewhere during the 16th century (p. 123). Antwerp is recorded as having had a glass-house operated by a Muranese from 1541, and its position as a seaport would have provided an excellent opportunity for developing a trade in glass alongside others already in existence. In addition, there were ready-made facilities for the importation of barilla from Spain; a product which provided the essential soda ingredient of the metal.

Liége had been for many centuries the seat of a Prince-Bishop, and was an important cultural centre. Its situation on the river Meuse gave it convenient water-borne access to Rotterdam and to much of the remainder of Holland. There were large forests growing near at hand for supplies of fuel, and when these gave out, or their use forbidden, there were ample nearby deposits of coal. Conditions favoured the establishment of glass-making enterprises in both cities, and they flourished in a manner to be expected.

The wares made at both of these centres, as well as at the others, are barely distinguishable. The metal was the same and the patterns are mostly alike, and not only are many of the products of the different towns liable to be confused, but there is no clear distinction between those of the Netherlands and those of Murano itself. For example, a goblet with the bowl of *cracked ice*, in the Victoria and Albert Museum, is catalogued by W. B. Honey as 'Probably Liége' (Fig. 285), while E. Barrington Haynes illustrates a similar (or perhaps the same) piece in his book, *Glass Through the Ages*, as 'Antwerp'. Both agree, however, that it originated in the Netherlands. It is not uncommon for similar differences of opinion to occur in the case of other factories, but as more evidence comes to light such divergences become fewer.

The Liége makers were fond of decorating their work with

**285. Goblet** with cracked ice decoration on the bowl: about 1600. Ht 8⅜ in.

applied masks and bosses, which were often embellished further with spots of pale blue enamel and gilding. At Antwerp they were addicted particularly to drinking-glasses with elaborately-scrolled stems. Covered goblets were given similar treatment, both stem and finial exhibiting snake-like coilings with added 'wings' in a contrasting colour (Figs. 286 to 289). Many of the Liége workmen were recruited from the Grand Duchy of Hesse, in Germany, where there was a liking for trailed work, and some of the so-called Netherlandish glasses of this type may have been made in that country.

To Amsterdam is assigned a group of glasses ornamented with so-called *beech-nut* moulding: a series of depressions in

**286–289. Drinking-glasses** with coiled stems: 17th century.

**290. Drinking-glass,** the bowl with beech-nut moulding: about
1600. **291. Tankard** with latticino ornament: about 1600. Ht 9⅜ in.
**292. Covered Roemer:** 17th century. Ht 12 in.

246

the bowl that are of that shape (Fig. 290). Otherwise, it would seem that the glass-houses of the city made wares that differed little from those made elsewhere.

The strong likeness to Venetian work is seen also in glass with latticino decoration. As in the example in Fig. 291, metal mounts have sometimes been added, and when they are present can be an indication of where a piece was made. On the other hand, they are not always to be interpreted in this way as it was not unlikely for an imported piece to have

**293. Bénitier:** 17th century.
**294. Ewer** in the form of a ship: 17th century. Ht 12¼ in.

been treated in the same manner. In the Netherlands, as well as in other countries, the employment of Venice-trained craftsmen must have led to a large output of pieces that imitated the forms and ornament current in Murano; the men could not have helped imparting a feeling of their homeland to all they made. This was not discouraged, as the whole purpose of having such men in the glass-houses was to compete with the imports from Murano. Thus, the tendency was for the native product and the imported to resemble one another as closely as possible, and while this pleased the buyer and saved currency it has bedevilled experts ever since.

The German influence on some Netherlandish glass was not confined to decorative treatment, but extended to a common demand for certain forms: notably the *roemer*. Undoubtedly many were imported from Germany, but quite as many, or more, were made in the Low Countries. At Liége in the late 17th century there was a mention of '*verrerie des Allemands*', which possibly refers to such articles. Of their popularity in Holland in particular there can be no doubt, for so many of these glasses are depicted in old paintings, and it is only reasonable to suppose that they should have been made there.

**295–297. Drinking-glasses** of Venetian type: 17th century.

Examples are illustrated in Figs. 150, 292 and 300, but their precise origin usually calls for the cautious addition of a question-mark.

Some of the less fanciful patterns of drinking-glasses are not greatly dissimilar to those assumed to have been made in England, and resemble somewhat those ordered from Venice by John Greene (p. 124). The Liége and Antwerp examples are noticeable for their stems, which are often built up with a series of hollow knops (Figs. 295 to 297), and may be compared in outline to the bobbin-turned woodwork seen on Flemish furniture of the period.

Flute-glasses of a particularly elongated shape were apparently favoured on both sides of the Channel (Fig. 298), but their lack of practicability in use would have given them a short life. Examples were made in Holland and no doubt exported from there, and it is argued whether specimens found in England were made in this country or brought in at some time. Also debatable as to origin are glasses of the type

**298. Flute drinking-glass:** 17th century. Ht 16¾ in.   **299. Drinking-glass:** 17th century. Ht 8½ in.   **300. Roemer** engraved by G. V. Nes: late 17th century. Ht 8 in.

in Fig. 299, which have been ascribed to both Netherlandish and French glass-houses.

All the foregoing pieces were made from soda glass, but although at Liége they are known to have been making *flint glass à l'anglaise* from about 1680, they did not make a wide use of lead oxide. The term would seem to have been applied to the shapes fashionable in the British Isles, rather than to the actual metal of which they were made. Both at

Middleburg and at Haarlem it is known that English crafts-men were at work, but their influence on design and formula is problematical. At the latter place, John Bellingham is said to have gained a knowledge of the secrets of looking-glass manufacture; a knowledge he put to use when he returned to England and became manager of the Vauxhall glass-house in 1671.

During the 18th century the successful introduction of lead glass and of glasses that made the best of its properties, gave the English industry an export outlet to the Netherlands. Dutch decoration is found on wine-glasses that are certainly of Newcastle manufacture, and there must have been a size-able trade across the North Sea. It has been suggested that many of the glasses of this distinctive baluster-stemmed type were made in Holland, but the fact that comparable examples were enamelled by the Beilbys of Newcastle makes it im-probable.

Wine-glasses made in the Netherlands during the 18th century are often closely similar to English ones, with colour-twist stems and other features that are deceptive at a first glance. The metal, however, is never as clear and colourless, lacks the bell-like ring when struck, and is immediately felt to be of much lighter weight. All these differences are because of the lack of lead, and a comparison between English and Netherlandish glasses makes the virtues of the former in-disputably obvious. Nonetheless, many an inferior glass changes hands every year and is accepted unthinkingly by its owner as of English make, whereas it is really a foreign imitation of inferior worth in every sense.

The decoration of glass in the Netherlands has been divided into three convenient groups: 17th-century diamond-en-graving, which was often the work of amateurs; replacement of it by professional engraving on the wheel from about 1690; and a revival of diamond-work by amateurs, but instead of by a 'drawing' technique of straight and curved lines it was done by stippling in the form of dots.

Dutch diamond-engraved glasses dating from as early as 1600 have survived, but most of these rarest of all specimens, and later examples that are little less scarce, are in Dutch museums. The names of many of the artists are known from the occasions when they signed their work. Among them are the following:

**Anna Roemers Visscher.** 1583–1651. Flowers, fruit and insects and inscriptions in copperplate and capital letters.

**Maria Tesselschade Roemers Visscher.** 1595–1649. Sister of the foregoing, who did similar work.

**Anna Maria van Schurman.** 1607–1678. Similar work to the two preceding.

**Willem Jacobsz van Heemskerk.** 1613–1692. Excellent lettering and curlicues.

Towards the middle of the 17th century, glasses were decorated with figures, of which a typical specimen in the Victoria and Albert Museum shows a woman being led by Cupid and bears amorous inscriptions referring to the scene. Slightly later in date are some glasses with royal portraits of which the origin has been much disputed. One in particular, a well-known flute of the type in Fig. 298, in the Royal Albert Memorial Museum, Exeter, bears on it a portrait of the monarch and the inscription: 'God Bless King Charles the Second'. For this reason it has been claimed as an English glass decorated here, but comparison with similar specimens makes it probable that it was made and finished abroad.

The engraved glasses are the more remarkable when it is remembered that they were decorated on a shaped surface, and that control of the cutting instrument must have needed considerable skill and patience. A few names, in addition to those noted above, have been recorded, but little is known about their bearers. They include:

**G. V. Nes.** On the *Roemer* in Fig. 300, which is engraved with the arms of the United Provinces and of William III.

**Willem Mooleyser.** A *Roemer* (like the above, in the Victoria and Albert Museum) shows the arms of William III as King of Great Britain and Ireland and of the United Netherlands. It is signed with the initials W M, and is dated 19th April, 1689, just eight days after the coronation of William and Mary.

**Jan Stam.** An 18th-century engraver who decorated a wine-glass in the Victoria and Albert Museum with a ship named '*D. Vergulde Walvis*'.

Dutch wheel-engraving resembled that of Germany, and the earliest examples date from the late 17th century. The best-known of the craftsmen is Jacob Sang whose signature appears on a number of glasses dated between 1752 and 1762. It is believed that he was related to some German engravers, A. F. Sang and J. H. B. Sang, but information about him is very scanty. His known works depict scenes with inscriptions to commemorate births and weddings, as well as a goblet decorated with a representation of the one-hundredth ship built by the Dutch East India Company, the 'Velzen', which he signed and dated 1757. Other glasses, unsigned, but in a similar style of cutting, show coats of arms as well as subjects like those used by Sang.

The introduction of stipple-engraving with a diamond-point is said to have been due to Frans Greenwood (1680–1761), who was born in Rotterdam perhaps of English parents, and worked in Dordrecht from 1726. He used a splinter of gem set in a handle and struck gently with a hammer to produce the small dots composing the design, which formed the lighter parts of the picture and left the untouched polished glass to form the shadows. The qualities of lead-glass were particularly suitable for the technique, and most of the pieces decorated in this manner were of English manufacture. It has been remarked aptly that 'in the hands of the more accomplished masters the method produced results of singular beauty, in which the engraving seems to rest like a scarcely perceptible film breathed upon the glass'.

Although Greenwood signed specimens of his stippling, which bear dates between 1722 and 1755, his earliest is a line-engraved wine-glass of 1720. It shows a group of figures from the Italian Comedy, and like most of his other subjects is not original, but copied from an engraving. Probably linked in acquaintance with Greenwood are two professional painters, both of whom were born in Dordrecht: Aert Schouman (1710–92) and G. H. Hoolart or Hoolarn (1716?–72). In addition to some signed glasses by Schouman, a wine-glass is known that bears a portrait of Greenwood in stipple. As it is after an engraving by Schouman himself it is supposed that he was responsible for the work on the glass. A stippled glass signed by Hoolart is in the Victoria and Albert Museum, but his supposed connection with Greenwood does not lie in its engraving. The maiden name of the latter's wife was Hoolart, and it is assumed that the artist was one of her relatives.

The name that occurs most frequently in conjunction with stipple-engraved glasses is that of David Wolff (1732–98), whose signed work is mostly dated between 1784 and 1795. Much inferior, as well as superior, work is without any signature and is often ascribed automatically to 'Wolff', without regard to the quality or style of the workmanship. Subjects which include naked children are invariably labelled as his, but, like Rembrandt and some other artists, he would have been unable to produce more than a fraction of the output assigned to him.

A number of artists who worked in stipple have had their names (or initials) recorded, and include: L. Adams, one glass dated 1800; Willem Fortuyn, and the date 1757; V. H., who signed a single glass with these initials in monogram and about whom nothing is known; and, finally, the names J. G. Smeyser and W. Sautyn, which are scratched on the feet of two glasses in the Rijksmusem, Amsterdam, and may be the names either of their engravers or of former owners. In the 19th century a collector of Wolff glasses, D. H. de Castro, revived the art of stippling which he practised until his death in 1863.

A late 18th-century Dutch artist, of whom only the surname is recorded, produced a number of attractive pictures in *verre églomisé*. His name was Zeuner, which appears on signed examlpes together with dates between about 1770 and 1810. He used both gold and silver leaf, and often painted the sky of a landscape in natural colours. Zeuner's subjects include scenes in Holland as well as in England, and he exhibited two of his pictures in London in 1778. Details of his career, as well as his Christian name, remain unknown.

# CHAPTER XIII

# French Glass

As in the other countries of Europe, Venetian craftsmen set up glass-houses in France, and made wares that are difficult to tell apart from those of Murano. The picture is complicated further by an acute dearth of surviving specimens; the incessant wars waged by the French having been fatal to the delicate material, and making it difficult to assess past work. The few ancient glasses accepted as being of French workmanship bear enamelled decoration, and their inscriptions in the tongue of that land are their most distinctive feature. Were it not for these words, usually good wishes on a presentation piece, they would be taken for Venetian. Indeed, it cannot be ruled out that they were made in that country and inscribed there to the order of French customers.

The mid-16th-century beaker in Fig. 301 is inscribed: FERME CUEUR CÕTRE FORTUNE and JE SUIS A VOUS, and is enamelled in colours and gilt. On it is an interesting sentence engraved with a diamond: 'Found in a hole behind the ivy at Stoke Curci Castle': the latter being an old way of spelling the name of the Somerset village of Stogursey. The enamelled chalice in Fig. 302 was made during the same century as the preceding piece; both of which are to be seen in London, the former at the Victoria and Albert Museum, and the latter in the Wallace Collection.

Equally confused is the allocation of a particular type of glass to the town of Nevers, south-east of Paris. The marriage of Henrietta of Cleves to Ludovico Gonzaga resulted in the bridegroom becoming Duke of Nevers, and the settlement in the town of some glass-makers from L'Altare. While they undoubtedly made all kinds of glassware, the town has given its name especially to small figures and objects, made from pieces of rod and tube softened at a lamp and formed with instruments to the desired shape.

There are a number of historic references to Nevers 'toys' (or trifles), including the statement that King Louis XIII (born in 1601) played with 'little dogs of glass and other animals made at Nevers' as a child. Later, in 1622, when he

**301. Enamelled and gilt beaker:** 16th century. Ht 6¾ in.

**302. Enamelled chalice:** 16th century. Ht 8⅞ in.

entered the town he was presented with 'an enamelled piece representing the victory gained by His Majesty against the rebels of the so-called Reformed Religion, the Ile de Ré, and also a hunting scene'. The range of subjects covered not only religious personages and scenes, but characters from the popular Italian Comedy and figures symbolical of the four Seasons (Figs. 303 to 305). Some of the more carefully modelled examples can be mistaken for porcelain, which those of later date must have imitated deliberately.

Although invariably attributed to Nevers, the work was by no means confined to that town. It is known that it was done also in Paris, Rouen, Bordeaux and Marseilles. While the earliest pieces date from the late 16th century, there was a

continuity of output and as late as 1845 a journalist of the day
wrote poetically:

'... the most terrible animals, the most pretty birds, the
fruits of the earth, the sweet flowers executed in glass of a
marvellous resemblance, by means of a lamp. Monsieur
Lambourd melts the glass, turns it, pulls it out, rounds it and
in five minutes his agile fingers have created two doves, an
elegant hare and a rose.'

It is perplexing, and often impossible to distinguish between

**303. Nevers figure of a priest:** 18th century. Ht 3 in.    **304. Nevers
group of rustics:** 18th century.   **305. Nevers figure representing
Winter:** 18th century. Ht 3 in.

work of this kind done in France, Germany, Venice or England,
but while this same problem of origin is common to much other
glass, that of Nevers is complicated also by the difficulty of
dating it. An example of this is seen in the work of a Paris
craftsman, Charles-François Hazard, who lived between the
years 1758 and 1812, but who modelled personages of the
16th and 17th centuries. Among them is a figure of Henry

IV of France, which is in a Paris museum, and if it was not known to have been made by Hazard might well be labelled 'late 16th century'.

Domestic glassware was not particularly distinguished in France either by the quality of the metal or by its originality of design. The nation spent so much of the 17th and 18th centuries engaged in wars with most of the rest of Europe, that such a peaceful art understandably suffered neglect. One branch of glass-making, however, was pursued with considerable success: the making of sheet glass by casting. This had been made there hitherto by the crown and broad processes (pp. 37–42), but in 1691 the new method was put into production in a factory in Paris.

Casting had been used earlier, most probably by the Romans, but had only been employed for small panes, whereas now it became possible to make plates 7 or 8 feet in height and 4 or 5 feet in breadth. Two years after opening, the casting side of the industry was removed to Saint-Gobain, in Picardy, where it operated as the *Manufacture Royale des Grandes Glaces*.

The important polishing department remained in the capital, and an English visitor to it in 1698 has left a record of what he saw and heard there. He mentioned that they already employed 600 men, with the prospect of further work for 400 more, and that the polishing was done with the same sandstone as was used for paving the Paris streets. It was ground to a powder, sieved, and used with water. The sheet to be polished was cemented to a flat table-top, and a small-sized piece of glass cemented to a weighted block of wood was pushed about on top of it while liberal supplies of sand and water were applied. Sometimes a strong and springy wooden 'bow' was fixed between the polishing block and the ceiling of the room, and this eased the task of the workmen by taking some of the backache out of the job (Fig. 306).

Not only were the front and back surfaces of the plate polished smooth, but the edges were treated in the same manner, and if required the latter were bevelled. It was reported that: 'The grinding the edges and borders is very troublesome, and odious for the horrid grating noise it makes, and which cannot be endured to one that is not used to it; and yet by long custom these fellows [the Paris workmen] are so easy with it, that they discourse together as nothing were.'

The opening years of the 19th century saw French glassmakers copying the English, and making pieces of heavy

306. Polishing plate glass.

weight decorated with elaborate cutting. Some of the work of this type, vases in particular, was mounted with bases, rims and handles of gilt bronze; a material which the French craftsmen in metal manipulated to a high state of perfection. The master bronze-worker of the period, Pierre-Philippe Thomire (1751–1843), occasionally ornamented glass in this manner, and the combination of matt and burnished gold with the silvery glitter of the glass is an effective one.

The *Crystallo-Ceramies*, popularised in England from about 1820 by Apsley Pellatt (p. 229), had been introduced in France some thirty years earlier. The name of a maker called Desprez, or that of his son, both of the Rue des Recollets du Temple, Paris, is found sometimes impressed on examples. Among other marks found occasionally is that of the famous glass (and china) shop *A l'Escalier de Cristal*, which traded in Paris from 1813 to 1910. Some of the cameos did not rely only on their modelling for decorative effect, but were coloured. Orders and decorations as well as religious emblems were embellished in this manner.

In the 1830's the fashion for coloured glass led to much experiment, and the French white and tinted opalines were the result. This semi-opaque glass was made in a wide range of colours, sometimes relying on gilt metal mounts for decoration and on other occasions painted in colours and gilt. The principal manufactories of opaline and other wares were:

**Baccarat:** situated to the east of Paris, and maker of clear as well as coloured glass during most of the 19th century.

**Choisy-le-Roi:** short-lived (1821–51), but it pioneered many new colours, shapes and ideas. It was directed by Georges Bontemps, who had to leave the country for political reasons in 1848 and came to England to work for Chance Brothers of Birmingham. He wrote an important book on the subject of glassmaking.

**Clichy:** at Billancourt, Paris, where it was started in 1837 for the making of cheaply-priced export wares. The factory moved to Clichy-la-Garenne by 1844, and soon began making coloured glass. It exhibited at the 1851 Great Exhibition in London, and showed coloured pieces, both plain and cased, as well as millefiore work.

**St Louis:** was the foremost maker of English-type cut-glass, and from 1839 made coloured wares of all kinds. The St Louis and Baccarat glass-works were the biggest throughout the 19th century.

The urn in Fig. 307 and the ewer in Fig. 308 both date from the first quarter of the century, and their gilt metal mounts may be compared in pattern with those on porcelain and furniture of the period. The shapes of both pieces can be paralleled in china made at Sèvres and the Paris factories. Lacking the classical outlines of the preceding, the vase in Fig. 309 has light-weight gilt metal mounts embellished further with coloured porcelain flowers. This piece is of later date than the preceding ones, and the attractive simplicity of design seen in the former is no longer present.

**307. Ormolu-mounted opaline urn:** early 19th century. Ht about 10 in.  **308. Ormolu mounted opaline ewer:** early 19th century.

The scent-bottles in Figs 310 and 311 both bear gilding: the first in the form of decorated gilt-bronze mounts on the stopper and the neck, and the latter has gold painted on the neck-rim, on the encircling snake and as a band round the body. The snake, incidentally, would seem to have been as popular as an ornament on glass in France as it was elsewhere in Europe. Also mounted in gilt metal is the box in

Fig. 312. This is cut with an all-over pattern of facets, and is complete with a lock and a chased escutcheon.

Vases and other pieces were made in a wide variety of patterns, many of them in direct imitation of German productions. Not only does the ubiquitous snake appear, but the pineapple cutting and the use of deeply cut and raised bosses are also seen in French work. Much of it, therefore, is not to

309. **Opaline vase** mounted in gilt metal with porcelain flowers: 19th century. Ht about 8 in. 310. **Ormolu-mounted moulded opaline scent-bottle.** 19th century. 311. **Opaline scent-bottle** with snake ornament: 19th century. 312. **Facet-cut opaline box** with gilt metal mount: 19th century.

be distinguished from contemporaneous work made in Germany and England.

The ornamental paperweights made at the Baccarat, Clichy and St Louis factories have become very well known during recent years because of the extravagantly high prices realised by the rarest of them at auction. They were made in a great number of different patterns, and only a brief indication of a few of them can be given here. The process of their manufacture was a complicated and highly-skilled one, and was achieved by placing thin sections of the selected *canes* (p. 23 and Fig. 15) and clear glass in a pattern within an iron mould. This was carefully heated to fuse them together, and then the whole was coated in successive layers of clear metal until it

**313. Mark on a Baccarat dated paperweight:** the B, green, centre numerals blue, and the outer numerals red.

was covered sufficiently. It was then annealed and polished, and the pontil-mark ground away from the base.

The earlier ones sometimes bear a date set casually among the colourful 'flowers' (Fig. 313), and these range from 1846 to 1849, inclusive. Baccarat examples occasionally add a capital B, Clichy used a cane in the form of a rose or the letters

**314. Baccarat paperweight** with entwined garlands: about 1850. Diam. 3⅜ in. **315. Baccarat paperweight,** the coloured overlay cut with 'printies'. Diam. 3¼ in.

CL, and St Louis the capital letters S L. Dates and identifying marks, which are present in only a small proportion of specimens, were placed to one side of the weight, and any that have such things at the top centre should be treated with great caution, as they are most probably not genuine.

Many of the paperweights were patterned with coloured canes either placed in a simple garland (Fig. 314), or completely covering the inner base: the 'close millefiore'. Another kind had the millefiore canes gathered in a central bunch encircled by a coloured corkscrew; a type named 'mushroom' from the resemblance to that fungus of its pattern when viewed from the side. These, and others, were sometimes cased in white and a colour, and then cut with windows (or *printies*) to reveal the interior (Fig. 315).

Others show realistically shaped and coloured flowers and

**316. Paperweight** with primrose-type flower. Diam. 1⅝ in.

**317. Baccarat paperweight** with a coiled snake. Diam. 3⅛ in.

leaves, ranging from pansies to dahlias and including a number that elude identification (Fig. 316). The period pet, the snake, is present sometimes, and usually has a green body with red markings (Fig. 317). It rests perhaps on a ground imitating rockwork, and less appropriately on broken pieces of corkscrew latticino known as *upset muslin*. Even rarer than the paperweight with a snake are the few recorded ones that show a salamander: the lizard-like reptile allegedly able to withstand fire.

The paperweight technique was adapted to other suitable forms, such as small vases for holding lead shot in which pens could rest (Fig. 318); egg-shaped hand-coolers; bell-pulls and pairs of door-handles. The bases and stoppers of scent-bottles were inset with millefiore, and even the occasional wine-glass is to be found with similar decoration.

A different technique was used at about the same period for the Pinchbeck weight. This had a heavy domed glass of the same shape as the conventional weights just described, through which showed a round disc of gilt metal embossed with a pattern. Several different designs have been recorded, many of them of romantic scenes with figures in ancient costume, and one features the head of Christ.

The artistic movement away from the factory and into the studio that took place in both Europe and America in the

**318. St Louis shot-vase.** Ht 3⅝ in. **319. Bowl** enamelled with branches of mistletoe by Joseph Brocard: about 1885. Ht 4½ in.

1870s, led to the emergence in France of a number of outstanding glass-workers. The earliest of them was Joseph Brocard, who first attracted attention with his imitations of Islamic mosque-lamps and other pieces in the same vein (p. 101). His more original work included some bowls with slightly-raised moulded designs of ingenious complexity, which were finished with careful painting in enamel. The example in Fig. 319 is patterned with branches of mistletoe rendered in natural colours.

The most prolific of the new men, in both inventiveness

and quantity of output, was Emile Gallé (1846–1904), of Nancy. His father was a maker of high-quality furniture and other luxury articles, and Emile inherited with his wife a looking-glass manufactory to which he added a department for table and ornamental glassware. The inspiration for his designs can be traced to a number of sources, but the chief of them was undoubtedly Japanese pottery and porcelain, which was then enjoying a great vogue. While some of the shapes

A: *E. Gallé Nancy*

B: *Gallé*

**320. Two of the marks used by Emile Gallé.** A: Engraved. B: In relief.
**321. Vase** by Emile Gallé: about 1890. Ht 4½ in.

and motifs were Oriental, he combined them with glass-making methods that had been devised over the centuries in the West. Thus, he will be found to have employed casing and cutting on a partially-tinted body that achieves a completely novel effect.

The contemporaneous liking for blues and mauves is visible in many of Gallé's pieces, on most of which he was proud to engrave his signature (Fig. 320). The signed vase shown in Fig. 321 is typical of his work when it was most strongly influenced by the Far East; it derives from an Oriental stem cup, with a mauve dragonfly poised on a soft brown ground. Finally, to close the century, is the vase in Fig. 322, which has a green body finished with a rough frosted surface beneath a rim moulded with 'drips', and is enamelled with a flower design.

Under the leadership of Georges Bontemps of Choisy-le-Roi, followed by the emergence of Gallé and his contempor-

**322. Vase** with frosted and enamel decoration by Emile Gallé: about 1900. Ht 5¼ in.

aries, French glass led the world. The great inventiveness in shape, pattern and colour, as well as the quality of its finish, raised it to a very high level, and it can be said that its progress in the 19th century compensated for its past failings.

# CHAPTER XIV

# Spanish Glass

The Spaniards began to make glass while the Iberian peninsula was under Roman rule. They imitated the wares imported from elsewhere in the Empire, and slowly learned to improve both the material itself and their methods of manipulating it. Most of the pieces were of simple design and intended for daily use; others, equally severe in pattern, were deposited in graves in the same manner as was common in many other lands.

Although it is known that a glass-blower named Guillem was working from 1189 at Poblet, near Tarragona, and fragments have been excavated on the site, there was little activity in glass-making throughout the country until the passing of two more centuries. In Barcelona and other cities there were strict regulations insisting that furnaces should not be built within the walls because, as was feared in Venice, there was the constant risk of fire, but nothing is known of what may have been manufactured.

The maritime operations of the Spaniards and their constant journeyings in the Mediterranean and elsewhere ensured a supply of foreign products being brought back by sailors, travellers and pilgrims. Among these were articles of glass from Syria and elsewhere, which served as inspirations to the home craftsmen. Thus, in spite of the fact that the peninsula was somewhat isolated from the rest of the civilised world by land, continual comings and goings by sea were a compensation.

Especially esteemed was the enamelled glass for which Damascus was noted. 14th-century documents contain records of specimens that were bequeathed in wills or listed in inventories, and in 1387 the city council at Tortosa ordered a glass lamp that was to be either of Damascus make or to be a close copy of one. A few distinctive specimens of Spanish manufacture have survived (Fig. 323), and, in addition, fragments of enamelled glass have been excavated on the site of an early furnace at San Feliú de Guixols, on the coast north of Barcelona. The patterns on these latter are strongly Islamic in character, and it is uncertain whether they were actually painted on the spot or were imported in the finished state.

**323. Enamelled sanctuary lamp:** Barcelona, 16th century. Ht 3⅛ in.

By the 1500s, the glass-making of the country had become divided: the manufactories in the north began to ape the prevailing Venetian styles, whereas the southern makers were less strongly influenced and took only what pleased them from the Italianate introductions. Thus, it is not always possible to differentiate between many of the products of Murano and Catalonia, but work in other parts of the country began to assume recognisably national characteristics. Many of the pieces remained in production over a period of several hundred years, and precise dating is not always possible.

There were numerous glass-houses, of which the principal ones were at Castril de la Peña in Granada, at Maria in Almeria, and at Royo Molino in Jaén, all of them in the south of the pensinsula, in Andalusia. The products of the various places are seldom distinguishable from each other, and the words 'perhaps' and 'probably' appear often when they are being described. Most frequently, such wares are termed by the name of the province where they may have been made, rather than by that of any particular town or village, but in many instances even those loose nomenclatures are open to argument.

Many of the pieces are of impure tinted glass, ornamented with trailing and pincered work of the types found in northern Europe (Fig. 324), and use was made of opaque white metal in the form of bands of latticino that originated in Venice and was imitated everywhere. An appealing rustic clumsiness is not uncommon, but this cannot be claimed as a feature exclusive to Spanish glass (Figs. 325 to 329).

A number of vessels are specifically of local pattern, and include the *almorrata* or *almorratxa*, used for sprinkling holy-water (Fig. 330); the *càntaro* or *càntir*, for holding drinking-water (Fig. 331); and the *porròn*, a long-spouted wine-vessel, from which the liquid is poured from above into the drinker's mouth without contact with the lips (Fig. 332).

Possibly much is claimed as Spanish that was made elsewhere: for instance, opaque white pieces with roughly-painted enamelled ornament resemble contemporaneous Bohemian examples, so they may have been imported and their true origin forgotten. It has been claimed, however, that some so-called 'Dutch' craftsmen, who settled on the coast between Valencia and Alicante, were responsible for work of this type (Fig. 333).

Toy pieces for sale at fairs were apparently made in large numbers, and surviving examples include models of animals (Fig. 334), hats (Fig. 335), shoes, and similar objects with a wide appeal that could be formed easily and sold cheaply. More complicated articles, such as oil-lamps for one or more wicks (Fig. 336), baskets of woven glass rod and even domestic trivialities like linen-smoothers (Fig. 337) were also attempted

**324. Yellow-tinted cup** with trailed ornament: late 16th/early 17th century. Ht 5½ in.  **325. Green-tinted vase:** Andalusia, 16th/17th century. Ht 7¾ in.

**326. Blue-tinted drinking glass** inscribed AVE MARIA: 17th century. Ht 3½ in.  **327. Vase** with winged handles: Andalusia, 17th century. Ht. 7 in.  **328. Green-tinted bottle:** 18th century. Ht 4 in.

with some success. Incidentally, these were all made in other lands as well, and it must not be assumed that examples of them are exclusively Spanish.

From the end of the 17th century a number of men were granted royal privileges so that an industry could be established to rival those of France and Germany. The most successful of them was a Catalan named Ventura Sit, who started a glass-house close to the palace of La Granja de San Ildefonso, near Segovia. Originally the factory received the encouragement of Queen Isabella, but ten years after the commencement the King himself, Philip V (1683–1746), gave it his patronage.

At first, production was concentrated on the making of sheet glass by the Broad process, but by the middle of the century cast plate was being manufactured successfully for

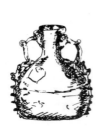  

**329. Yellow-green tinted bottle:** Granada, 18th century. Ht 4 in.
**330. Almorrata:** Catalonia, 17th or 18th century. Ht 3¾ in.
**331. Càntir:** Southern France, 18th century. Ht 7¼ in.

the various palaces and in due course for other great houses in the country. The plates were described at the time as being of great size and larger than those made elsewhere, some examples measuring thirteen feet by eight. A writer of 1867 noted: 'During the reign of Ferdinand VII (who died in 1833), there was found in a storage room of the factory a mirror so large that a mounted horseman could have seen his reflection in it.'

The enterprise flourished in spite of high costs, and in due course its activities embraced all kinds of glass ware and also lenses. Chandeliers were made, and some of these still hang in the Palace at Madrid for which they were made originally. In style they resemble those made in England during the later years of the 18th century, with curved and facet-cut arms and festoons of drops. Occasional use was made of gilt metal for the central vase-shaped shaft and other weight-bearing parts, and the contrast between this and the glass is a pleasing one.

Sit took charge of the plate-glass side of the manufactory from 1740, and a Frenchman, Dionisio Sivert, managed the remainder. Ten years later there was a further change and a Swede named Laurence Eder succeeded the Frenchman (the Swede's father, Joseph Eder, worked in the plate-glass department). A further change in the mid-1760s saw Sigismund Brun, a German, in the post of director. This somewhat cosmopolitan series of comings and goings has resulted in a situation where most glass from San Ildefonso shows strong French, Scandinavian or German characteristics.

The most obvious of these is the decorating of clear glass articles with deep cutting embellished with gilding. Its introduction in Spain is accredited to Brun, who naturally would have had a good knowledge of the types of ornament popular in his native land. The work rarely approached the quality of the original either in design or execution. Floral motifs were the most popular subjects, with sprays of rather stiff leaves centred on a sunflower or some other bloom less easy to identify (Figs. 338 to 341).

During most of this time, the factory had enjoyed royal patronage in return for supplying the needs of the palaces, or otherwise carrying out the orders of the monarch. Some of the productions were sent abroad as presents, no doubt to enhance the prestige of the giver and his subjects, and one such gift comprised a quantity of looking-glass which was sent by

332. **Porròn:** probably Valencia, 18th century. Ht 7¼ in.  333.
**Opaque white mug** with enamelled decoration: 18th century.
Ht 4 in.  334. **Lizard:** late 18th/early 19th century. L. 11¼ in.
335. **Hat** with blue and white decoration: late 16th century. Ht
3 in.  336. **Oil lamp** with four burners: 18th century. Ht 4¼ in.
337. **Green-tinted linen-smoother:** Granada, 18th century. Ht 5¼ in.

Charles IV in 1782 to the Sultan of Turkey in celebration of a treaty. However, before this date, in about 1760, it had been decided that the whole venture was too extravagant, and a retail showroom was opened in Madrid. To assist it, a decree forbade the selling of all glass other than from San Ildefonso within a radius of 26 miles of the capital city. In addition,

**338. Wine-glass** with cut and gilded decoration: La Granja de San Ildefonso. Ht 4½ in. **339. Saltcellar,** patterned similarly to Figs. 338 and 341: La Granja de San Ildefonso. Ht 1½ in. **340. Bowl** with cut and gilded decoration: La Granja de San Ildefonso. Ht 3 in. **341. Bottle,** patterned similarly to Fig. 338: La Granja de San Ildefonso. Ht 5 in.

attempts were made to start a trade with North and South America, but for one reason or another success was not achieved. Finally, in 1829, the concern was sold and the new owners turned their attention to making wares that would produce a worthwhile profit, but which were both commonplace and uninteresting.

# CHAPTER XV

# Scandinavian and Russian Glass

The story of Scandinavian glass is concerned primarily with that of Sweden, where the industry, as in most other countries of Europe, was started by Italians. Some were there in the late 16th century, but no traces remain of their activities nor of the output of the glass-makers who followed in their footsteps. There is the same lack of information concerning a factory started by a man named Melchior Jung at Stockholm in 1641, and which closed in 1678. Finally, another Italian pursued a more successful course; some of the output of his glass-house has survived and to all intents and purposes he must be considered the first glass-maker in Sweden.

Giacomo Bernardini Scapitta founded the *Kungsholm Glasbruk* at Stockholm in 1676, and although he left the country two years later, the manufactory remained in operation until 1815. As the works were situated in the capital city they enjoyed the patronage of royalty and the nobility, and the wares produced were of a comparatively sophisticated type to appeal to such clients. The output was not a large one, and specimens are rarely to be found outside their country of origin.

Venetian influence is to be seen in the earlier pieces made at the factory. Not only is the glass blown thinly but the shapes and decoration are obviously based on those current in Murano and, it may be added, on those current everywhere else that Italians had established themselves. Many pieces show signs of crisselling, which is not uncommon on first efforts before practice had revealed weakness in the formula in use.

While the general tendency was to follow Venetian patterns, certain features were local. Thus, the initials of the king, Charles XI (1655–97) or Charles XII (1697–1718), were sometimes used to form an unusual stem for a goblet, and a crown was very often employed as the finial or knob of a cover (Fig. 342).

As the 18th century progressed there were increasing signs of German inspiration. It took the form of thicker metal and a

342. Goblet and cover: Kungsholm, late 17th century. 343. Crowned monogram of Charles XI. 344. Engraved wine-glass: Kungsholm, mid-18th century. 345. Engraved wine-glass: Kungsholm, mid-18th century.

general air of solidity enhanced by cutting, in place of the earlier elaborate trailed and pincered ornament. As early as 1698 a German, Christoph Elstermann, was recorded as working at the factory, and he stayed there until 1715. He was probably responsible for the introduction of cutting and engraving, which persisted as the most popular decoration during the remaining decades of Kungsholm's existence.

Engraved ornament on drinking-glasses and other pieces

frequently took the form of the monarch's monogram beneath a crown and within formal floral mantling. The example in Fig. 343 shows the crowned monogram of Charles XI, but this type of device was by no means exclusive to the Kungsholm Glasbruk. The use of such royal emblems was not confined to pieces intended for palace use, but was put on wares for public sale to patriotic citizens.

**346. Engraved rœmer:** Kungsholm, late 17th century. Ht 7¾ in.
**347. Engraved decanter,** dated 1761: Skånska Glasbruket.

The shapes of pieces can also cause confusion. The glasses in Figs. 344 and 345 exhibit the high domed foot that remained current in Scandinavia after it had passed out of fashion in England, and they are engraved with crowned initials. Pieces of this type are often attributed to Kungsholm, but it will be found that they are sometimes claimed for other factories. Of more certain ascription is the rœmer in Fig. 346, which is engraved with a scene showing a huntsman in a landscape, with birds overhead and a hound (or is it a fox?) in the background. It compares favourably in both metal and shaping with its German or Dutch counterpart.

A few years after the start of the Kungsholm factory another was opened in the north of Scania, which is situated in the very south of the country. The *Skånska Glasbruket* was founded in 1691 and for its first twenty-five years made purely utilitarian articles. From 1715 attention was paid to the decorative aspects of the wares, and this endured until the factory was destroyed by fire in 1762. Much of the output consisted of imitations of Kungsholm products, and engraving was used in a similar manner to that practised in Stockholm.

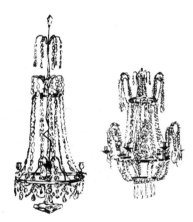

**348. Candelabrum:**
Swedish, late 18th century.
Ht 35½ in.

**349. Chandelier:**
Swedish, early 19th
century. Ht 43 in.

On the whole, Skånska pieces reflect the rustic area in which they were made; the decanter, dated 1761, in Fig. 347 is a typical example.

To the north, in the district of Småland, a factory was opened in Kosta in 1742 and remains in production to this day. From time to time workers left and started their own glass-houses in the area, but they made little, if anything, of interest. The famous modern Orrefors factory is near Kosta and has helped to bring to fruition the great skills that had attempted, without avail, to find full expression in the past.

The chandeliers, wall-lights and candelabra made in Sweden in the late 18th/early 19th century have a distinctive lightness of design shared with those made in Norway. In both instances, the patterns followed contemporaneous English

**350. Chandelier:** Danish, late 18th century.

ones, but were often elaborated by the addition of further cascading festoons of cut drops (Figs. 348 to 350).

The first Norwegian factory was opened in 1741 and from the start was under the personal patronage of the king, Christian VI of Denmark and Norway. It was situated at Nöstetangen, near the town of Drammen, which lies a short distance to the south-west of Oslo, a city then named Christiania. While most of the first productions were utilitarian wares including bottles and window-glass, a number of more ambitious and artistic specimens were supplied to royalty and the nobility. The craftsmen were probably from Germany, and itinerant engravers from the same country were responsible for adding any decoration that was required.

The newly-introduced industry showed signs of prospering, and in 1753 it was decided to reorganise it so that it could cater fully for the needs of both Denmark and Norway. To this end, the making of ornamental and table glassware was concentrated on Nöstetangen, and the various buildings were enlarged and modernised for the purpose. More Germans were engaged, and an Englishman, James Keith, with his assistant, William Brown, were offered sufficiently attractive terms to induce them to leave Newcastle upon Tyne in 1755 and join the expanding staff.

A year or so later, a German engraver, Heinrich Gottlieb Köhler, was brought from Copenhagen to direct the newly-introduced engraving workshop and to become artistic manager of the whole concern. Under his able command, the English and German characteristics were merged to produce an individual Norwegian style. Köhler's pupil, Villas Vinter, started his career as a glass-blower, but learned the art of engraving with such success that he took it up. Signed pieces by both men have been recorded (Fig. 351).

One of the innovations for which the Englishman, Keith, was responsible was the introduction of the coveted lead-glass as an alternative to the German soda-glass, which had been the only available metal. Following a further modernisation of the industry and its factories in 1760, a royal decree stopped all importations of glassware and gave a monopoly to Nöstetangen for supplying Norway and Denmark. The following years were the most important and prolific in the history of the factory, but the death of Frederik V in 1766 was followed by a gradual decline which culminated in closure in 1777.

The wares produced at Nöstetangen covered a wide range, the wine-glasses often with stems comparable with those of Newcastle, of baluster shapes and with air-twists within them, and the covered articles topped with the crown, popular also

**351. Covered goblet** engraved by H. G. Köhler: Nöstetangen, 1764.

in Sweden (Figs. 351–4). Similarly, the king's monogram was placed on articles for general sale, and the example on a wine-glass bowl in Fig. 355 shows the crowned monogram of Frederik V.

Many of the Nöstetangen pieces of the 1760s show a revival of Venetian techniques that had been popularised widely in Europe during the late 17th century. These include trailing, either plain, pincered or 'nipt diamond waies', which was employed with skill and taste (Figs. 356–7). Some use was made, also, of tinted metal, and the simple stoppered decanter in Fig. 358, engraved with initials and an inscription, is an example.

**352 to 354. Wine-glasses** with air-twist stems: Nöstetangen, mid-18th century.   **355. Crowned monogram of Frederick V,** King of Denmark.

Following the closing of the factory, production was transferred farther north to *Hurdals Verk* whence followed most of the craftsmen, including James Keith. The same types of wares manufactured previously continued to be made,

**356. Ewer** with trailed ornament: Nöstetangen, about 1760.
**357. Covered jar** with trailed ornament: Nöstetangen, about 1760.
**358. Red-tinted decanter and stopper:** Nöstetangen, about 1760.

but there was a large proportion of coloured pieces from about 1780. Blue and purple predominated, and were sometimes enhanced with engraving and gilding.

The Hurdals factory was closed in 1809, and there was yet

another transfer of production and workers. Keith had retired in 1787, but his descendants, under variations of his surname (Kith, Keth, and so forth), figure in the records of Scandinavian glass-works in later times. The *Gjövik Verk* was started in 1809 and continued until 1847 making and developing the types of wares suited to the tastes of its clients. Amongst them was the decanter known locally as a *Zirat-fladke*, of which a specimen with trailed decoration that includes initials and the date 1832 is shown in Fig. 359. The

**359. Decanter** with trailed ornament, dated 1832: Gjövik Verk.

*fladke* inspired the making of a very similar-looking bottle which is not uncommon in England, but whether these were imported or made in the latter country remains a matter of argument.

Glass-making in Russia is lacking in details of its history and there are few specimens. There would seem to have been numerous attempts to start glass-houses in various parts of the country, but each ended in failure and in most instances there is all too little knowledge of what they may have made. Finally, in 1760, a Moscow merchant named Thoma Maltzoff opened a factory which succeeded to the extent that his brother, who followed him in ownership, was ennobled by Catherine the Great. In 1777 the *Manufacture Impériale de Cristal*, the property of Prince Gregoire Potemkine, was started and is known to have made fine wares for the Court, as well as more ordinary pieces for sale to the public. Contemporary with it was the Bakhmeteff glass-house in Moscow, which remained in operation until the early 20th century.

It is known that in the early 19th century there were more than a hundred privately owned factories, mostly small in size and making principally utilitarian wares. A few of them did, however, compete with the State-run establishments in catering for the Court and wealthy citizens who demanded high quality articles.

Among pieces that have been recorded are some enamelled examples inscribed so that their origin is beyond doubt, and dated between 1722 and 1767. On the whole, much remains to be discovered about the glass made in Russia. Like so much else produced there, the identified glassware seldom differs much from that made contemporaneously in Europe. The more ambitious specimens exhibit a high standard of craftsmanship, but as very little of it appears to have been exported it can be studied in quantity only in the land where it was made.

# CHAPTER XVI

# American Glass

Glass-making began in America very soon after the early colonists arrived from England in 1607 and began to settle at Jamestown, Virginia. The intention was to make wares for export, but this laudable and ambitious idea did not succeed. A further attempt at the same place had a similar ending, and modern excavations on the sites of the furnaces have revealed only evidence that they existed; fragments of glass were plentiful, but too small in size to reconstruct. Additional evidence is to be found in the words of Captain John Smith, one of the party of settlers, who wrote later: 'We sent home ample proofs of pitch, tar, glass . . .'. The four other glass-houses recorded as having been in existence during the 17th century have left equally slight traces of their operations.

The 18th century, when the country was being colonised rapidly and living standards were advancing at an equivalent pace, saw a number of glass-houses established. Several of them produced wares that were sufficiently distinctive to be identified, although much is now attributed to them that was imported at the time—or more recently. The fact that the craftsmen came principally from England and Germany, and brought with them the skills and traditions of their native lands, meant that most or all of their output was closely similar to what they had made in their homelands. Thus, these early surviving American pieces can have been made in that country, or they can have been among the thousands of boat-loads of goods that crossed the Atlantic to supply the needs of a new continent. Only in rare instances has it been possible to authenticate the origin of specimens; sometimes the precise history of a piece enables it to be traced from family to family, or an inscription positively links it with a particular manufactory.

A German, Caspar Wistar (1695–1752), came to America in 1717 and settled in Philadelphia, where he manufactured brass buttons. In 1739 he sent to Germany for four glass-blowers and established them in a factory built on the banks of Alloway's Creek on the south of New Jersey. His son, Richard, continued the business after the death of Caspar until it finally closed in 1780.

The principal output at Wistarburg was common glass in the form of bottles and sheets, but it is said that 'a small corner pot was always set up for the personal use of the blowers'. From this, it seems they would make for their families and friends anything that they fancied in the way of ornamental or useful pieces. The metal was either the greenish one in everyday use, or it was tinted agreeably in blue or some other shade. Ornament on these wares took the form of applied trailing or prunts (Fig. 360), and their simplicity and spontaneity reflect the unsophisticated demands of a pioneering people, as well as the somewhat haphazard conditions of manufacture.

Pieces of similar appearance were produced in a factory started in about 1781 by some former Wistar employees, brothers of the name of Stanger. The opening of further factories in the 19th century, both in Jersey, New York, and farther afield, where comparable work was done, has led to the term *South Jersey type* being applied nowadays to all wares of this kind. It is so very rarely possible to allocate any particular piece to any particular factory, that some general name for them all had to be found, and it is now given to specimens irrespective of their origin in that state and over a wide range of years.

The South Jersey bowl and cover in Fig. 361 is of aquamarine-blue tint, the ornament is trailed and tooled into the shapes known as 'lily-pads': the name in the United States for the floating leaves of water-lilies. In the hollow knops of the stem and cover are coins dated 1829 and 1835, and the finial is in the shape of a seated hen. The bowl in Fig. 362 is

**360. Aquamarine-blue mug:** South Jersey type, about 1850. Ht 4⅜ in. **361. Aquamarine-blue bowl and cover** with lily-pad decoration and coins of 1829 and 1835 in stem and finial: South Jersey type, about 1840. Ht 11 in. **362. Pale green bowl:** South Jersey type, about 1850. Ht 5 in.

pale green in colour, again with 'lily-pads' and the foot is crimped. Much research has been carried out into the various types of American glass, which is collected very keenly in the United States, and the several popular decorative motifs have been carefully listed. There are, for instance, three distinct styles of 'lily-pad', each of which came into use at a different date. It has been noted that finials did not always take immediately recognisable forms: swans were sometimes given a crest, as the example in Fig. 363.

Another German, Henry William Stiegel (1729–85), settled in Lancaster County, Pennsylvania. He, too, began work in another trade, iron-founding, before taking up the manufacture of glass. His first glass-works was opened in 1763, and within two years he owned three of them, but this rapid ex-

363. **Swan finial.**  364. **Stiegel type tumbler** with enamelled decoration: late 18th century.  365. **Stiegel type engraving:** late 18th century.

pansion terminated after a few years in his imprisonment for debt and the closing in 1774 of his factories.

Stiegel brought over Venetian, English and German craftsmen, and their various national styles blended, more or less, in their work. Coarsely-painted bottles and jugs, with patterns of flowers and birds on them, were made by these men, but it is not possible to distinguish those that may be American from examples of European origin (Fig. 364). Also attributed to the Stiegel factories are pieces with simple engraved designs on them, which are to be seen also on continental cheaply-made wares (Fig. 365). The third type of Stiegel product was blown in moulds to give a patterned surface (Figs. 366 and 367), and these employed metal of several colours: blue, green or amethyst, in numerous shades. As with the South Jersey glass, the name Stiegel is applied loosely to anything resembling the key pieces.

Decorative and useful glassware was made also by the Philadelphia Glass Works, Kensington, and at the New Bremen Glass Manufactory, near Frederick, Maryland, by John Frederick Amelung. Whereas a few pieces of the latter's make have been preserved, nothing from Kensington is now known. Not surprisingly, because he came also from Germany, Amelung's output comprised much that is similar to Stiegel's. He, too, suffered financial failure.

**366. Amethyst-colour salt:** early 19th century. Ht 3 in.

**367. Bottle** moulded with daisy pattern, attributed to Stiegel.

The start of the 19th century saw no more than a dozen glass-houses in the entire country, but within twenty years the number had trebled and by 1830 as many as ninety were in operation. Whereas blown, hand-made wares of South Jersey type continued to be made, especially in Ohio (Figs. 368 to 372), there was a keen demand for cut pieces of European style. These were far too expensive for the majority of would-be buyers, but the demand for them was met by an increase of mould-blown wares. The hinged metal mould into which a bubble of molten glass was blown by the operator was used increasingly, and the variety of patterns was very large. The decorated bottle or flask, which attained an immense popularity in the United States, is a typical blown article that was made in several hundred different designs as well as in many single and mixed colours (Figs. 373–375).

**368. Sugar-bowl and cover:** South Boston, about 1825. **369. Clear glass covered bowl:** Pittsburgh, 19th century. Ht 7¾ in. **370. Blue covered bowl:** Pittsburgh, 19th century. Ht 7 in.

**371. Amber-coloured dish on foot:** Ohio, 19th century. Ht 4½ in. **372. Jug with red and white looped decoration:** Pittsburgh, 19th century. Ht 11 in. **373. Flask with ribbed pattern moulding:** early 19th century.

Moulds were used in combination with hand-finishing: the body of the decanter in Fig. 376 would have been moulded and the neck shaped afterwards. A similar mould was used for the jug in Fig. 377; a fact made clear because the word GIN is partly concealed by the base of the handle, whereas it would have been borne proudly on the front of a decanter. Some of the pocket-flasks were made also by this combined method, and the example in Fig. 373 was moulded and then twisted while hot, so as to give the ribbing a spiral effect. Others were blown into a mould, twisted, moulded with a further imprint and then again blown, to produce unusual surface effects.

A clever and energetic glass technician, Deming Jarves (1790–1869), was in charge of the New England Glass Company, whose factory was at East Cambridge, Boston. He left

374. **Aquamarine pocket flask** with sunburst motif: inscribed 'M'Carty & Torreyson, Wellsburg, Va.,' 19th century. 375. **Aquamarine pocket flask** with portrait of the singer, Jenny Lind. 376. **Moulded 'Whiskey' decanter.** Ht about 10 in. 377. **Moulded water jug.**

it in 1825 and founded a rival, the Boston and Sandwich Company, at Sandwich, near Cape Cod (Fig. 378). Two years later, a worker at his former manufactory, Enoch Robinson, produced a machine for pressing (p. 27), and Jarves himself soon introduced one at Sandwich.

While blown moulding usually set out to imitate as closely as possible the complexities of cut-glass, pressing was able to exploit designs created especially for itself. Before very long, these new, so-called 'lacy', patterns were current in innumerable variations; although pressing was used to some degree in England it was exploited more fully in the United States. There, on one article alone, the cup-plate on which the teacup stood while the tea cooled in the china saucer, several hundred different patterns have been recorded (Fig. 379).

The process was able to employ patterns that could not possibly have been realised by the old method of cutting on the wheel, which was, on the whole, most successful in geometric straight-line designs. The 'lacy' pressed patterns made

**378. The Boston and Sandwich Glass Works,** about 1830.

considerable use of small dots or beads, which not only formed a glittering background, but made imperfections in manufacture much less noticeable. The designs featured such patriotic emblems as the American Eagle (Fig. 380) and the heads of presidents, as well as flowers and leaves and compositions incorporating classical motifs like honeysuckle and husks (Fig. 381).

A twining branch of ivy is used against a ribbed background for the goblet in Fig. 382, but the employment of the process for drinking-vessels must have been limited. The thickness of body necessary for a successful product would have made such pieces very clumsy, if not unpleasant, in use. It was much more appropriate when applied to lighting devices: candlesticks and oil-lamps, of which there are examples in Figs. 383 to 385. The first two have hand-made top sections affixed to moulded bases by means of a blob of molten glass (known as a *merese*) which is shaped to conform with the general outline of the article. Some of the larger lamps are on bases from the same moulds as cup-plates, which were inverted (pattern uppermost) with the oil-container applied with a merese irrespective of the pattern in the centre. The candle-sticks in Figs. 385 and 387 are each made in two parts and

**379. Pressed cup-plate.** Diam. about 3½ in.   **380. American eagle.**
**381. Motif** used on pressed pieces.

joined, and it is interesting to notice that both employ the same pattern of nozzle.

A proportion of pressed pieces were marked with their maker's name and address. Thus, *B & S Glass Co.* and *Sandwich* are to be found on a salt-cellar in the inappropriate shape of a paddle-steamer which bears its name, LAFAYET, on the side. The milk-jug or creamer in Fig. 386 is marked *R. B. Curling & Sons, Fort Pitt*; a firm established in Pennsylvania in 1826. Another salt-cellar, this time of simple rectangular shape decorated with flowers, is marked *Jersey Glass Co. Nr. N. York*; a product of New Jersey, where there were no fewer than forty glass-houses operating in 1836.

The majority of the earlier pressed pieces were of clear

**382. Pressed goblet** with ivy pattern on a ribbed ground : about 1850.
Ht 6 in.    **383. Blown lamp** on a pressed base. Ht 8 in.    **384. Blown candlestick** on a pressed base. Ht about 6 in.

**385. Pressed candlestick** with column support. Ht. about 9 ins.
**386. Milk jug.** marked *R. B. Curling & Sons, Fort Pitt.* **387.
Pressed candlestick** with dolphin support. Ht about 10 in.

metal, but as the century progressed colour was introduced and every attempt made to emulate the rainbow. There were shades to please every taste, and variegated effects in imitation of tortoiseshell, marbled effects in purple and white (*Slag glass*), and the use of two separate colours in a single article, vied in popularity with opaque white *milk glass* (Fig. 388).

In spite of the enormous success of cheap pressed wares, there remained a public for the more costly hand-blown specimens. A visitor to the Massachusetts factory of the New England Glass Company, wrote: 'We are repeatedly struck with the fact, new to us, that most of the exquisite, richly colored and decorated glass ware, which is so much admired under the name of "Bohemian Glass", is manufactured at these works'. Indeed, this was not the only place where overlay and other complex processes were used, and most of the novelties then current in Europe were quickly copied at one or more factories.

The esteemed French paperweights were produced with varying success (Fig. 389), by factories which included the New England Glass Company, who employed an ex-Baccarat man, François Pierre; the Boston and Sandwich Company where another Frenchman, Nicholas Lutz from St Louis, was on the staff; and the Brooklyn manufactory of John L. Gilliland. Others also helped to satisfy this eager market, but on the whole few examples were produced that competed seriously with the excellent French ones. Less exotic-looking weights took many forms, and a typical example is the hexagonal specimen in Fig. 390, which bears impressed on the underside a portrait of Daniel Webster (1782–1852), the American statesman.

Some of the different styles of glassware produced during the last thirty years of the 19th century include the following:

**Agata:** a mottled surface finish applied often to Amberina.

**Amberina:** shades from dark red to amber produced by partial re-heating. Made by the New England Glass Works from 1883.

**Burmese:** shades from rosy-pink to the palest of yellow, and made by the Mount Washington Glass Company, New Bedford, Massachusetts, from 1885. Some examples were sent to Queen Victoria and following the publicity resulting on her paying £250 for them, Thomas Webb & Sons of Stourbridge obtained a licence to manufacture it in England.

**388. Opaque white covered dish:** Pennsylvania, about 1880. Ht 7 in.
**389. Millefiore paperweight,** attributed to the New England Glass Company. Diam. about 2½ in.  **390. Paperweight** with portrait of Daniel Webster: 1850–60.

**Kewblas:** a three-layer technique involving the application of a coating of coloured glass over opaque white with clear glass on top. Made by the Union Glass Works, Somerville, Massachusetts, in the 1890s.

**Mother-of-pearl:** a two-layer process with opaque white glass coated with transparent and etched with acid to give a matt surface. Made by the Phoenix Glass Company, Pittsburgh, Pennsylvania, 1885.

**Peach Glass:** known also as Peachblow, shades from cream to rose, yellow to red, or blue to pink. Made by the New England Glass Company in 1885 and by Hobbs, Brockunier

297

& Company of Wheeling, West Virginia, in the following year. The latter firm popularised this when they copied in it a Chinese porcelain vase sold by auction in 1886 for $18,000. Their product (Peach Glass) is a coated one on opaque white glass, whereas the other is solid throughout. It is comparable to Burmese (q.v.), and the two wares are often confused. They are sometimes found with a matt surface finish and in that case it has been suggested they come into the category of Satinware (Fig. 391).

**Pomona:** a partially stippled effect achieved with acid and

391. Peachblow water jug: 1885–90.

usually with an applied garland of flowers in contrast to the rough background. Made by the New England Glass Company, Cambridge, Massachusetts, 1884.

**Satinware:** with a matt surface and sometimes used to describe all pieces with such a finish: mother-of-pearl, peach, etc.

**Spangled:** known also as Spattered, contains particles of metal or mica which gives a glittering effect. Made by Hobbs, Brockunier & Company, 1883, and known by them as 'Vasa Murrhina'. The latter name had been applied the year before to a similar product patented by Webbs of Stourbridge.

Parallel with end-of-the century developments on a large commercial scale was the more limited, but nonetheless lucrative, enterprise of Louis Comfort Tiffany (1848–1933). He was the son of New York's most eminent jeweller, and became the leader in America of the *Art Nouveau* movement. In company with a Venetian glass-blower named Andrea Boldini he started a glass-making firm, and by 1880 had patented his 'Favrile' glass. This has an irridescent surface equalled only on pieces that have lain buried for centuries, and was achieved by placing the heated articles in an enclosed chamber where they were subjected to chemical fumes.

Similar effects had been obtained earlier in Vienna and in London, but Tiffany eclipsed them. Perhaps it was because his

392. **Vase** in rough-surfaced Lava Favrile. Ht 5½ in.   393. **Favrile vase** with clematis decoration. Ht 17½ in.   394. **Tulip-shaped Favrile vase.** Ht 11½ in.   395. **Vase** by Louis Comfort Tiffany. Ht 6¼ in.

publicity was better and the prices he charged much higher, but it was more probably on account of his original designs. Certainly, his name and work are remembered, while his competitors have not received anything like the acclaim.

He produced a wide range of articles, including many vases or, as one critic has written 'decorative pieces of blown glass vaguely resembling some plant, flower or vegetable form which were made in the shape of a vase, but were hardly ever suited to holding flowers'. Typical pieces are in Figs. 392 to 394, the latter, called a 'Tulip' vase, exemplifying the words quoted. Fig. 395 is an example of one of Tiffany's other types of glass, made by sandwiching opaque metal between layers of clear, but this and other innovations did not attain the popularity of 'Favrile'.

A large proportion of the glass is marked with the initials of the maker and a serial number, but some of the more important examples are without any indication of their origin. It had an international sale at the time of its manufacture and examples may still be seen in many countries, both in homes and museums. While the galleries in New York have a plentiful variety on display, in England the Haworth Art Gallery, Accrington, possesses what is probably the best collection in Europe. It reached its home in the provinces from the family of one of Louis Tiffany's English assistants, Joseph Briggs, and comprises no fewer than 73 'Favrile' vases and numerous other pieces.

# CHAPTER XVII

# Chinese Glass

Glass has not played the part in Chinese life that it has played in the life of Western peoples. The early invention by them of porcelain, and the development of near-porcelain that led up to it, ensured there was an acceptable medium available for making vessels and other articles that otherwise needed glass. Indeed, they themselves doubt whether it was in use there prior to the end of the 5th century A.D., and it is admitted that their knowledge of it was acquired from traders who entered the country from outside.

In spite of this, there are in existence a number of specimens of glass datable to as far back as the Han dynasty (206 B.C. to 220 A.D.), for which the material was perhaps imported in block form from Alexandria. As in the Middle East and in Europe, there is the same effort to counterfeit Nature, and these early pieces are close copies of carved jade of the period. No attempts were made to blow hollow articles, but the glass was treated as if it was a stone and cut by lapidaries who dealt habitually with the latter.

The first pseudo-jades were reproductions of the Han funeral jades: the stones disposed about the dead body of an important person and which were provided for the purpose by the Master of Sacrificial Ceremonies. These amulets were intended to prevent, or at least delay, the complete decay of the corpse, and were used to close all the openings of the body. It was said that 'If there is gold and jade in the nine apertures of the corpse, it will preserve the body from putrefaction', thus the event of decease would be only temporary and resurrection could take place in due course. Some of the

301

surviving glass objects are in the form of a cicada, an insect well-known in the East, of which a stylised model was placed in the mouth of a dead person. Others take the form of a flat disc with a central hole, known as a *pi*, which is a symbol of Heaven and also plays its part in funerary ceremony.

The majority of surviving examples of Chinese glass do not date before the reign of K'ang Hsi (1662–1722), by which time it is certain that blowing had been attempted and manufacture was being carried out by this means. The emperor ordered a number of factories to be set up in 1680 within the

**396. Crisselled whitish bowl:** late 17th century. Ht 8¾ in.

boundaries of the Palace in Pekin, and among them was one for glass-making.

As in European experimental pieces, the first efforts show signs of crisselling and this evidence of decay has led to many of the surviving examples being given an age greater than they merit. Some specimens incorporate latticino in their ornament, and the Western origin of this and other features is obvious. It probably came about through the activities at court of the Jesuit missionaries, whose artistic prowess was placed at the command of the emperor as a means of gaining his interest in their religion. In this way, not only glass-making, but many other Western skills were taught to Chinese craftsmen.

A bowl with ribbed ornament on the body (Fig. 396) is a

typical example of the K'ang Hsi wares, and the whitish metal is obviously suffering from too much alkali in its composition which has resulted in its being crisselled.

Following a period of blown and manipulated work, during which pieces like the above were made, the industry returned to openly imitating stone and much else. Remarkable objects were made that closely simulated lacquer or tortoiseshell, in addition to every known stone as well as many imaginary

**397. Snuff-bottle** carved with a carp: 18th century. Ht $2\frac{7}{8}$ in.
**398. Yellow glass vase.** Ht $4\frac{1}{2}$ in.    **399. Snuff-bottle** in blue on white glass: 18th century. Ht $2\frac{1}{2}$ in.

ones. Most of the articles are of small size, and in this category come the snuff-bottles on which much of the greatest craftsmanship was expended. The red and white example in Fig. 397 is a close imitation of chalcedony, and the blue and white one in Fig. 398 is not like any known stone, but is nonetheless attractive. Both exhibit the symbolism dear to the Chinese and present in every facet of their Arts. The grotesque-looking carp (Fig. 397) is an emblem of perseverence, and the *pa-kua* or eight trigrams with the *yin-yang* in the centre

(Fig. 399) would preserve the owner from misfortune and ensure his future prosperity.

Both the snuff-bottles illustrated are examples of the skill of the Chinese glass-maker in applying one layer of glass on another, and ensuring that although they adhere perfectly the colours do not mingle. In addition, they show the mastery of the cutter in this difficult medium and on a small scale.

Not only were they able to control the colours so that they remained quite separate, but they were able to blend them, if required, and also to make cameos of more than one

**400. Inscribed glass amulet.** Diam. 1⅝ in.

colour superimposed on another. In addition they decorated opaque white glass with enamel painting and one man, named Hu, was so clever at this particular work that some of his pieces were sent by order of the emperor Ch'ien Lung to be copied at the porcelain factories. He adopted the pseudonym *Ku Yüeh Hsuän*, which means 'Ancient Moon Pavilion', and specialised in extremely delicately painted scenes which often include European figures.

Other painted snuff-bottles are of clear glass, with the pictures applied on the inside by carefully using a brush through the narrow neck opening. It has been remarked that this shows 'great if misapplied skill', and examples of it have delighted the Western world since they first reached it a century or so ago. Most of them are of average size, about 2½ to 3 in. in height, but larger ones exist and these have been decorated through an equally restricted orifice.

Just as the porcelain makers copied successful essays in glass, so did the reverse happen, and many earthenware vase shapes were rendered by the glass-makers (Fig. 398). The range of colours in which the latter worked was a very wide one, and many of them rivalled in brilliance anything that could be attained by means of a glaze. Particularly, a strong yellow, the imperial favourite, and pale green-blues were rarely equalled in any other medium.

The ancient manufacture of amulets to place with the dead was succeeded eventually by the making of those to be worn by the living. The inscription on the example in Fig. 400 is an appropriate one with which to close this book: 'May the celestial mandarins be propitious to man'. In allowing mankind to create so much beauty from such a simply-compounded material as glass, it must be agreed that the mandarins have served him well.

# Select Bibliography

### General Works

(which deal with the technique of glass-making and with the products of more than one country)

| | |
|---|---|
| Neri, A. | *L'arte vetraria*. Florence, 1612. (Translated into English as *The Art of Glass*, by Christopher Merret. London, 1662.) |
| Dossie, Robert | *The Handmaid to the Arts*. 2 vols. London, 1758 (revised 1764) |
| Hartshorne, A. | *Old English Glasses*. London, 1897; reprinted, New York, 1967. (Despite its title contains information about glass from other countries.) |
| Schmidt, Robert | *Das Glas*. Berlin and Leipzig, 2nd edition, 1922. |
| Hudig, F. W. | *Das Glas*. Vienna, 1925. |
| Buckley, Wilfred | *European Glass*. London, 1926. |
| | *The Art of Glass*. London, 1939. |
| Honey, W. B. | *Glass: a Handbook and Guide to the Museum Collection*. Victoria and Albert Museum, 1946. |
| Haynes, E. B. | *Glass through the Ages*. London, 1948; revised 1959. |
| Polak, Ada | *Modern Glass*. London, 1962. |
| Kämpfer, F. and K. Beyer | *Glass, a World History*. London, 1966. |
| Harden, D. B. and others | *Masterpieces of Glass*. British Museum, 1968. |
| Douglas, R. W. and S. Frank | *History of Glassmaking*. Henley-on-Thames, 1972. |
| Schack, Clementine | *Die Glaskunst*. Munich, 1976. |
| Beard, Geoffrey | *International Modern Glass*. London, 1976. |
| Newman, Harold | *Illustrated Dictionary of Glass*, London, 1977 |

### Egyptian, Roman and Medieval Glass

| | |
|---|---|
| Kisa, A. | *Das Glas in Altertume*. 3 vols. Leipzig, 1908. |
| Neuberg, F. | *Ancient Glass*. London, 1962. |

### Islamic Glass

| | |
|---|---|
| Schmoranz, A. | *Old Oriental . . . Glass Vessels*. London and Vienna, 1899. |

# BIBLIOGRAPHY

## Venetian Glass

Lorenzetti, G.     *Vetri di Murano*. Rome, 1931.
Gasparetto, A.     *Il vetro di Murano*. Venice, 1959.
Mariacher, G.     *Italian Blown Glass*. London, 1961.

## German and Bohemian Glass

Pazurek, G. E.     *Gläser der Empire-und Biedermeierzeit*. Leipzig, 1923.
Rademacher, F.     *Die Deutschen Gläser des Mittelalters*. Berlin, 1933.
Egg, Erich.     *Die Glashütten zu Hall und Innsbruck im 16 Jahrhunderts*. Innsbruck, 1962.
Meyer-Heisig, E.     *Der Nürnberger Glasschnitt als 17 Jahrhunderts*. Nuremberg, 1963.

## English and Irish Glass

Houghton, John.     *A Collection of Letters for the Improvement of Husbandry and Trade*. London, 1681–83 and 1692–1703.
Powell, Harry J.     *Glass-making in England*. Cambridge, 1923.
Buckley, Francis.     *A History of Old English Glass*. London, 1925.
Francis, Grant R.     *Old English Drinking Glasses*. London, 1926.
Thorpe, W. A.     *A History of English & Irish Glass*. 2 vols. London, 1929.
    *English Glass*. London, 1935 (third edition, 1961).
Ruggles-Brise, S.     *Sealed Glass Bottles*. London, 1949.
Elville, E. M.     *English Table Glass*. London, 1951.
    *English and Irish Cut Glass*. London, 1954.
Beard, G. W.     *Nineteenth Century Cameo Glass*. Newport, 1956.
Wakefield, Hugh.     *19th Century British Glass*. London, 1961.
Davis, Derek C.     *English and Irish Antique Glass*. London, 1964.
Warren, Phelps     *Irish Glass*. London, 1970.
Godfrey, Eleanor S.     *Development of English Glassmaking*. Chapel Hill, N. Carolina, 1975.
Wills, Geoffrey     *English Looking-Glasses*. London, 1965.
    *English and Irish Glass*. London, 1968.
    *Victorian Glass*. London, 1976.
    *Bottle-Collector's Guide*. London, 1977.

*Some of the books noted above under 'General Works' include important chapters on English glass, notably Albert Hartshorne's pioneer volume.*

# BIBLIOGRAPHY

## Netherlandish Glass

| | |
|---|---|
| Pholien, F. | *La verrerie au pays de Liége*. Liége, 1899. |
| Chambon, R. | *L'histoire de la verrerie en Belgique*. Brussels, 1955. |

## French Glass

| | |
|---|---|
| Imbert. R., and Y. Amic. | *French Crystal Paperweights*. Paris, 1948. |
| Amic, Yolande. | *L'Opaline française au 19e. siècle*. Paris, 1952. |
| Barrelet, James. | *La verrerie en France*. Paris, 1953. |
| Jokelson, Paul. | *Antique French Paperweights*. New York, 1955. |
| McCawley, Patricia K. | *Antique Glass Paperweights from France*. London, 1968. |
| Hollister, Jr., Paul | *Encyclopaedia of Glass Paperweights*. New York, 1969. |
| Cloak, E. Campbell | *Glass Paperweights*. London, 1969. |

## Spanish Glass

| | |
|---|---|
| Riaño, J. F. | *The Industrial Arts in Spain*. London, 1879. |
| Frothingham, A. W. | *Hispanic Glass*. New York, 1941. |
| | *Spanish Glass*. London, 1964. |

## Scandinavian Glass

| | |
|---|---|
| Seitz, H. | *Äldre svenska glas med gravered dekor*. Stockholm, 1936. |
| Wettergren, E. | *Orrefors glasbruk*. Paris, 1937. |
| Polak, Ada. | *Old Norwegian Glass*. 1954. |
| Larsen, Alfred. | *Dansk glas, 1825–1925*. Copenhagen, 1963. |

## Russian Glass

| | |
|---|---|
| Bezborodov, M. A. | *Steklodenie v drevnei Rusi (Glass-making in Russia)*. Minsk, 1956. |

## American Glass

| | |
|---|---|
| McKearin, G. S. & H. | *American Glass*. New York, 1941. |
| | *Two Hundred Years of American Blown Glass*. New York, 1950. |
| | *American Historical Flasks*. Corning, 1953. |

## BIBLIOGRAPHY

| | |
|---|---|
| Lee, Ruth W. | *Early American Pressed Glass.* Northboro, Mass., 1946. |
| Belknap, E. McC. | *Milk Glass.* New York, 1949. |
| Watkins, L. W. | *American Glass and Glass Making.* New York, 1950. |
| Revi, A. C. | *American Pressed Glass.* New York, 1964. |
| Papert, Emma | *Illustrated Guide to American Glass.* New York, 1972. |

### Chinese Glass

| | |
|---|---|
| Bushell, S. W. | *Chinese Art.* 2 vols. London, revised edition, 1909. (Vol. II includes a chapter devoted to the subject). |

Much information on glass of all countries is printed from time to time in magazines dealing with antiques and collecting, and in such specialised journals as *The Transactions of the Society of Glass Technology* (Sheffield), and the *Journal of Glass Studies* (Corning Museum of Glass, New York).

# Index

311